A TACTICAL ANALYSIS

SURVIVAL LESSONS FROM ONE OF LAW ENFORCEMENT'S DEADLIEST SHOOTINGS

Written by Mike Wood

Foreword by Massad Ayoob

Published by

Gun Digest® Books, an imprint of Caribou Media Group, LLC

Gun Digest Media
5600 W. Grande Market Drive, Suite 100
Appleton, WI 54913
www.gundigest.com

To order books or other products call 920.471.4522
or visit us online at www.gundigeststore.com

Cover photo courtesy of Los Angeles Sheriff's Department

ISBN-13: 978-1-4402-4099-7

Edited by Corrina Peterson
Cover & Design by Kevin Ulrich

Printed in the United States of America

10 9 8 7 6 5 4

DEDICATION

I'd like to dedicate this book to my mom, Kathleen. For the three decades that my dad patrolled the highways as a "Road Warrior," she faithfully kept the light burning for him at home. While he chased bad guys, tended to the wounded, and cleaned up the grisly wrecks, she worked, raised the boys, and anxiously awaited his safe return. She patched his wounds, physical and emotional, kept his Thermos filled with hot coffee for those long Graveyard nights, and never forgot to put an "I Love You" note in the cup. Being a highway patrolman is tough work. Being the wife of a highway patrolman is tougher. I love you, Mom. You made it look easy even when it wasn't.

I'd be remiss if I didn't mention Dad's fellow patrolmen, his "Band of Brothers." They looked out after each other and kept each other laughing when times were tough. They grew close in that special way that only men who face dangers and horrors together can. I know that Dad was proud to serve with them, to be among them, to call them his friends. To Gary, Bob, Pat, Ken, Tom, Roger, Bud, Phil, Gil, Jay, Bubba, and all the rest, you have my everlasting respect and thanks. I'm proud to have been a part of the CHP Family with you.—M.W.

CONTENTS

SECTION 3: ANALYSIS OF THE NEWHALL GUNFIGHT

SECTION 4: WHERE ARE WE NOW?

APPENDIX

FOREWORD

By Massad Ayoob

The slaughter of four young California Highway Patrol Officers at Ne-whall, in 1970, was a watershed experience in the history of American law enforcement. It was the slap in the face that awoke the profession to the fact that its training, collectively, had stagnated. Newhall became the dawn of officer survival training for modern police.

Many lessons were learned in the sacrifice of those four brave men at the hands of two classic examples of feral homo sapiens. Lessons of risk assessment and tactics. The realization that there is a time to approach and a time to fall back and contain. The importance of adequate weapons and of reality-based training and policy.

CHP's honest self-assessment led to sweeping changes in the way police were equipped and in the ways high-risk policing was accomplished. We will never know how many police lives have since been saved by the lessons that grew from the martyrdom of Patrolmen Alleyn, Frago, Gore, and Pence.

Time went on. Memory dimmed. This writer became a law enforcement trainer two years after Newhall, when the tragedy was fresh in the collective mind of the police establishment; CHP's training film on the incident was practically mandatory viewing for cops nationwide. By the twenty-first century, though, we had a generation of young officers for whom Newhall had dropped from the radar screen.

One observer who recognized this was Mike Wood. Not wishing to see the lessons of the tragedy blurred, he began to dig. His fresh eye uncovered details that had not been widely known. Mike reached far beyond the crime scene and into politics and mores of the time. He uncovered salient points that helped us gain a fresh understanding of why four productive lives had been cut so tragically short that night in Newhall.

Mike Wood's book is, I think, the best and most comprehensive analysis of the incident yet. It reminds us that the keys to surviving violent encounters must be in place long before they occur. That, in macrocosm, institutional policy must stay focused on reality and not be shaped by "political correctness." That in microcosm, those whose duties take them into harm's way must be prepared early and constantly to face the worst, and must be trained and equipped to neutralize the most violent and well-equipped human adversaries a dangerous high-tech world can produce.

Mike's analysis of the evidence resolves at least one controversy about the issue. It also gives us a better look at the histories of the four victim officers and the best profile yet of "the face of the enemy," with his in-depth reconstruction of the background of the two cop-killers. And, thanks to Mike Wood, another generation of America's finest has a better opportunity than ever to learn from the sacrifice of those four young state policemen.

Alleyn. Frago. Gore. Pence.

Remember.

Massad Ayoob has been teaching firearms and officer survival tactics since 1972. He served 19 years as the chair of the Firearms and Deadly Force Training Committee of the American Society of Law Enforcement Trainers, serves presently on the Advisory Board of the International Law Enforcement Educators and Trainers Association, and for more than 30 years has been Law Enforcement Editor of American Handgunner magazine. He may be reached through http://massadayoobgroup.com.

PREFACE

It has been more than 40 years since the last shots were fired in the driveway of the Standard station and J's Coffee Shop in Newhall, California, so it is only natural for some to question the need for and timing of this book. Why this book? Why now?

It's immediately apparent that the Newhall shooting was an action of great historical significance, as it was the deadliest law enforcement shooting in American history to date. Never before had America seen so many law enforcement officers perish in a single action, and it would be almost four decades before this kind of carnage would be revisited (sadly, twice in the course of a few months[1]). The significance of this event alone justifies an exhaustive reporting, but I had more specific goals in mind when I started on this project.

Foremost in my mind was the desire to honor these brave officers who lost their lives while acting in defense of their community. Each of these men was in the spring of their lives, having just embarked on promising new careers

Officer George M. Alleyn. Photo courtesy of the California Highway Patrol Museum.

Officer Walter C. Frago. Photo courtesy of the California Highway Patrol Museum.

that would allow them to provide for their growing young families, when all was cut short by the gunfire of felons. They left behind wives, children, extended families, and friends that were left holding the shattered pieces of unfinished plans and unfulfilled dreams, and who were forced to endure the long, solitary pain that lives on well after the loss has been erased from fleeting public consciousness.

It didn't seem right that their valorous sacrifice was largely forgotten by the very people they died to protect, and I was determined to reignite a consciousness of that gift. These men and their families deserve our thanks and respect, not only for what they did and what they gave, but for what they represent as defenders of the public against the forces of evil that would otherwise destroy it. They deserve to be honored.

It's with this goal in mind that I gingerly, cautiously approached my second motivation of delivering a thorough tactical analysis of the incident to determine the lessons that could be learned from the action.[2] I am entirely cogni-

Officer Roger D. Gore. Photo courtesy of the California Highway Patrol Museum.

Officer James E. Pence, Jr. Photo courtesy of the California Highway Patrol Museum.

zant that any criticisms of the officers and their actions could be misconstrued as a degrading, personal attack on them, but I want to assure the reader that this is not my motivation or intent. These officers acted with great heroism and performed to the very limits of their training and abilities in a frightening, fluid, confusing, and violent action unlike anything most of us will ever face. My evaluation of their actions is not intended to demean them, discredit them, or treat them with any kind of dishonor. Instead, I propose that a thorough analysis that aims at identifying mistakes so that their fellow warriors can learn from them and increase their own survival quotient is the best way to honor their sacrifice. Absent this kind of analysis, the loss of these officers would be purposeless and merely tragic, which is a much greater insult to the memory of these fine men.

To a certain extent, this process of analysis began many years ago. In the immediate aftermath of the shooting, the California Highway Patrol (CHP) and some allied agencies attempted to distill the lessons learned, disseminate them throughout the law enforcement community, and incorporate them into their training and education processes. However, we now have the benefit of an additional 40 years worth of experience, maturity, study, and insight into the dynamics of personal combat, and this provides us the opportunity to derive new observations and challenge the validity of some old accepted ones. The fact remains that Newhall is more than just a footnote in the history of American law enforcement. It is a schoolhouse fully capable of educating a new generation of warriors in the mechanics of survival.

All of this brings us to the third motivation for this book, which is to ensure that the lessons of Newhall, once identified, are fully integrated into the training and education of today's warriors.[3]

The American law enforcement community was left severely shaken in the wake of Newhall, and it is axiomatic that Newhall was a watershed event that changed the nature of law enforcement tactics, procedures, equipment, training, and education. However, four decades later, the corporate knowledge on the incident is spotty within law enforcement circles, and while Newhall plays prominently in the training of some law enforcement cadets, many officers complete basic and advanced training without ever being exposed to the shooting and its survival lessons. Even among officers exposed to the Newhall shooting, there is a great inconsistency on the quality of the information they receive. Myths and misunderstandings abound.

More importantly, there is ample evidence to indicate that some of the lessons of Newhall have yet to be fully incorporated into the training and education process for America's law enforcement officers. Some agencies appear content to declare that they learned the lessons, fixed what needed to be fixed at the time, and have moved on, leaving Newhall behind as a distant memory, irrelevant to today's law enforcement operations. I submit that there is still a great amount of work to be done on this front, and I hope this book, in some small way, will force agencies and instructors to reevaluate their training mechanisms through the lens of Newhall.

So, back to those original questions: Why this book? Why now? I submit that while the gunsmoke that filled the parking lot of J's Coffee Shop has long since drifted away, the echoes of the gunfire should still be ringing in our ears. The survival lessons of that desperate night some 40 years ago are just as relevant today as they were then, and we would be wise to note them.

The study of combat and self-defense is big and complex. It's been said that each of us has a piece of the puzzle, but that no single person can truly wrap his hands around it all and see the entire "blind man's elephant" for what it is. I respectfully submit to you this book, my own small, personal piece of the puzzle, and hope that it will somehow help you to become better prepared for your own fight against evil.

Semper Vigilans!
Mike Wood
June, 2011

ENDNOTES

1. The fatal shooting of 4 Oakland police officers on March 21, 2009 was quickly followed by the shooting of 3 Philadelphia police officers on April 4, 2009, reopening many of the old emotional wounds from Newhall.

2. Others before me have attacked the issue to some degree. Chief John Anderson's The Newhall Incident offered less in the way of tactical analysis, and instead focused more on the historical backgrounds of the killers and the officers, and the overall narrative of the story. Massad Ayoob's "Ayoob Files: The Newhall Massacre" was much more tactically focused, but suffered from limitations of the abbreviated magazine article format, which prohibited the use of extensive figures, photographic evidence, and detailed analysis.

3. I should take special care to note that I use this term broadly, purposely including not only our law enforcement and military professionals, but also Lieutenant Colonel Dave Grossman's aptly-named civilian "sheepdogs" as well (On Combat, Lt Col Dave Grossman with Loren W. Christensen). After all, as we shall see, it was one of these civilian sheepdogs who valiantly fought alongside the officers on that fateful night and inflicted the most significant wounds on the enemy.

ACKNOWLEDGEMENTS

I'd like to thank the following people for their critical assistance in the preparation of this book.

Jay Rice (CHP Officer, ret.), for answering all my silly questions about CHP history, policies, training, and equipment in great detail, for putting me in contact with other valuable sources to interview, and for graciously letting me have access to his priceless library of notes and manuals from his days as a CHP Cadet. I appreciate all the support and encouragement you gave me.

Gil Payne (CHP Officer, ret.), for his equally important and detailed inputs on CHP training, vehicles, and firearms of the era, and for his encouragement on the project. Keep sending those great emails, Gil.

George Nuttall (CHP Captain, ret.), for his invaluable contributions about training and leadership issues at the CHP Academy, CHP policies and procedures of the era, CHP firearms history, and for his razor-sharp memory about all things CHP. Those with an interest in the CHP will want to check out his book, Cops, Crooks and Other Crazies, which is superb.

Harry Ingold (CHP Sergeant, ret.) and Richard Robinson (CHP Officer, ret.) for sharing their critical first-person accounts of the shooting, their memories of the officers, and their valuable time, but most of all for risking their own safety to help their fellow officers. Harry, Richard, you did everything you possibly could for those guys, and I respect you greatly for it. Thank you for being willing to revisit some painful memories. I'm grateful for the opportunity to help you tell your story.

Massad Ayoob, my teacher, mentor, and friend, for more than three decades of cutting edge instruction in how to defend and preserve life against the evil in this world. You have taught me and inspired me, Mas, as both a teacher and author, and I'm grateful for your example, guidance, friendship, and assistance on this project. I'm honored to know you, learn from you, and work with you.

Bruce Siddle, my new friend and the "Father of Combat Human Factors," for his exceptional insight and his enthusiasm and support for my project. Your vote of confidence was the best endorsement I could ever ask for. Thank you for carrying the torch to light the way for the rest of us.

The gang at Mollies, for all their encouragement and support ever since I was a little kid picking up brass on the range and posting targets, for always making a seat available for me when I visit, and for keeping my Dad alive in the stories they tell about him—I'm always happy and proud to be with you guys and wish I could be there more often.

Tom Vetter (LASD Lieutenant, ret.), for sharing his memories of the officers and providing valuable insight about the details of the shooting.

Captain Dave Smith (LASD Homicide), for allowing me access to his outstanding people and resources. Thank you for your trust and assistance.

Detective Sergeant Paul Delhauer (LASD, ret.), for his gracious and generous assistance with the project. Thank you for your kind reception, for your special efforts with the pictures, for allowing me to pick your brain, and for allowing me to invade your crowded office. I hope you'll enjoy a well-deserved retirement.

Detective Pat Dorris (LASD), for his thorough review of the manuscript and for his valuable insights to working the street. Thank you for going the extra mile to put me in touch with Homicide—it was a breakthrough that made the book possible, and I can't thank you enough. Your dad's excellent work on this case, now more than 40 years ago, made this researcher's job much easier.

Mike Havstad (LASD Scientific Services Bureau), for all of his wonderful efforts with the photographs and for his patience with me as I sent him back into the negatives time after time to look for microscopic details and find the right images.

Michael Fratantoni (LASD Historian), for his gracious help and assistance.

Detective Scott Lusk (LASD Homicide), for shepherding me while I did my research.

Pat Saletore and the folks at the Santa Clarita Valley Historical Society, for their gracious help and assistance, for putting me in contact with Harry, and for their outstanding work in preserving the history of the Newhall Shooting;

California Highway Patrol Commissioner J.A. Farrow, for authorizing the use of CHP images with this work.

Officer Craig Kuehl (CHP Solano Area Training Officer), for his valuable time, keen insights of today's CHP, and gracious assistance with the project. Your officers are safer because of your talented and dedicated efforts.

Officer Fred Oakes (CHP Academy, Enforcement Tactics Unit), for graciously hosting me at the CHP Academy and providing a window into modern-day cadet training at one of the world's foremost law enforcement academies. I appreciate all your efforts to pave the way for me, Fred—you went above and beyond and are a true professional in every sense. Thanks also to Fred's team of highly talented, highly motivated instructors: Officer Jake Steel, Officer Kevin Jeffcoach, and Officer Ryan Dore. Thank you for what you do, gentlemen. I was honored to spend time with you.

Sergeant Mike Green (CHP Academy, Weapons Training Unit) for his generous time and for running a world-class training program for the men and women who protect our communities.

Sergeant Linda Powell (CHP Academy, Administrative Services Unit) for opening the doors to the CHP Museum archives and for her support and help.

Sergeant John Owen (Media Relations, CHP Headquarters) for his assistance with coordinating image releases and a review of the manuscript;

The CHP Museum Foundation Board of Directors, to include Commissioner (Retired) Spike Helmick, Chief (Retired) Keith Miller, and Officer (Retired) Rick Mattos. Thank you for allowing me access to the treasures in your archives, for your exceptional support and trust, and for keeping the history of the Patrol alive through your dedicated efforts. I owe special thanks to Rick Mattos for paving the way with his own book, California Highway Patrol (Images of America), published by Arcadia Publishing, which is a fascinating pictoral history of the Patrol. Readers are highly encouraged to visit the newly-remodeled CHP Museum, located on the grounds of the CHP Academy in Sacramento.

Mr. Dan Fowler, for his exceptional work with the historic images from the CHP Museum and for catching my last-minute "Hail Mary" pass with ease. You brought these pages to life with exciting images of days past, and I'm grateful;

Lieutenant John Whitney (Vallejo, California PD), for his careful review of the manuscript, detailed answers to my questions, and for his friendship and encouragement. I respect you greatly. Be safe out there, my friend.

Lieutenant Colonel Paul Wood (USAF), for his critical review of the manuscript, his valuable operational and tactical expertise, and his encouragement with the project. He even came up with the title. We took much of this journey through CHP history together, and I enjoyed it even more because he was there with me. I'm proud to be your brother. Thank you for your dedicated service to our great nation.

Jim Schlender and Corrina Peterson at F&W Media, for taking a chance on an unknown wannabe author, and giving him the opportunity to achieve a dream. Thank you both for allowing me to share this book with the law enforcement profession I respect so much.

The "Quiet Professionals," for their selfless service to our nation. Semper Vigilans!

Lastly, my loving family, for their patience and support as I took valuable time away from them to pursue this project. Thank you for your understanding and love. I'm so proud of each of you and love you with all my heart. I hope I can make you equally as proud, and want you to know that you are the greatest gifts in my life.

INTRODUCTION

Car trips in the Wood family were different than they were in our friend's families. In their cars, favorite restaurants, scenic views, unique buildings, or entertaining billboards were the waypoints that allowed them to track the progress of their journeys. Their cars sped idly down the road, often with little thought about the territory they passed or the events that happened there once upon a time.

For my highway patrolman father, each journey was marked by memories of fiery crashes, the routes of high-speed chases, "deuces" who had to be wrestled into handcuffs, and countless citations. Mileposts and freeway exit signs served less to guide the traveler than they did to define the boundaries of patrol beats and mark the locations where battles of life and death had been fought by motorists, outlaws, and lawmen, much like battlefield monuments or tombstones.

Dad would share some of these memories with us along the way and would include a lesson here and there when appropriate: A sharp curve in the highway served as an opportunity for an impromptu lesson in the operation and handling of a vehicle at high speeds. A highway merge became the focus of a lesson on defensive driving. A dip in the freeway was a physics lesson about the areas that would block radio signals from transmitting cries for backup.

As young boys eager to join the law enforcement profession and follow in our father's footsteps, we wouldn't have had it any other way. Indeed, much of the discussion was at our insistence and due to our constant questions. We found it fascinating, exciting, and educational and secretly made notes to ourselves to remember this or that fact because it might save our lives someday when we were grownups.

Our mother, ever indulgent, let our father weave the tales, while she tried to think about something else other than the dangers and horrors faced nightly by her husband on patrol. Dad was cautious to edit the narrative for young ears and sensibilities and didn't talk about the gruesome details of what happened to God's finest creations when they slammed into a 100-year-old oak tree at 95 miles per hour, or when they mindlessly drifted into an accident scene full of officers and firemen because they were attracted by all the flashing lights on the emergency vehicles—but Mom filled in the blanks automatically in her mind.

She remembered the gray look on Dad's face that night, early in his career, when he swung by the house for a quick dinner in the middle of his shift. He had just come from working a particularly gory accident scene and she had innocently served spaghetti; he could barely look at it and left after taking in nothing but coffee.

Like most wives of rookie cops, she had helped him through the sometimes painful and horrifying early days of his career, when everything was new and confusing and he was still building the emotional skills necessary to handle the job and make sense of all that he saw and experienced. She would listen to the stories of what he had seen and done during his shift, giving him someone to lean on when he needed it and easing the burden by sharing the pain. She heard about the kids thrown from cars as they rolled over, about the false reassurances he had to give to people about those he knew wouldn't make it, and all the other things that give cops nightmares long after they're over. She was relieved that he didn't share these stories often anymore, didn't need to, but she remembered them like she had been there herself, the details vivid in her mind.

Those memories weren't as difficult as the night she got the phone call telling her he was in the hospital because he had been hit by a drunk driver. He had been working an accident scene, standing in front of a tow truck with his boot on the front bumper to form a knee rest for the report book he was taking notes with, when the car slammed into the rear of the truck and flung him like a rag doll a hundred feet away into the iceplant. She did her best to forget that and the nagging thought that it could happen again at any time, but the sometimes crippling back issues that would lay him up for days in the years that followed would always remind her.

She also remembered the night when he called to say he would be home late, because he'd had to shoot at a man and the investigators would be talking to him for a while longer. The man eagerly surrendered at the shot, unharmed by the bullet that lodged in the object he was taking cover behind, and the shooting was declared in-policy. They would later joke about the "Great Gunfight at the Mission Trading Post," but behind her smile was a worried wife who knew that someday her husband might encounter an armed man who didn't want to surrender so easily.

Thus, it was with great determination and grit that Mom would endure our family journeys to the Magic Mountain amusement park and points north, because the highway always took us past a special place, with a special story for Dad to tell and a special set of lessons for us to catalog. It was a story of fear, courage, sadness, sacrifice and valor. It was a story that began and ended for four brave men near a freeway exit sign simply marked "Henry Mayo Drive."

The events of that night would be remembered not by the street name, but by the name of the city in which they occurred: Newhall. In time, that name would become loaded with a special meaning for law enforcement, spoken with a tone of reverence by those who knew what happened there. Unfortunately, that circle has grown smaller and smaller over the years, and the site itself has been razed and remodeled so that no trace of the original killing field remains.

We can't allow the memories of what happened that day to fade away, and we can't allow the lessons written in blood to be forgotten. As such, it's time to go back to rural Los Angeles County and a young freeway that snaked through its canyons and the unincorporated city of Newhall . . .

The Shooting

Introduction

The following narrative of the Newhall shooting[1] is drawn from multiple sources, including interviews with participants, a thorough examination of the homicide investigation files completed and maintained by the Los Angeles County Sheriff's Department, and official California Highway Patrol (CHP) documents, photographs, and film.

Unfortunately, the reconstruction of a complex event is often limited by the fallible memories of the participants and witnesses. It's a matter of extensive research, investigation, and discussion within medical and legal circles that witnesses often don't remember the details of an event, particularly a dramatic and life-threatening event such as a gunfight, with total accuracy.[2] Since a memory is "a record of people's experiences of events, not a record of those events themselves," it is bound to be influenced by a host of physical, spatial, cognitive, environmental, and emotional factors that affect those personal experiences and place their own imprints on the individuals' perception of the true action that occurred.[3] This leads to the inevitable result of conflicting testimony and complicates the investigator's and author's task of understanding the incident as it truly happened.

This general tendency is made even worse by the nature of a large-scale gunfight such as the Newhall shooting, because the action is fast, dispersed, and constant, and because multiple storylines are being played out simultaneously in a way that none of the participants or witnesses can actively track each of them with any fidelity as they occur. Gunfights are not tidy, linear actions that can be neatly recreated in sequence, but rather messy, confused events in which the participants are keenly aware of their immediate situation, but largely unaware of their place in the larger picture.

This is certainly the case in the Newhall shooting. While the general narrative is agreed upon, there are certain aspects of the event for which information is not clear. The physical evidence is incomplete, and witnesses provided conflicting testimony about various aspects of the shooting. While we can hazard our best guess of the situation, based on known evidence and a preponderance of testimony, we may never know exactly what happened during portions of this fluid, fast-paced action. The task of recreating the sequence of the Newhall shooting is further complicated by the fact that five of the seven principal players were killed during or shortly after the incident occurred. Fortunately, there are also many factors that helped to mitigate these concerns.

To begin with, there was a large number of witnesses to the event, as it occurred in a brightly lit area within the visual range of a parking lot and restaurant full of people.[4] The volume of reports allowed investigators to separate the wheat from the chaff and assemble a reasonably consistent picture of the events as they took place.

One of the perpetrators, Jack Twining, spoke to Los Angeles County Sheriff's Department personnel via phone during the hostage crisis that ensued as he attempted his escape from the scene of the shooting. He also discussed the shooting via monitored phone call with his partner, Bobby Davis, who had been captured and was in Sheriff's custody. Lastly, Twining completed a phone interview with media personnel (which was monitored by law enforcement), prior to his suicide.[5] During these conversations, Twining recounted valuable details about the shooting, which assisted investigators in their reconstruction efforts. The other perpetrator, Bobby Davis, also provided information to investigators in the wake of his capture, interrogation, and trial.

The civilian hero of the shooting, Gary Dean Kness, also provided vital firsthand knowledge of a portion of the events. As an active participant in the gunfight, Mr. Kness was certainly subject to a host of physiological reactions that might have affected his memory of the events, but as the only surviving close range witness to some of the happenings, his testimony was critical to a complete understanding of some of the most desperate moments of the battle.

Besides witness testimony, the shooting investigation team had a host of physical evidence to draw upon as it prepared its reconstruction of the shooting. Much of this evidence has been well preserved and was still accessible during research for this project. Some of the evidence was incomplete from the beginning (such as the information on the number of shots fired during the incident), but we are fortunate that the majority of the physical evidence was properly documented and preserved.[6]

With these limitations in mind, the following narrative represents the most comprehensive, accurate account of this watershed event to date. Where inconsistencies or unknowns exist, they will be recognized and explained to the best extent possible.

CHAPTER 1

Prelude

Bobby Augustus Davis and Jack Wright Twining were violent, career criminals who had recently been released from prison. They had befriended each other in prison, and in the wake of their release, they traveled to California, where they began to plan a series of crimes, including the takedown and robbery of an armored car.

On the evening of April 5, 1970, Davis and Twining were in the coastal mountains of the Angeles National Forest, between the towns of Gorman and Castaic, California. (Fig. 1) They were there for several purposes, all of which

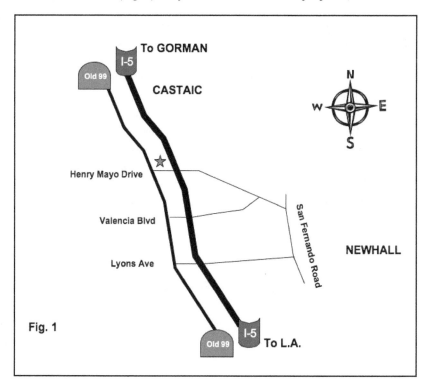

Fig. 1

related to their planned crimes. Their primary objective was to locate and steal explosives from a construction site, those explosives intended for use in their attack on the armored car. Additionally, they wanted to troubleshoot and test-fire some weapons, as well as perform an operational test on some portable radios (five-watt CB transceivers) that they planned on using during the heist.[7]

At one point, Twining was away from the vehicle in search of the explosives, while Davis remained behind to safeguard it and the cache of weapons in the rear seat and trunk of the two-door, 1964 Pontiac Gran Prix. Davis parked the vehicle on the shoulder of the northbound side of the interstate (Interstate 5, formerly Highway 99), but attracted the attention and suspicions of some stranded motorists ahead and felt compelled to leave quickly. He made a large, sweeping U-turn across the highway and headed southbound, cutting off another southbound motorist in the process, who had to slam on the brakes to avoid a collision. The time was approximately 23:22.[8]

The motorist who'd been cut off by Davis was Ivory Jack Tidwell, a U.S. Navy sailor returning home with his wife, Pamela, after a family reunion. Tidwell became irate with Davis and sped up to catch him. To Tidwell's surprise, the reckless driver pulled over to the shoulder and stopped, allowing Tidwell to pull up alongside him. Through the open window on his wife's side of the vehicle, Tidwell cussed out the errant driver.

Davis responded by pointing a two-inch .38 caliber Smith & Wesson revolver at Tidwell and his wife. Desperate to escape, Tidwell tricked Davis by claiming that a vehicle approaching from behind was a California Highway Patrol car. Davis fell for the ruse and told Tidwell to "Git!" Tidwell sped away down the highway and was relieved to see he had not been followed. He soon found a phone at a service station on Violin Canyon Road and reported the incident to the Highway Patrol at 23:36, giving the license plate and description of the car and driver. One minute later, Officers Roger D. Gore and Walter C. Frago, Unit 78-8, were notified by dispatch about the misdemeanor brandishing incident.[9]

In the meantime, Davis located and picked up Twining, and they proceeded southbound on Interstate 5 towards the town of Castaic and their home further

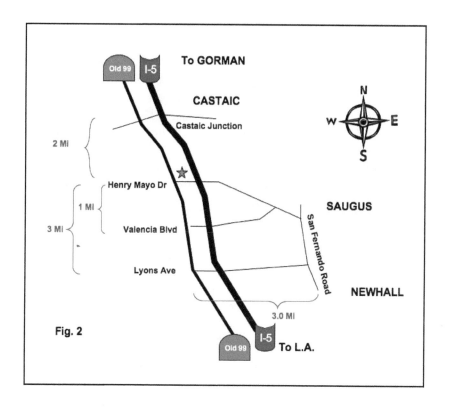

Fig. 2

south in Long Beach. Davis relayed the details of the incident to Twining as they drove.

Officers Gore and Frago established an observation position south of Castaic at Castaic Junction (Fig. 2) and picked up a visual on the suspect vehicle less than 20 minutes later, at 23:54. They radioed to dispatch that they were behind the Pontiac, southbound at the semi-truck scales, and asked for assistance with stopping the vehicle.

CHAPTER 2

The Stop

At the time of Unit 78-8's request, several CHP units were nearby in a position to assist with the stop.

Officers Ed Holmes and Richard Robinson, Unit 78-16R, were patrolling about five miles southeast of Castaic, near the town of Saugus. They were southbound on Route 126 East (San Fernando Road), near the Saugus Café. (Fig. 3)

Officers Harry Ingold and Roger Palmer, Unit 78-19R, were just a few miles further south, near the town center of Newhall. They were heading southbound on the same road (San Fernando Road, Route 126 West) near the Way Station Coffee Shop in downtown Newhall, when 78-8 radioed that they were in position behind the Pontiac. (Refer again to Fig. 3)

Unit 78-12, Officers James E. Pence and George M. Alleyn, were in position about three miles south of Unit 78-8, on the southbound entrance to Interstate 5 at Valencia Boulevard. In coordination with Unit 78-8, they planned to

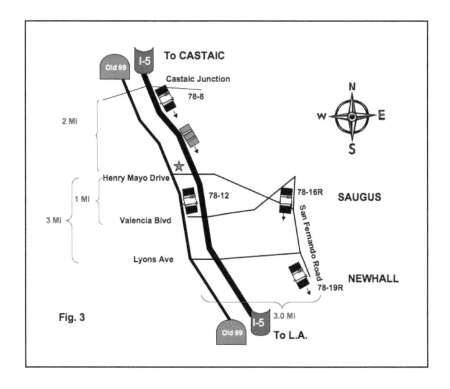

Fig. 3

join the pursuit there and assist 78-8 with the stop shortly thereafter. (Refer again to Fig. 3)

The plan was good, but it was not meant to be. Having spotted 78-8 in his trail, Davis unexpectedly chose to exit Interstate 5 at Henry Mayo Drive, a little more than one mile north of Unit 78-12's position, shortly after 23:54. Unit 78-8 followed the Pontiac westbound on Henry Mayo Drive as Unit 78-12 reversed direction, raced across the overpass, and hurried northbound on Interstate 5 to join 78-8 a mile north on Henry Mayo. (Fig. 4)

When Unit 78-16R heard Unit 78-8 broadcast that they were exiting the freeway at Henry Mayo Drive and were going to make the stop, they made a U-turn in front of the Thatcher Glass Company on San Fernando Road and began to respond. Unit 78-19R also made a U-turn and proceeded northbound on San Fernando Road from Newhall to assist. (Refer again to Fig. 4.) Moments later, the responding units heard a transmission from Unit 78-12 saying that they were approaching the scene and would back up 78-8 with the stop— "We're with them now." Feeling that two units would be enough to cover the call, Units 78-16R and 78-19R both discontinued their response. Unit 78-16R made another U-turn near the intersection of Henry Mayo Drive and Boquet Canyon Road, and continued travel back in their original direction, southbound on San Fernando Road. Unit 78-19R continued northbound on San

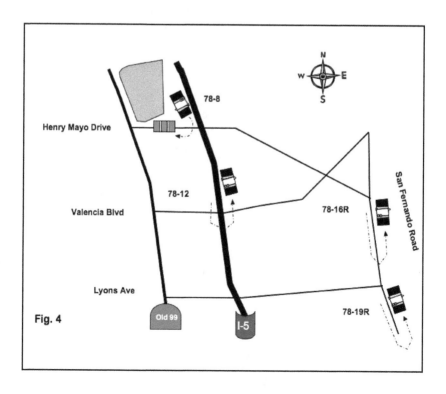

Fig. 4

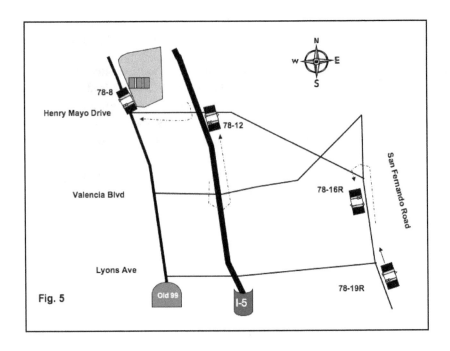

Fig. 5

Fernando Road from Newhall, towards Unit 78-16R. (Fig. 5)

With Unit 78-12 one minute behind, the Pontiac turned northbound on The Old Road (the old, pre-freeway Highway 99) from Henry Mayo Drive and immediately into the driveway that led into the Standard Gas Station and the parking lot of J's Coffee Shop. (Fig. 6) As they pulled into the driveway, Officer Frago trained the white spotlight on the passenger side of the patrol car onto the Pontiac.

Instead of pulling deep into the parking lot, Davis suddenly stopped the red Pontiac, just past the throat of the driveway and about 55 feet short of the gas pump island of the Standard Gas Station. This left Unit 78-8 stuck in the middle of the driveway, a little over one car length behind the Pontiac, with a low (approximately three- to four-foot deep) ditch to either side. (Fig. 7)

Officers Gore and Frago elected to proceed with the stop from this constrained position and made no attempt to direct the driver of the Pontiac to move the vehicle to another location in the parking lot. The time was just a few seconds before 23:55. As Officer Gore put the transmission of the 1969 Dodge Polara patrol vehicle into "Park," Unit 78-12 was approaching the northbound Henry Mayo Drive exit, just a minute behind.

Davis and Twining were already proceeding with their plan.

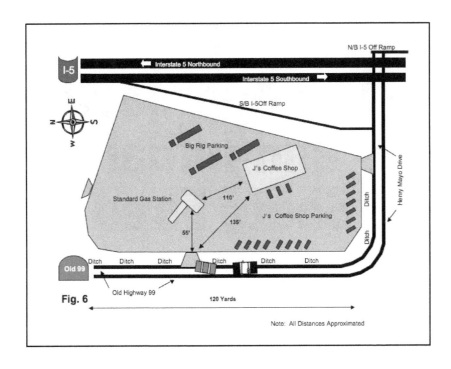

Fig. 6

Note: All Distances Approximated

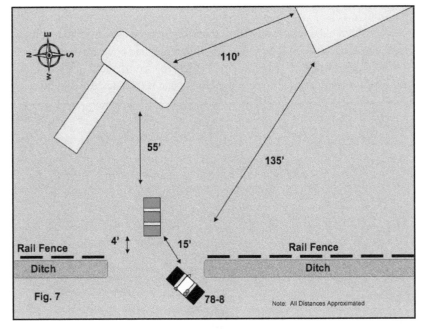

Fig. 7

Note: All Distances Approximated

CHAPTER 3

The Approach and Initial Shots Fired

When Davis brought the Pontiac to a stop, he did so in an area bathed with light from the gas station ahead and the restaurant parking lot to the right. With the additional light provided by the headlights of the CHP cruiser and the passenger side-mounted white spotlight, Officers Gore and Frago could clearly see that the vehicle contained two occupants, not the single occupant reported by the complainant, Tidwell. Davis was behind the wheel, and Twining was in the right front passenger seat of the Pontiac. They remained inside the vehicle. (Fig. 8)

The CHP Dodge was located at the five o'clock position from the Pontiac, approximately 15 to 20 feet behind—a little more than one car length away. The Dodge was angled away from the Pontiac towards the left, in a way that exposed the right side of the patrol car to anyone who exited the passenger

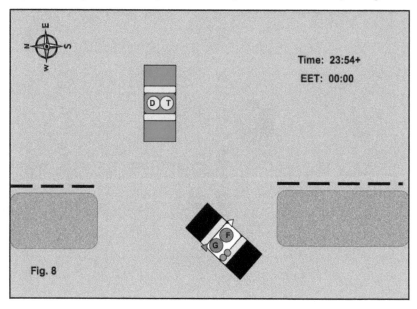

Fig. 8

side of the Pontiac. (Refer again to Fig. 8.)

The officers got out of their patrol car and took up initial positions with weapons drawn, as was standard procedure for a high risk or "hot" stop. Officer Gore exited the driver's side, drew his six-inch Colt Python .357 Magnum revolver from his swivel holster, and pointed it at the vehicle from a "leaning" position across the left front fender and hood of the Dodge. Officer Frago, armed with the Remington 870 12-gauge shotgun from the patrol car's Lektro-Lok rack, donned his hat and established a position just aft of the right front headlamp of the patrol car, in accordance with the tactics he had been taught for routine vehicle stops as a cadet less than a year and a half prior. (Fig. 9)

Officer Gore ordered the occupants out of the car with the command, "Get out with your hands up." When neither Davis nor Twining complied with the command, he repeated it a second and third time before the driver, Davis, finally exited the vehicle. Witnesses reported that Gore had to order the non-compliant Davis an additional time to raise his hands, stating, "We told you to get your hands up." Against directions, Twining remained in the car.

Officer Gore ordered Davis to spread his legs, place his hands on top of the Pontiac, and lean on the car. When Davis assumed the directed search position, Officer Gore advanced the short distance between them (about 10 to 15 feet) to search the suspect. (Fig. 10) The time was just prior to 23:55.

Meanwhile, Officer Frago abandoned his covering position at the front of the Polara and approached the passenger side of the Gran Prix with the shotgun in a "port arms" position. Nearing the vehicle, he reportedly shifted the butt of the shotgun to his right hip and held the firearm with the muzzle in the air with his right hand only, as he reached for the door handle of the Pontiac

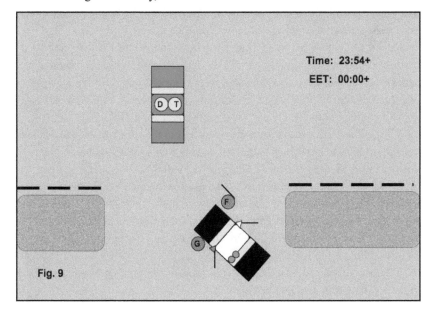

Time: 23:54+
EET: 00:00+

Fig. 9

with his left hand to remove the noncompliant passenger, Twining (Refer again to Fig. 10)[10]

As Officer Frago reached for the door handle, Twining suddenly opened the door and spun to face Officer Frago with a four-inch Smith & Wesson Model 28 .357 Magnum revolver in his hand.[11] Officer Frago was reported to have yelled "Hold it!" before Twining fired twice with the revolver, striking him in the left armpit area with both shots. The bullets from the Western-brand .357 Magnum cartridges traversed Officer Frago's upper chest, killing him instantly, and he fell where he stood. (Fig. 11)[12]

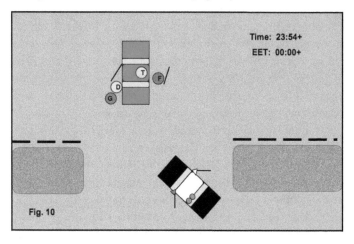

Time: 23:54+
EET: 00:00+

Fig. 10

Twining quickly exited the vehicle and turned to fire two shots at Officer Gore, who was near Davis on the other side of the vehicle. In his haste, Twining triggered both shots low, into the right rear side of the Pontiac's body and roof as he tracked the gun upward towards Officer Gore. (Fig. 12) As this happened, Officer Gore turned away from Davis, aimed his revolver, and fired a single round of Remington-Peters .357 Magnum ammunition at Twining across the deck lid of the car. The shot went wide and missed Twining, striking the right rear window of a Ford Mustang parked in the restaurant parking lot and exiting out that car's rear window. (Refer again to Fig. 12.)

With Officer Gore focused on the threat across the car from him, Davis had the opportunity to push back from the car, spin to his right, and pull a two-inch Smith & Wesson Model 38 Bodyguard Airweight .38 Special revolver from his waistband (the same gun he had used to threaten the Tidwells with earlier). Davis shot the distracted officer twice in the chest at arm's length, the bullets traveling from left front to right back. Like his hapless partner, academy classmate, and childhood friend, Officer Frago, Officer Gore was dead before he hit the ground. (Fig. 13)

The time was 23:56. The Pontiac had stopped just a little more than one minute earlier, and help had just arrived.

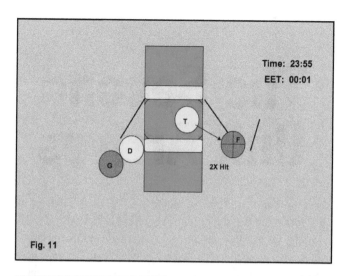

Time: 23:55
EET: 00:01

2X Hit

Fig. 11

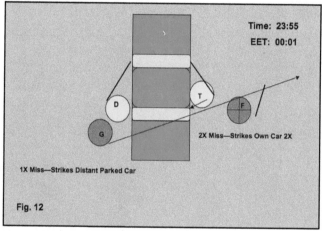

Time: 23:55
EET: 00:01

2X Miss—Strikes Own Car 2X

1X Miss—Strikes Distant Parked Car

Fig. 12

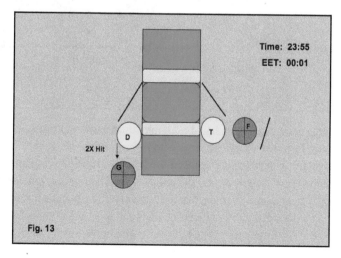

Time: 23:55
EET: 00:01

2X Hit

Fig. 13

CHAPTER 4

The Second Unit Arrives

As Officer Gore fell, mortally wounded, Unit 78-12 was pulling into position roughly parallel and to the north of Unit 78-8. The nose of 78-12 was ahead of 78-8 by about half a car length and angled slightly towards 78-8, and the two cruisers were separated by just eight to 10 feet. The newly arriving patrol car was caught in the same chokepoint as the previous vehicle, only slightly more than a car's length behind the Pontiac. (Fig. 14)

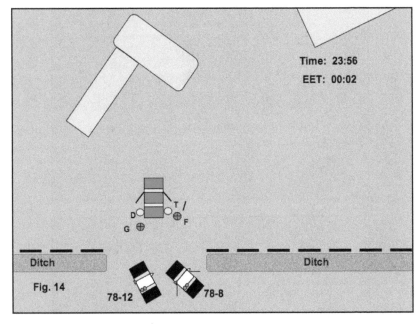

Time: 23:56
EET: 00:02

Ditch

Ditch

Fig. 14

78-12

78-8

Officers Pence and Alleyn had driven into an ambush and came under immediate fire from Davis and Twining, who had moved to the front of the car for cover. Davis placed his left hand on the hood of the car for support and triggered the remaining three rounds in the Model 38 revolver from an outstretched right arm, and Twining shot the remaining two rounds in the Model 28 revolver at the responding officers as their car approached (Fig. 15) [13]

At 23:56, Officer Pence grabbed the radio microphone and broadcast an

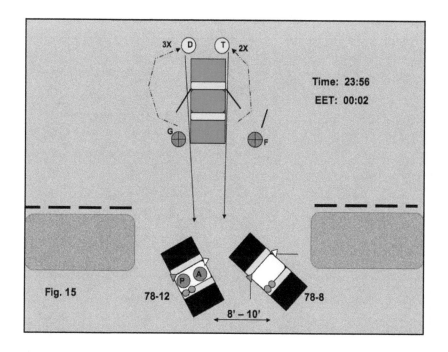

Fig. 15

Time: 23:56
EET: 00:02

urgent message to Newhall Dispatch in an excited voice. Using the CHP brevity code for "Officer Needs Help," Officer Pence broadcast: "11-99! Standard Station at J's! Shots fired!"[14]

As Officer Pence was sending the desperate call for help, Davis and Twining reentered the Pontiac from the passenger side and armed themselves with new weapons from the back seat. Davis selected a 12-gauge pump shotgun with a sawed-off barrel and stock (loaded with six rounds of Remington-Peters 00 Buckshot), and Twining selected a Remington-Rand 1911A1 .45 ACP semi-automatic pistol loaded with a full magazine of seven, 230-grain FMJ cartridges and an eighth round in the chamber. (Fig. 16)[15]

As Officers Pence and Alleyn prepared to exit their patrol car, Davis moved to the front of the Pontiac and fired a shot from the shotgun, which raked pellets across the hood of the vehicle from a point near the center of the right fender and extending across the hood to the center of the windshield.[16] Simultaneously, Twining attempted to fire, from a position near the driver's side door of the Pontiac, a single shot from his pistol at the officers. The pistol failed to fire, and Twining ejected a live round from the pistol to clear it. In doing so, another live round jammed in the pistol and prevented the slide from going into battery. The malfunction prevented Twining from firing the gun, and he ditched it in the rear of the Pontiac on the floorboard behind the driver's seat. (Fig. 17)[17]

After making the 11-99 radio call, Officer Pence exited the CHP cruiser, drew his six-inch .357 Magnum Colt Python revolver from its crossdraw hol-

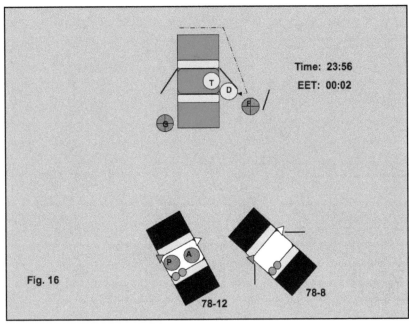

Time: 23:56
EET: 00:02

Fig. 16

78-12

78-8

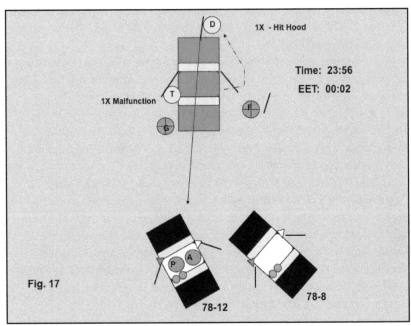

1X - Hit Hood

Time: 23:56
EET: 00:02

1X Malfunction

Fig. 17

78-12

78-8

ster, and began to fire at Davis and/or Twining, using the patrol vehicle's open door as cover. (Fig. 18)

Just prior to this, as Officer Pence was bringing the vehicle to a halt and making the 11-99 call, Officer Alleyn was deploying the car's Remington 870 12-gauge shotgun from the Lektro-Lok cradle. As Officer Pence exited the driver's side and began to fire, Officer Alleyn exited the passenger side of the vehicle, with his issued hat securely in place, and pumped a round into the chamber of the shotgun as he made his way aft in the narrow channel between the two patrol cars.[18] He rounded the back of Unit 78-8 and took up a position on the right side, behind the open passenger door of that unit. (Refer again to Fig. 18.) This "end run" was surely prompted by the fact that Officer Alleyn had been under fire since his arrival, and he felt unprotected due to the angle of Unit 78-12, which exposed the entire right side of the unit to the shooters.

As Officer Alleyn was moving, Twining climbed into the Pontiac and fished around in the back seat for a second 1911A1 pistol of Colt's manufacture. As he was doing this, Officer Alleyn reached his position at the door of 78-8, and, apparently, having forgotten that he had already done so in the stress of the moment, racked the slide of the shotgun again to chamber a round. This ejected an unfired round of buckshot onto the ground, which was discovered later during the post-shooting investigation.[19]

Officer Alleyn fired two rounds of Western Super-X buckshot at Twining while he was inside the Pontiac arming himself with the second 1911A1 pistol. One of the pellets from these two shells penetrated the rear window

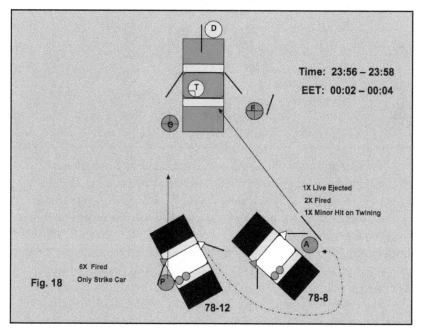

Time: 23:56 – 23:58
EET: 00:02 – 00:04

1X Live Ejected
2X Fired
1X Minor Hit on Twining

6X Fired
Only Strike Car

Fig. 18

78-12

78-8

of the Pontiac and, having spent its energy in doing so, struck Twining in the forehead. The pellet did not significantly wound him, but Twining would later complain that he had a "terrible headache" from the "hunk of buckshot in my scalp." The wound "hurt like hell" and angered him, but while it made him bleed, it would not slow him down during the fight. (Refer again to Fig. 18.)[20]

Officer Alleyn also fired one shot from the shotgun at Davis while he was still at the front of the Pontiac, leaving marks on the passenger side of the vehicle.[21] In doing so, Officer Alleyn ran the Remington 870 shotgun dry. Unfortunately, Davis' shotgun was still loaded, and he fired at Officer Alleyn twice with the sawed-off shotgun, leaving a pattern of 13 pellet streaks alongside the right rear passenger door and right rear quarter panel of the CHP cruiser. The white passenger-side spotlight also took three hits at some point, probably from Davis' buckshot blasts. (Fig. 19)

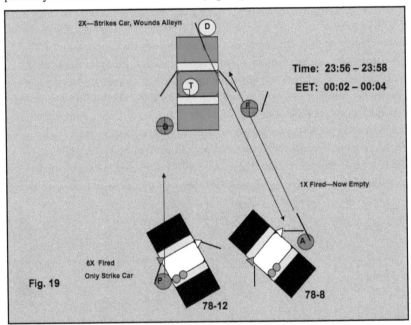

Fig. 19

After being grazed by Officer Alleyn's shotgun pellet, Twining exited the Pontiac through the open driver's side door, leaving blood stains inside the vehicle on the left sidewall and the rear of the driver's seat. He began to engage Officer Pence (and possibly Officer Alleyn) with the new pistol from a position somewhere near the forward driver's side of the vehicle.[22] Officer Pence continued to fire his revolver from his position behind the driver's side door, apparently striking the left rear of the Pontiac near the area where Twining emerged. (Fig. 20)[23]

After running the shotgun empty, Officer Alleyn retreated from his position at the right door of Unit 78-8 to a position at the rear left corner of the vehicle. (Refer again to Fig. 20.)As Officer Alleyn turned to the rear to begin this movement away from the door, several witnesses saw him with blood on his face, indicating he had already been wounded during the exchange of fire with Twining and Davis.[24]

After ditching the empty shotgun on the ground at the rear of the patrol car, Officer Alleyn drew his six-inch Smith & Wesson Model 19-2 .357 Magnum revolver from its crossdraw holster and began to fire at Davis, who had rounded the front of the Pontiac on the passenger's side and had begun to advance to a position in front of and between the two CHP units with his sawed off-pump shotgun.[25] As he moved, Davis possibly fired one round from the shotgun at Officer Pence, striking the side of the unit. (Refer again to Fig. 20.)[26]

Officer Alleyn fired three rounds of .357 Magnum ammunition at Davis (and possibly Twining, according to a witness), from the left rear of Unit 78-8, firing from the time that Davis was at the front of the Pontiac to when he advanced on the patrol cars. Witnesses indicated that he fired with a single hand, using the other (his left) to brace himself on the trunk. Unfortunately, none of his bullets hit the highly mobile target that some witnesses later described as "bobbing" and "restless." (Refer again to Fig. 20.)[27]

Officer Alleyn raised himself up above the trunk of Unit 78-8 to locate and target Davis during this phase of the battle and was shot in the face and chest by Davis, who had reached the front of the vehicle by this point. In mortal agony, Officer Alleyn attempted to prop himself up on the trunk lid of

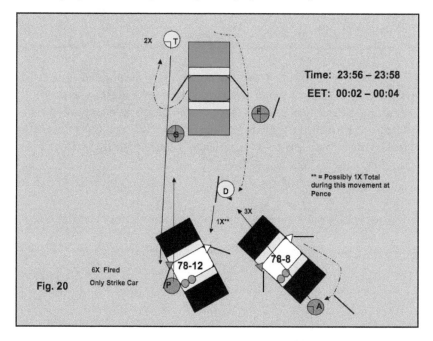

Fig. 20

Time: 23:56 – 23:58
EET: 00:02 – 00:04

** = Possibly 1X Total during this movement at Pence

6X Fired
Only Strike Car

the vehicle, whereupon he was shot again in the chest by Davis at the length of the car. This caused Officer Alleyn to reflexively trigger a round from his revolver into the rear window of 78-8, turning the glass into a frosty haze.28 Near death, Officer Alleyn fell forward onto the trunk then slid off to his right. He landed with his feet towards the centerline of the car and his upper body extending past the right side of the car, a total of 10 .33-caliber 00 Buckshot pellets in his face and chest. (Fig. 21)

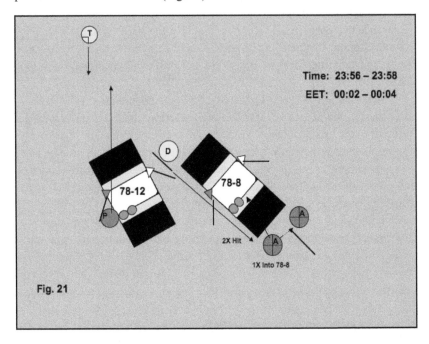

Fig. 21

With his shotgun finally empty, Davis retreated to the position of the fallen Officer Frago and stripped him of his weapons. He placed the unfired CHP Remington 870 shotgun inside the Pontiac, along with his empty sawed-off shotgun, and armed himself with the fallen officer's six-inch Colt Officer's Model Match .38 Special revolver, which he'd taken from Officer Frago's crossdraw holster. (Figs. 22 and 23)[29]

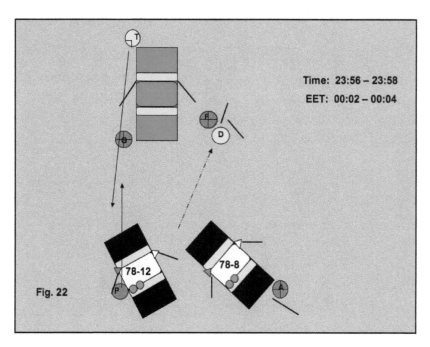

Time: 23:56 – 23:58
EET: 00:02 – 00:04

Fig. 22

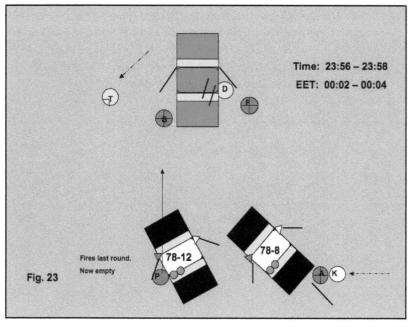

Time: 23:56 – 23:58
EET: 00:02 – 00:04

Fires last round.
Now empty

Fig. 23

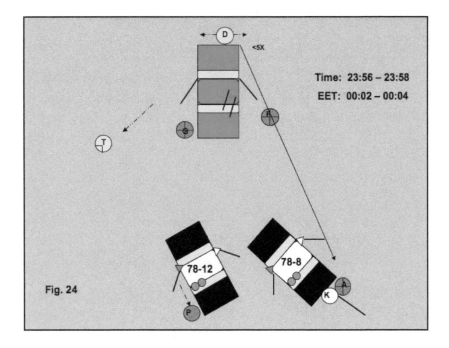

Fig. 24

Time: 23:56 – 23:58
EET: 00:02 – 00:04

Thusly armed, Davis began to fire at the stricken Officer Alleyn, whose prone body was exposed at the right rear of the Polara. Witnesses would later recount (and blood evidence would confirm), that Davis maneuvered along the entire front of the Pontiac, firing from various positions, and that he rested his left elbow on the hood to brace his right hand, which held the revolver. (Fig. 24)

CHAPTER 5

A Heroic Attempt

Earlier, as Officers Pence and Alleyn raced down the northbound off-ramp and turned westbound onto Henry Mayo Drive, they passed a car on their right waiting at the westbound Henry Mayo Stop sign. The car contained a single citizen by the name of Gary Dean Kness, who was on his way to work the night shift as a computer operator at Hydraulic Research and Manufacturing Corporation, in the nearby Rye Canyon industrial park.

After Unit 78-12 sped past with amber deck lights flashing, Mr. Kness continued ahead on Henry Mayo Drive, turned right on The Old Road, and followed the vehicle towards the Standard Station. As he approached, it occurred to him that the lights of the gas station were usually off at this time of evening, but tonight they were on for some reason. As he got closer, he saw a pair of CHP cruisers in the parking lot and flashes of gunfire from Officers Pence and Alleyn at the rear of Units 78-12 and 78-8. His first thought was that a movie was being filmed on location, but as he neared the scene and saw Officer Alleyn go down, he realized it was a real gunfight and thought to himself, "Somebody has got to do something."[30]

The former Marine stopped his car along The Old Road, bailed out, and ran about 70 yards to assist Officer Alleyn. His first thought was that he had to get the officer back behind cover, because he was lying in an exposed position at the right rear of the Dodge and the gunman ahead was still firing at him. (Refer again to Figs. 23 and 24.)

Upon reaching Officer Alleyn, Mr. Kness grabbed him by the gunbelt and attempted to pull him to cover, but he found he could not move him. As Mr. Kness attempted to rescue Officer Alleyn, Davis stepped around the right front of the Pontiac and began to advance on the pair. (Fig. 25)

Seeing the CHP shotgun on the ground at Officer Alleyn's feet, Mr. Kness grabbed the weapon, aimed it around the right rear fender of the CHP car (resting his left hand on the fender) at the advancing Davis, and pulled the trigger on an empty chamber. He immediately racked the slide of the shotgun and pulled the trigger again on an empty chamber.[31]

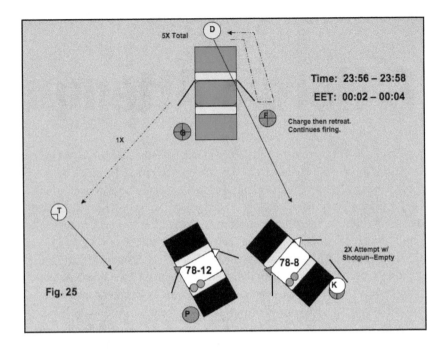

Fig. 25

5X Total

Time: 23:56 – 23:58
EET: 00:02 – 00:04

Charge then retreat.
Continues firing.

1X

78-12

78-8

2X Attempt w/
Shotgun--Empty

At the sight of Mr. Kness aiming the shotgun at him, Davis abandoned his advance and immediately retreated back to the front of the Pontiac. However, once it became apparent that the shotgun was empty, Davis began another advance on Mr. Kness and Officer Alleyn, continuing to fire the .38-caliber revolver he had taken from Officer Frago. (Refer again to Fig. 25.)

When he saw Davis retreat, Mr. Kness ditched the useless shotgun and resumed his work of trying to pull Officer Alleyn to cover behind the vehicle. However, when he saw Davis again step out from the right front of the Pontiac to initiate a new charge on his position, Mr. Kness found and picked up Officer Alleyn's blood-soaked revolver. He obtained a two-handed grip (a "combat grip" in his description), cocked the weapon, braced his elbows on the trunk of the patrol car, and fired a single round at Davis, who had already fired five of the six Super-Vel .38 Special rounds in Officer Frago's revolver at Officer Alleyn and Mr. Kness by this point. (Fig. 26)[32]

Mister Kness would later report that the impact of the fired shot spun Davis around, but there was no significant wound from the shot.[33] Davis was later found to have two copper-jacketed fragments imbedded in the upper middle portion of his chest, so it is presumed that the bullet struck the Pontiac first and broke into pieces before it struck Davis. The fragments, depleted of most

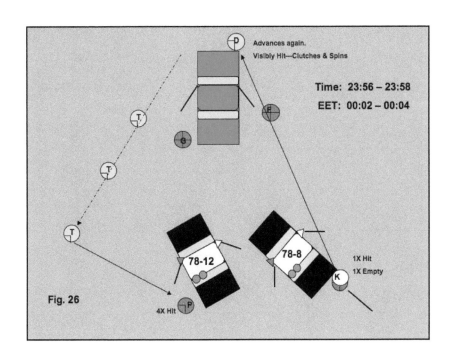

Advances again.
Visibly Hit—Clutches & Spins

Time: 23:56 – 23:58
EET: 00:02 – 00:04

78-12

78-8

1X Hit
1X Empty

4X Hit

Fig. 26

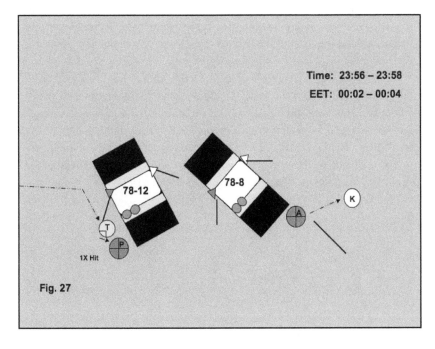

Time: 23:56 – 23:58
EET: 00:02 – 00:04

78-12

78-8

1X Hit

Fig. 27

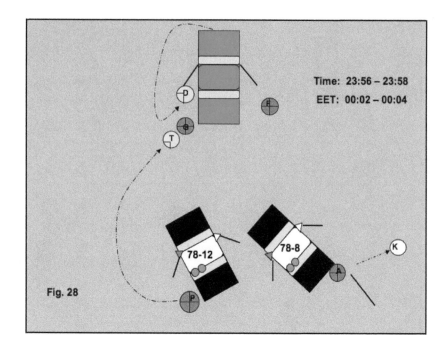

Time: 23:56 – 23:58
EET: 00:02 – 00:04

78-12

78-8

Fig. 28

of their energy and mass, failed to significantly wound him, but it was enough to cause Davis to break off the attack a second time.[34] Davis disengaged and headed around the front of the Pontiac to enter the vehicle via the driver's side door. (Fig. 28)

Mister Kness immediately attempted another shot at Davis after the first, but for the third time in the fight, Mr. Kness pulled the trigger on an empty chamber.[35] He heard additional shooting on his left, but also heard a more reassuring sound—the sirens of additional CHP cruisers approaching from the south along The Old Road.[36] Faced with the prospect of being outnumbered in the middle of an active gunfight with two empty weapons and hearing the sound of "the good guys" approaching, he fled to his right, towards the safety of the ditch. (Fig. 27) (Also, refer again to Fig. 28.)[37]

CHAPTER 6

The Flanking Movement

As the drama played out at the rear of Unit 78-8, Twining had been shooting at Officer Pence (and possibly Officer Alleyn) from a location near the front left of the Pontiac, using it for cover. It is probable that Twining fired two rounds from his .45-caliber 1911A1 pistol at Officer Pence from this position, while Officer Pence returned fire with his .357 Magnum revolver from behind the door of the patrol car. (Refer again to Figs. 20, 21 and 22.)

At some point, Twining left his position at the Pontiac and began a wide flanking movement to Officer Pence's left, in order to get a better angle of fire on the officer. One witness reported that he yelled out a warning from across the parking lot that Twining was on the move, but his message was undoubtedly drowned out by the gunfire and the phenomena of auditory exclusion that was certainly affecting the officers. (Refer again to Fig. 23.)

Officer Pence had fired all six rounds from his revolver and it was now empty. Instead of attempting to reload the revolver in the position from where he was taking fire, he elected to move to the left rear corner of the patrol car and complete his reload there, where the car could offer greater protection. (Refer again to Fig. 24.) On his way to the rear of the car, he opened the cylinder of his Colt Python and dumped the six spent .357 Magnum cases on the ground, roughly abeam the rear door on the driver's side of the vehicle.[38]

As Officer Pence's fire slackened off, Twining pressed the offensive, concealed by the shadows, and advanced along a line that would bring him wide and to the north of Unit 78-12, where he could flank and get a better shot at Officer Pence. The pattern of recovered spent cases suggests that Twining fired one round during the early portion of this movement. (Refer again to Figs. 24 and 25.)

As Officer Pence knelt behind the patrol car and began to reload his empty revolver from the right side of his dump pouch, Twining fired four rounds at him from the left flank, striking him twice in the legs (inducing a compound fracture of the left femur and a wound to his right lower leg), and twice again in the lower torso (striking Officer Pence in the left hip and left abdomen). Terribly wounded, Officer Pence struggled to complete his reload of the empty revolver and get back into the fight. (Refer again to Fig. 26.)[39]

Twining pressed his advantage by closing in on the left rear of the patrol car. Drops of Twining's blood would later mark the spot near the left rear door handle where he leaned over the fender of the car and extended his pistol at Officer Pence as he reloaded. Twining fired the pistol once from a few feet away, hitting Officer Pence in the back of the head and killing him instantly at the same moment Officer Pence was preparing to close the cylinder on his freshly loaded revolver.

As Twining fired the execution-style shot, the escaping citizen-hero, Gary Kness, heard Twining exclaim, "I've got you now, you dumb son of a bitch!" (Refer again to Fig. 27.)[40]

After killing Officer Pence, Twining retreated to the Pontiac, stopping on his way at Officer Gore's lifeless body to take his revolver. Davis had made his way around the front of the Pontiac and entered the driver's side of the vehicle to prepare for their escape. (Refer again to Fig. 28.)

CHAPTER 7

More Backup Arrives

At 23:56, when Officer Pence arrived on scene, took fire, and broadcast the 11-99 call, Unit 78-16R (Officers Ed Holmes and Richard Robinson), made another U-turn south of Thatcher Glass Company, directly in front of the oncoming Unit 78-19R (Officers Harry Ingold and Roger Palmer), and the pair of CHP cars responded northbound, Code 3. (Fig. 29)

Officer Ingold would later recall that, as they approached the Saugus Café and began the sweeping left turn onto Henry Mayo Drive, they were exceeding speeds of 130 miles per hour, taking every advantage of the legendary performance of the Dodge Polara Pursuit vehicle.[41] They likewise hit the "Edison Curve," just east of the interstate on Henry Mayo Drive, at 90 mph. To navigate that turn (which was marked at 35 miles per hour), the officers had to drive into the opposing lane, entering high and coming out low as they

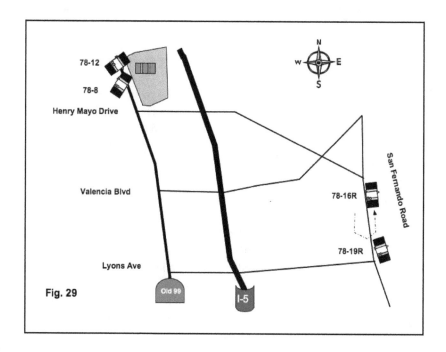

Fig. 29

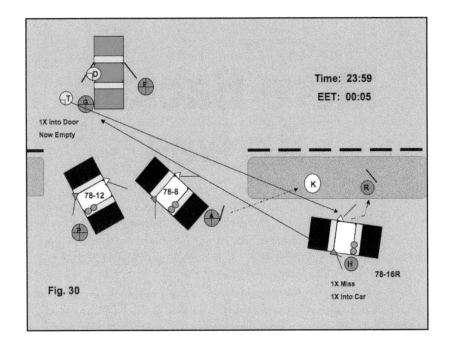

Fig. 30

Time: 23:59
EET: 00:05

1X Into Door
Now Empty

78-12

78-8

78-16R

1X Miss
1X Into Car

had been taught in the Emergency Vehicle Operations Course (EVOC) at the Academy.

Less than three full minutes from the start of their response, the units came to a screeching halt and joined the fight, just as Davis and Twining reached their Pontiac in flight, having killed Officers Alleyn and Pence moments earlier.

The total time since Officers Gore and Frago first stopped the Pontiac was only four and a half minutes.

The first unit on scene was 78-16R, who stopped about three car lengths short of Unit 78-8, facing north and slightly east on The Old Road. Gun smoke still hung in the air as Officer Robinson exited the passenger side of the patrol car with a Remington 870 shotgun in hand, narrowly missing being struck by the last .45-caliber bullet from Twining's handgun, which hit the door of the car after Twining took a shot at his fifth CHP Officer that night. (Fig. 30)[42]

Officer Robinson hadn't seen Twining yet, however. The first man that he confronted was the escaping Mr. Kness, who pointed the way to the fleeing felons with one hand, while the other still clutched Officer Alleyn's empty revolver.[43] Officer Robinson crossed the ditch and leveled his Remington 870 shotgun over the top of the fence at the escaping Pontiac, too late to fire a shot. (Fig. 31). It was at this time that he saw the bloody Officer Alleyn, moving slightly on the ground in his green "Ike" uniform jacket, and he realized one of his fellow officers had been hurt.

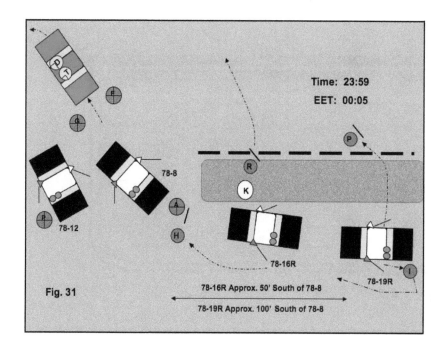

Fig. 31

Time: 23:59
EET: 00:05

78-8

78-12

78-16R

78-19R

78-16R Approx. 50' South of 78-8

78-19R Approx. 100' South of 78-8

Meanwhile, Officer Holmes had exited the driver's side of 78-16R and had seen Twining fire at them. Holmes fired one shot at Twining with his revolver as he was getting into the driver's side of the vehicle, then once more through the already shattered rear window of the escaping vehicle as it sped off northeast through the gas pump islands with Davis at the wheel and Twining in the rear seat. (Refer again to Figs. 30 and 31.)[44]

Concurrent with the sound of Officer Holmes' shots, Officer Robinson saw the Pontiac speeding away through the gas pump islands and noticed that the rear window was "disappearing," either due to Officer Holmes' gunfire, or because the movement of the vehicle dislodged the damaged glass that had been destroyed by Officer Alleyn's shotgun blasts. He crossed the rail fence and went around the backside of the gas station to begin his search for the fleeing vehicle, whose escape he knew would be cut short by the fence and riverbed at the rear of the lot.

Officer Holmes moved forward and saw three of the fallen officers. He checked them out, turned off the motors on the two patrol cars and called Newhall dispatch on the radio, advising that there were three officers down; two were "11-44" (deceased, coroner required), and a third was seriously wounded. He went back to render aid to the dying Officer Alleyn and soon noticed the fourth slain officer. (Refer again to Fig. 31.)[45]

Arriving on the bumper of 78-16R, Officers Ingold and Palmer also stopped their car northbound on The Old Road, about 100 feet south of the shooting. Officer Palmer exited the passenger side of his unit with a Reming-

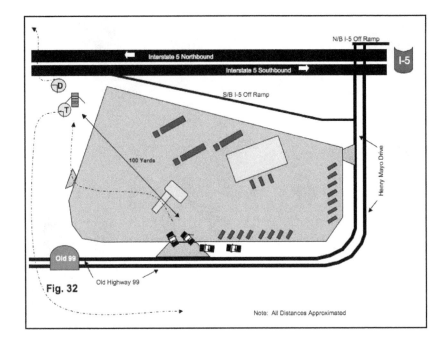

ton 870 shotgun, crossed the ditch and fence to his right, and entered the parking lot outside of J's Coffee Shop. He approached a red Chevrolet Camaro, where a witness pointed to the northeast and told him that two officers had been killed in that direction and the suspects were beyond the gas station. Another pair of men behind a black Cadillac told him that two officers had been killed by the people in the departing red Pontiac. (Refer again to Fig. 31.)[46]

After parking Unit 78-19R and exiting, Officer Ingold initially went to the rear of his unit for a few seconds, seeking cover from the gunfire he heard while he assessed the situation. He quickly moved forward to join the other officers, as the Pontiac was speeding off. (Refer again to Fig. 31.)[47]

Officers Robinson, Ingold and Palmer began a sweeping search of the parking lot for the offenders, moving in the direction of the escaping vehicle. They were joined by additional officers who'd arrived on the scene from the CHP's Castaic truck scales facility and other beats. There were a number of large commercial trucks behind the Standard Station that were searched before the officers saw the Pontiac, parked at the end of a dirt road about 150 yards to the northeast of the scene of the shooting. (Fig. 32)

When the Pontiac was spotted, CHP Officer Tolliver Miller cautiously approached the passenger side of the vehicle to clear it for suspects, with Officer Robinson close behind, shotgun at the ready. As they approached the vehicle, they heard Officer Holmes make his "11-44" call to dispatch via the external speakers on each CHP unit at the scene. The officers realized for the first time that their brothers had been killed by the men they were hunting; the men who could still be in the Pontiac they were now approaching. Crouching down below the level of the window, Officer Miller steadied himself with his left hand on the car and slowly raised up to peer through the passenger side window with his revolver in his right hand, its muzzle clearing the bottom edge of the window at the same time as his eyes.[48]

The car was empty.

In their haste to escape, the felons had chosen a dead-end road that ended with a heavy rail fence at the Santa Clara River. With nowhere else to go, they bailed out of the vehicle on foot, moving towards a dry wash to the north that ran roughly along an east/west axis. The pair split up when Twining returned to the vehicle to get additional weapons, grabbing the shotgun that had been taken from Officer Frago and the revolver that had been taken from Officer Gore. Davis followed the wash to the northeast across the freeway to San Francisquito Canyon, while Twining moved to the southwest, across The Old Road and an open field (now Magic Mountain amusement park), and then south along the foothills that paralleled the highway. (Refer again to Fig. 32.)[49]

As other officers split up into search teams and fanned out to the north from the Pontiac in search of the escaping felons, Officer Ingold returned to the scene of the shooting, took out a piece of yellow chalk that he used to mark accident scenes, and outlined the fallen bodies of his fellow officers, marking each with the name of the deceased.[50]

The deadliest law enforcement shooting of the modern era had come to a close.

It had taken four-and-a-half minutes. Learning the lessons from it would take decades.

ENDNOTES

1. I'll refer to this event as the "Newhall shooting," not the "Newhall incident" or "Newhall massacre" as others have. Calling this event an "incident" seems to downplay the significance of this historic lethal encounter, and terming it a "massacre" is equally misleading, since the term conjures images of unarmed or defenseless victims being killed by brutal, armed opponents. While the ruthless and violent nature of the offenders is not in question, the slain officers were certainly not unarmed nor defenseless during the encounter—they were merely overwhelmed by opponents who were better prepared to win the fight.

2. Simply do an Internet search using the keywords "witness memory" for a taste of the voluminous research and literature that exists on the subject.

3. Gibb, F. (2008, July 11) You can't trust a witness's memory, experts tell courts. The Sunday Times, <http://www.timesonline.co.uk/tol/news/uk/crime/article4312689.ece>.

4. The shooting occurred within approximately 100 to 150 feet of J's Coffee Shop, which had a large crowd of approximately 40 patrons and employees inside. Many of these people witnessed the shooting from the windows of the restaurant. Meanwhile, in the parking lot, motorists and truck drivers saw the events go down from different vantage points within 150 feet or less of the

action. Anderson, J., & Cassady, M. (1999) The Newhall Incident. Fresno, CA: Quill Driver Books. pp.151-153 and Lanning, Rick. Los Angeles Herald Examiner. Los Angeles, CA. 6 Apr 1970.

5. These media contacts were alternately described as reporters from the San Francisco Chronicle by the CHP, reporters from radio station KFWB by print media, and reporters from KNEW radio station by Anderson. Anderson, J., & Cassady, M. (1999) The Newhall Incident. Fresno, CA: Quill Driver Books. p.177.

6. The CHP's report said that "more than 40" shots had been fired during the incident, with 15 of them by the officers, but the research conducted for this account of the shooting indicates that the number is closer to 45, with 14 fired by officers and one fired by the responding civilian. Los Angeles County Sheriff's Department Homicide investigation files.

7. One of those weapons, a Ruger .44 Magnum Deerstalker carbine, was later recovered from their vehicle with a live round jammed in the chamber and four live rounds in the magazine. A second weapon, a Colt 1911A1 pistol, would later malfunction in the middle of the gunfight. Unfortunately, the remainder of the weapons worked as designed. Los Angeles County Sheriff's Department Homicide investigation files and Anderson, J., & Cassady, M. (1999) The Newhall Incident. Fresno, CA: Quill Driver Books. p.137.

8. Elements of the following narrative sourced from: Los Angeles County Sheriff's Department Homicide investigation files; interview with Gary Dean Kness; personal interviews with CHP Sergeant (ret.) Harry Ingold and CHP Officer (Retired) Richard Robinson; California Highway Patrol. (1970) Information Bulletin (July 1, 1970): Shooting Incident—Newhall Area. Sacramento, CA, and; Anderson, J., & Cassady, M. (1999) The Newhall Incident. Fresno, CA: Quill Driver Books. p.131-141, and; California Highway Patrol. (1975) Newhall: 1970 [Film]. Sacramento, CA, courtesy of Santa Clarita Valley Historical Society and SCVTV, < http://www.scvtv.com/html/ newhall1970-chp1975btv.html> and; Santa Clarita Valley Historical Society. (2010) The Newhall Incident: A Law Enforcement Tragedy [Film]. Santa Clarita, CA, courtesy of Santa Clarita Valley Historical Society and SCVTV, <http://www.scvtv.com/html/scvhs040510btv.html>. Individual source references will only be provided by exception for the remainder of the narrative.

9. In the CHP's report of the shooting, they went to lengths to explain that brandishing calls were routine in this rural area and the reported crime was a misdemeanor, not a felony, which may have affected the response and mindset of the officers. California Highway Patrol. (1970) Information Bulletin (July 1, 1970): Shooting Incident—Newhall Area. Sacramento, CA.

10. Alternate versions of Frago's approach exist. In the CHP Information Bulletin of 1 Jul '70, the CHP noted simply that Frago approached the passenger side of the vehicle in a "port arms" position and made no mention of him reaching for the door handle, but several witnesses (among them Joseph Tancredi) specifically recalled seeing Officer Frago extend his left hand to open the door while his right held the shotgun with muzzle up in the air in the "hip rest" carry position taught to CHP cadets at the Academy. In the 1975 training film produced by the CHP (with the full benefit of access to the detailed investigation report from Los Angeles County Sheriff's Office Homicide investigators, the CHP's own investigation report, the official record of the October 1970 trial of Bobby Davis, and the interviews and testimony of the involved parties and witnesses), Frago is specifically described as having reached to operate the handle on the door of the Pontiac with his left hand, so that is the accepted version for this narrative. Los Angeles County Sheriff's Department Homicide investigation files, California Highway Patrol. (1970) Information Bulletin (July 1, 1970): Shooting Incident—Newhall Area. Sacramento, CA, and California Highway Patrol. (1975) Newhall: 1970 [Film]. Sacramento, CA, courtesy of Santa Clarita Valley Historical Society and SCVTV, <http://www.scvtv.com/html/newhall1970-chp1975btv.html>.

11. Ironically, this model was known as the "Highway Patrolman," and in a previous life it had been a duty weapon for the Texas Department of Public Safety (DPS) The weapon had been sold as surplus by the DPS and purchased as one of a group of 50 weapons by Glenn Slade's Texas Gun Clinic, a wholesaler in Houston. Salesman Henry Fontenot reported that he had sanded the DPS serial numbers off the guns in compliance with a DPS requirement of sale. Davis had purchased the firearm on March 6, 1970, using an alias. Ten days later, he bought the Smith & Wesson Model 38 Bodyguard Airweight revolver that he used to threaten the Tidwell's from the

same dealer. Los Angeles County Sheriff's Department Homicide investigation files.

12. It has been reported from reliable sources close to the investigation that Twining admitted to watching Officer Frago in the side and rear view mirrors as he exited the patrol car. During his phone conversation with Los Angeles County Sheriff's Department investigators from the Hoag house, Twining supposedly stated he unlatched his door prior to Officer Frago's advance, but did not push it open, in a preparatory move for the ambush he was planning. When Twining saw Officer Frago near the car and shift his shotgun from "port arms" to what the CHP training manuals described as a "hip rest" position, he knew he could attack Officer Frago before the officer could get the gun into action. As Officer Frago reached for the door, Twining threw it open and ambushed the unsuspecting officer. Personal interview with a confidential source, July 2011.

13. Davis' Model 38 revolver would be recovered from the rear seat of the Pontiac after the shooting was over, with five spent cases in the cylinder.
Twining's Model 28 revolver would be recovered later that morning at another crime scene along the escape path of suspect Davis, in San Francisquito Canyon. When the weapon was recovered by Los Angeles Sheriff's Deputy Thomas L. Fryer, it had a single spent case in the weapon, which was not resting under the hammer. No other cartridges or cases were in the weapon. Because it was known that a single round had been fired at that second crime scene, LASD investigators initially assumed that it had been fired from this weapon. If this were true, then it would indicate that Twining fired all but this one cartridge in the Standard Station parking lot, instead of emptying the revolver as indicated in the narrative, because the suspect Davis did not have spare ammunition on his person to reload the gun when he fled the original crime scene with it. However, it was later determined that Davis had another gun in his possession at the San Francisquito Canyon crime scene (Officer Frago's Colt Officer's Model Match revolver), and this gun was also found empty with the exception of a single spent case, making it possible that this was the gun that fired the shot instead. The CHP felt that this was the gun used by Davis against Schwartz.
In the wake of inconclusive evidence to prove which gun fired the shot during the escape, it is suggested that it is much more likely the round was fired from Officer Frago's Colt. It is hard to imagine that Twining would have stopped shooting at the arriving Unit 78-12 prior to running his Model 28 dry, because he did not have another weapon on his person at this stage of the gunfight. It is much more likely that Twining fired all six shots from this revolver at the initial scene, then ditched the weapon in the car when it proved to be empty, whereupon it was later taken away from the scene by Davis. Davis likely dumped the spent brass (save one, perhaps because he mistakenly thought it was a live cartridge in the darkness or thought it could be used to bluff an opponent) sometime during his escape, because the five spent cases were never recovered at the scene of the shooting. Los Angeles County Sheriff's Department Homicide investigation files.

14. This is the phraseology attributed to Officer Pence in the 1975 CHP training film, but the 1 Jul '70 CHP Information Bulletin quotes Officer Pence as saying a slightly altered form: "11-99, shots fired, at J's Standard." The official CHP radio log, maintained by Dispatcher Jo Ann Tidley, records the call as, "2356: 78-12, 11-99 Standard Station J's." Los Angeles County Sheriff's Department Homicide investigation files, California Highway Patrol. (1970) Information Bulletin (July 1, 1970): Shooting Incident—Newhall Area. Sacramento, CA, and California Highway Patrol. (1975) Newhall: 1970 [Film]. Sacramento, CA, courtesy of Santa Clarita Valley Historical Society and SCVTV, <http://www.scvtv.com/html/newhall1970-chp1975btv.html>.

15. Davis' shotgun was a Western Field 550AD, a re-branded Mossberg 500 12-gauge shotgun with deluxe furniture manufactured for the Montgomery Wards department store chain. This shotgun had a six-round capacity, with one round in the chamber and five rounds in the magazine. Six spent blue Remington-Peters shotgun shells were found at the scene of the shooting, and the Los Angeles County Sheriff's Evidence Lab technicians verified that they had been fired from this weapon. Los Angeles County Sheriff's Department Homicide investigation files.

16. A single spent shotgun shell, Sheriff's Crime Lab evidence number JHC #24, was found lodged in the front grille of the Pontiac after the shooting. None of the remaining five shotgun shells that were fired from this weapon were found at the front of the Pontiac, so it appears that Davis only fired a single round with the Western Field 550AD from this position.

17. The sequence of events for Twining's malfunction and his position during this stage of the fight is driven by the physical evidence at the scene. The Remington-Rand 1911A1 pistol was found on the floorboard behind the driver's seat with six live rounds in the magazine and a seventh live round jammed in the chamber. An eighth live round was recovered from the ground on the driver's side of the Pontiac (evidence placard "JHC #8" for Sheriff's Crime Lab employee Jack H. Clark), the only live .45 ACP round found in the vicinity. An accounting of the evidence indicates that eight other spent .45 ACP cases were found at the scene, all of which were determined to be fired in a second 1911A1 pistol of Colt manufacture that was recovered as evidence. No other .45 ACP spent cases were found at the scene. Therefore, it is likely that the Remington-Rand 1911A1 was not fired at the scene and the JHC #8 live round that was booked into evidence was probably the eighth cartridge that had originally been loaded into the pistol. This is supported by Twining's testimony as well. During his phone conversation with Los Angeles County Sheriff's Detective (Sgt.) John M. Brady, Twining was asked if one of the .45 ACP pistols had jammed on him. Twining responded, "Yeah, I may have got one shot, then it jammed and I got the other." When asked if he then emptied the second 1911A1 pistol, Twining answered, "Yeah." Los Angeles County Sheriff's Department Homicide investigation files.

18. The CHP's shotguns were carried in "cruiser ready" condition, meaning they had a full magazine of four Winchester Super X 00 Buckshot shells and an empty chamber. Officer Alleyn had to rack the slide of the shotgun initially to prepare it for firing.

19. Throughout the years, critics have argued the case that the ejected round was an indicator that Officer Alleyn was not competent with the weapon and his training was deficient, but this does not seem like a reasonable conclusion. Forty plus years of experience since the event has shown that officers in gunfights make decisions and take actions that they normally wouldn't under less stressful conditions, when their minds are not under the effect of powerful, naturally occurring chemicals like adrenalin, which flood the body during periods of peak stress.
Given the extreme stress that Officer Alleyn was under during the initial moments of the ambush, it's likely that his system was being flooded with stress hormones that effected normal cognitive processes like memory. It's probable that Officer Alleyn honestly didn't remember if he had already charged the weapon, so he took the steps required to ensure it was loaded, ejecting the live shell in the process. Because early versions of the Remington 870 shotgun were sometimes prone to double feeding (where an additional round is inadvertently released from the magazine tube at the wrong time in the sequence), it is possible that the live round was intentionally ejected as part of a malfunction clearance, but it's more likely that the round was simply accidentally ejected as a byproduct of survival stress.
The live round, found near Officer Alleyn's position at the door of Unit 78-8, was temporarily secured with the shotgun by CHP officers who found it on scene, and was later delivered to Los Angeles County Sheriff's Department Crime Lab Sergeant James Warner by CHP Sergeant Cable, along with the CHP shotgun (CHP #39), Officer Pence and Alleyn's revolvers, and the live cartridges and spent cases from those revolvers. Los Angeles County Sheriff's Department Homicide investigation files.

20. The Pontiac's trunk lid bore the scars of Alleyn's two shotgun blasts, which ran from the right rear corner of the vehicle to the left rear corner of the rear window. The two tracks were 15 inches apart, and the right track showed five paint chip spots and eight skid marks, while the left track showed four paint chip spots and seven skid marks. Additional pellet strikes were seen on the roof pillar, between the left side rear glass and the rear window. The blasts tore out the rear window, leaving only a small rim of shattered, hanging glass along the top edge and left vertical edge of the window. Los Angeles County Sheriff's Department Homicide investigation files.
Twining made the remarks to reporters and Sheriff's Department personnel during the phone calls that took place later, after the shooting had evolved into a hostage crisis. Blood from his wound would allow investigators to recreate his movements during the fight later on.

21. While it was not reported by the CHP in either its 1 Jul '70 Information Bulletin or in its 1975 training film, it appears that Officer Alleyn may have nicked Davis with one of the pellets and came very close to stopping the fight. The lead homicide investigator, former Los Angeles County Sheriff's Office (LASO) Homicide Detective (Sgt.) John Brady, reported that:
"The whole thing almost ended right there. Officer Alleyn hit both Davis and Twining with the shotgun blasts. A pellet from Alleyn's shotgun streaked across the top of Twining's scalp, ripping

an angry red gash. If it had been just a little lower, it could have opened the top of his skull, or at least knocked him down. Davis was turned sideways to Alleyn. A shotgun pellet tore right over the bridge of his nose. If he had been looking directly back at the officer, the pellet would have hit him right between the eyes."

The LASO booking pictures of Davis clearly show the wound to his nose. Thus, it was only by the slimmest of margins that Officer Alleyn's shots were unsuccessful. It's an appealing exercise to ponder what might have happened if he hadn't ejected the unfired round prior to shooting and had been able to fire it at Twining after the rear window was ballistically compromised by the previous shots. Kolman, J., Capt.. (2009) Rulers of the Night, Volume I: 1958-1988. Santa Ana, CA: Graphic Publishers, pp. 132-133.

22. The number of spent .45 ACP cases at the scene indicates Twining had the second (Colt) 1911A1 pistol loaded similarly to the first; that is, with a fully loaded magazine of seven rounds and an eighth in the chamber. Based on the pattern of spent cases recovered at the scene, Twining fired three shots from a position somewhere between the driver's side door of the Pontiac and the left front fender of the Pontiac with the Colt 1911A1 pistol (Los Angeles Sheriff's Department evidence tags JHC #4,5,6) Some witness accounts (Ball, Barth) place Twining back at the front of the Pontiac during this phase of the gunfight, but other witness accounts (Tancredi) contradict that. The pattern of spent cases suggests that he may have fired from a position that was closer to the side of the car than the front, but blood evidence indicates that Twining may actually have been closer to the front of the car. Of note, in the CHP's account of the shooting, Twining fires on Officer Pence from the front left corner of the Pontiac, using it for cover during this phase of the shootout.

Witness accounts indicate it is possible that Twining engaged both Officer Pence and Officer Alleyn with these pistol shots. A spent .45-caliber bullet was found by investigators on the ground between Unit 78-12 and Unit 78-8, on the right side of 78-12 (Sheriff's Evidence Tag #23). California Highway Patrol. (1975) Newhall: 1970 [Film] and Los Angeles County Sheriff's Department Homicide investigation files.

23. Crime scene photos show a pair of bullet strikes on the left side of the Pontiac that were likely fired by Officer Pence, due to the angle of impact. One strike is above the gas door at the junction of the rear deck lid and the roof pillar, and another is forward, underneath the left rear side window. The left rear side window itself was also hit near the top center, shattering that window, perhaps by Officer Pence or perhaps by one of Officer Alleyn's shotgun pellets. It's likely the pair of rounds that struck the body of the car were fired at Twining as he emerged from the driver's side and began to engage Officer Pence. There were additional bullet strikes in the dash of the Pontiac that could also have been caused by Officer Pence, Officer Alleyn, or Officer Holmes. The left rear tire of the Pontiac was also flattened when the car was recovered, and it's possible that Officer Pence or Officer Holmes could have struck it with gunfire. Los Angeles County Sheriff's Department Homicide investigation files, California Highway Patrol. (1975) Newhall: 1970 [Film]. Sacramento, CA, courtesy of Santa Clarita Valley Historical Society and SCVTV, <http://www.scvtv.com/html/newhall1970-chp1975btv.html>.

24. The white spotlight on Unit 78-8 was raised and had been hit three times during the fight, presumably by shotgun pellets fired from Davis' gun. This spotlight would have been directly in front of Officer Alleyn's face as he kneeled and fired the Remington 870 shotgun in the crotch between the vehicle and the frame of the open door. It is possible that Officer Alleyn was injured by debris from the spotlight after it was struck, or by an actual pellet from Davis' shotgun, before he left his position at the door.

25. A bullet struck the dashboard of the Pontiac forward of the steering wheel from the rear at some point during the gunfight. The bullet skidded for seven inches along the dash and struck the windshield from the inside, approximately 16.5 inches to the right of the left side moulding, leaving a piece of the bullet jacket in the dash (Los Angeles Sheriff's Department evidence tag #JW3, collected by Sergeant James Warner). Another bullet struck the dash, above the glovebox on the passenger side of the Pontiac. Bullet fragments from this strike were recovered under the hood of the vehicle, about 15 inches towards the center of the vehicle from the right fender (Los Angeles Sheriff's Department evidence tag #JW2). It's unknown if these two bullets were fired by Officer Alleyn, Pence or Holmes. Los Angeles County Sheriff's Department Homicide investigation files.

26. Multiple witnesses reported seeing Davis shoot at Pence with the shotgun, and a pattern of three ejected shotshells (Los Angeles Sheriff's Department evidence tags JHC #10,12,13) suggests that one round could have been fired during Davis' advance on the patrol cars (the other two were known to be fired at Officer Alleyn). Unit 78-12 was struck on the right side by multiple projectiles at some point during the fight, but it is unknown if these strikes were from the revolver gunfire of Davis and Twining as 78-12 arrived on scene, or the single shotgun blast fired by Davis from the front of the Pontiac, which streaked across the hood of the CHP car. It's possible that none of the earlier shots caused the damage and that it was the result of Davis firing at Pence while he advanced. The right rear window of 78-12 was completely shot out with no glass hanging, and the center of the right passenger window was also shot out, but a rim of shattered glass hung around the edges of the window. There was a hit between the two windows on the vertical portion of the pillar, as well as a hit on the right front fender, about 12:30 to 1:00 position from the tire. There was also a hit on the bottom edge of the door above the running board, at about 5:30 position from the CHP star on the door. The left rear tire was also flat, perhaps due to Twining's gunfire as he shot at Officer Pence from the left flank, or because a projectile struck the ground and skipped underneath the car at some point during the fight.

27. As previously discussed in Endnote 24, Officer Alleyn may have been wounded at this point, with blood running into his eyes and disrupting his vision and his ability to place accurate fire on Davis.

28. The round fired by Officer Alleyn struck the rear window of Unit 78-8 about 2.75 inches above the moulding and 18.75 inches to the right of the left moulding. The bullet was later recovered from the rear of the driver's seat, about three inches below the top edge of the seat and in line with the hole in the window. Los Angeles County Sheriff's Department Homicide investigation files.

29. There are multiple contradictions in witness testimony during this phase of the battle. Some witnesses claimed that the CHP shotgun had been retrieved earlier in the fight, and there is confusion about whether Davis or Twining was the person who picked it up. However, the preponderance of evidence suggests that the shotgun had not been retrieved prior to this point and that Davis was the one to recover it.
A witness claimed that Davis struggled with the CHP shotgun and inadvertently fired it while trying to work the gun. After the accidental discharge, the shotgun was placed in the car, according to the witness. Importantly, this testimony matches the CHP's version of the event, as well.
The physical evidence tends to discredit this narrative, however. An accounting of the ammunition from this shotgun indicates that one spent CHP shotgun shell and three live CHP shotgun rounds were found with the weapon at the Hoag house, where Twining had taken hostages later in the day during his escape attempt. The spent shell was found in the hallway of the Hoag house next to Twining's dead body, along with two other spent shells supplied from Twining's own stock. (Fortunately, the brand and hull color of the CHP's shotgun ammunition differed from the ammunition that the felons brought to the fight, making it easy to identify the source—the CHP issued Western Super-X ammunition with red hulls, while Davis and Twining had brought Remington-Peters ammunition with blue hulls to the fight.) Because Twining had engaged Los Angeles County Sheriff's deputies with multiple shots from the shotgun in that location during two raids on the house, it is believed that the CHP shotshell was fired in the hallway of the Hoag house and not at the Standard Station location. Furthermore, it is inconceivable that the weapons-savvy Twining would have waited to eject the spent CHP shotshell and make the gun ready with a live round until starting the gun battle with Los Angeles County Sheriff's deputies in the hallway of the Hoag household. He most certainly would have ensured the gun had a loaded chamber at some time during his three-mile flight from the scene, particularly before he used the gun to take the Hoag family hostage. This makes the accidental discharge theory even less plausible and tends to confirm the accounts of witnesses who did not see the accidental shotgun discharge occur.
There is an additional matter that Davis should not have been confused by the operation of the CHP shotgun, which was virtually identical to his own. The location of the button that releases the fore-end and the safety button are different on the Remington 870 and Western Field 550 designs, but it's unlikely this would have confused the weapons-savvy Davis enough to cause an accidental discharge.
Interestingly, other witnesses claim that Davis fired Officer Frago's shotgun or revolver at the

fallen officer, at contact range, after he had taken them away from him. However, the coroner who performed the post-mortem examination on Officer Frago found no evidence of additional wounds beyond the two gunshot wounds from Twining's revolver. Additionally, there was no physical evidence that indicated such a shot was taken (spent cases, impact marks on the asphalt, etc.). It is much more likely that these witnesses saw the muzzle blast from Twining's handgun, which was simultaneously being fired beyond Davis on the opposite side of the Pontiac, and mistook it for fire from Davis. Los Angeles County Sheriff's Department Homicide investigation files.

30. Interview with Mr. Kness and Officer (Retired) Richard Robinson, who was present when Mr. Kness made his initial statement to Los Angeles County Sheriff's Department investigators after the shooting. Santa Clarita Valley Historical Society. (2010) The Newhall Incident: A Law Enforcement Tragedy [Film]. Santa Clarita, CA, courtesy of Santa Clarita Valley Historical Society and SCVTV, <http://www.scvtv.com/html/scvhs040510btv.html> and personal interview with Richard Robinson.

31. In Mr. Kness' own words, Officer Alleyn "was dead weight to me" when he attempted to drag him to cover and he couldn't move him. Because Davis was still firing at them, Mr. Kness tried to shoot him with the shotgun, but when it clicked on an empty chamber he "got a sick feeling." When the shotgun clicked on an empty chamber the second time, he "really got a sick feeling." Interview with Mr. Kness. Santa Clarita Valley Historical Society. (2010) The Newhall Incident: A Law Enforcement Tragedy [Film]. Santa Clarita, CA, courtesy of Santa Clarita Valley Historical Society and SCVTV, <http://www.scvtv.com/html/scvhs040510btv.html>.

32. Mister Kness reported that, when he first picked up the revolver and attempted to cock it, his thumb had a hard time finding the hammer spur. He then grabbed the revolver by the barrel with his left hand, placed his right hand on the grip, and successfully thumb-cocked the revolver. He then mated his left hand to the right in a "two-hand combat position" to fire the shot over the trunk with his elbows resting on the vehicle. Mister Kness later told investigators that he was a little surprised the weapon fired, because after having two dry fires on the shotgun earlier, he didn't know if the revolver would dry fire, too. Interview with Mr. Kness. Santa Clarita Valley Historical Society. (2010) The Newhall Incident: A Law Enforcement Tragedy [Film]. Santa Clarita, CA, courtesy of Santa Clarita Valley Historical Society and SCVTV, <http://www.scvtv.com/html/scvhs040510btv.html> and Los Angeles County Sheriff's Department Homicide investigation files.

33. Several witnesses would recount that Davis clutched his chest or armpit area and spun away like he had been hit, and Mr. Kness said that, "I knew I had him, because he spun around." Davis was later found to have a 1" long wound under the armpit at the hospital, but it's not clear if this wound came from Mr. Kness' shot or from one of Mr. Schwartz's shots later.
The "wing window" trim on the passenger's side door of the Pontiac was hit by a bullet at some point during the fight, and bullet core and jacket pieces were later recovered from the vehicle in this location (Los Angeles Sheriff's Department evidence tag #JW1). A hit in this area would have been in line with Mr. Kness' position at the right rear of Unit 78-8 and Davis' position at the front bumper of the Pontiac, and it is possible this is where Mr. Kness' bullet struck, sending fragments into Davis. Los Angeles County Sheriff's Department Homicide investigation files.

34. There has been some limited discussion as to whether or not Mr. Kness wounded Davis with his revolver shot, or if the wounds were sustained during Davis' later encounter with another civilian after he fled the scene. The evidence indicates that the wounds Davis received in the later fight were to his neck and collarbone area. Also, since Mr. Kness was shooting at Davis from a very close distance and saw him spin away as the shot was fired, and since Davis disengaged at this point of the fight, it is most likely that Mr. Kness did indeed hit Davis with a fragment of a bullet, as indicated in the narrative. California Highway Patrol. (1975) Newhall: 1970 [Film]. Sacramento, CA, courtesy of Santa Clarita Valley Historical Society and SCVTV, <http://www.scvtv.com/html/newhall1970-chp1975btv.html> and Anderson, J., & Cassady, M. (1999) The Newhall Incident. Fresno, CA: Quill Driver Books. p.157-158, and Interview with Mr. Kness. Santa Clarita Valley Historical Society. (2010) The Newhall Incident: A Law Enforcement Tragedy [Film]. Santa Clarita, CA, courtesy of Santa Clarita Valley Historical Society and SCVTV, <http://www. scvtv.com/html/scvhs040510btv.html>.

35. Although he could not have known it at the time, it appears that Officer Alleyn's gun was not

empty and that Mr. Kness actually had one additional live round left in the cylinder.

When the fight was over, Officer Alleyn's Model 19-2 revolver was recovered by CHP Officer Jack Burniston and placed in CHP Sergeant P.M. Connell's car, along with Officer Pence's loaded revolver and Officer Alleyn's empty shotgun. One live round of .357 Magnum ammunition was recovered with Officer Alleyn's gun, in addition to five spent cases.

It's conceivable that Officer Alleyn tried to cock or fire the revolver earlier in the fight, but did not work the hammer or trigger all the way, perhaps because the bloody revolver was so slippery. This short stroke could have advanced the cylinder far enough to line up the next round, but since the hammer was not brought fully back (in either single- or double-action), or the trigger was released forward before the sear tripped, the round under the hammer was not fired. A subsequent trigger stroke or manual cocking of the hammer would have advanced the cylinder again, skipping this live round.

In such a sequence, rounds numbers one through three were fired by Officer Alleyn, round number four was somehow skipped, round number five was fired into the rear window of 78-8, and round number 6 was fired by Mr. Kness at Davis.

It's plausible that such an action occurred after Officer Alleyn was shot by Davis with the shotgun, at the rear of Unit 78-8. The horrible wounds suffered by Officer Alleyn could have caused him to short stroke or release the trigger as he clung to life and desperately tried to continue fighting. The live round would have been skipped immediately before Officer Alleyn was struck a second time by Davis' buckshot and before he triggered his final round into the rear window of Unit 78-8.

Alternatively, the round may have been skipped by Mr. Kness himself, who reported difficulty with cocking the gun properly after he picked it up from the ground. After reacquiring a better grip, Mr. Kness was able to cock the revolver and fire it once at Davis, before a spent case found its way under the hammer for the subsequent attempt.

Again, Mr. Kness could not have known there was another live round in the gun. After two unsuccessful attempts to shoot the empty shotgun, it's entirely reasonable that he assumed the revolver was also completely empty when it clicked dry on the second attempt. It's simply a shame that fate and the friction of war intervened to deprive him of a second chance to fire at Davis. Los Angeles County Sheriff's Department Homicide investigation files.

36. Unit 78-16R (Officers Holmes and Robinson) in the lead with Unit 78-19R (Officers Ingold and Palmer) behind.

37. When he attempted to fire the revolver a second time and the hammer fell on an empty chamber, Mr. Kness decided to leave the scene. Simultaneously, he heard a boom "like a 105mm howitzer going off, but it was only a .45." The boom was the 1911A1 pistol being fired by Twining at Officer Pence. Interview with Mr. Kness. Santa Clarita Valley Historical Society. (2010) The Newhall Incident: A Law Enforcement Tragedy [Film]. Santa Clarita, CA, courtesy of Santa Clarita Valley Historical Society and SCVTV, <http://www.scvtv.com/html/scvhs040510btv.html>.

38. Officer Pence's reload has been the subject of much discussion and debate. It has been widely reported that Officer Pence reflexively pocketed his spent brass as he had been conditioned to do in range training at the CHP Academy. It has been reported that the spent brass was found in his pants pocket during the post-mortem examination, and this supposed "fact" has been used to support a multitude of theories about the quality of CHP training and Officer Pence's presence of mind during the fight.

It is categorically false that Officer Pence pocketed the spent .357 Magnum brass during the gunfight. His pile of spent .357 brass, marked by Los Angeles Sheriff's Department evidence tag JHC #18, was found on the ground abeam the rear door on the driver's side of the vehicle, right where Officer Pence was reloading his weapon before he was murdered. Evidence photos show the brass in that location, and the witness testimony of retired CHP Sergeant (then, Officer) Harry Ingold, who checked on Officer Pence and marked the spot he had fallen in the immediate moments after the fight, supports it. Sergeant Ingold specifically recalls seeing the spent brass on the ground in that location; the same location reported by Los Angeles Sheriff's Department Criminalist Jack H. Clark when he tagged it "found by side of vehicle #2" and had it photographed as evidence item #18 (JHC #18), hours later.

This brass was also mentioned in the report of the lead investigator, Los Angeles County Sheriff's Department Homicide Sergeant John Brady, who said that when they arrived at 00:50 hours (less than an hour after the shooting ended), and began their inspection of the crime scene, he noted "several expended shell cases, possibly .38 or .357" on the ground.

It's critical to note that the only spent revolver brass found loose on the ground at the crime scene was the brass near Officer Pence's location.

The spent .38 Special revolver brass in Davis' Model 38 revolver was still in the revolver, which was left in the rear seat of the Pontiac. The spent .357 Magnum revolver brass in Twining's Model 28 revolver was dumped during the flight from the crime scene and never recovered, except for the one case that remained in the gun as it was found at the scene of the Schwartz robbery by Los Angeles County Sheriff's Deputy Thomas L. Fryer. The spent .38 Special revolver brass in Officer Frago's Officer's Model Match revolver was also dumped during the flight from the crime scene and never recovered, except for one case that was found in the gun when it was located in the camper of Schwartz's vehicle and booked into evidence by Los Angeles County Sheriff's Deputy Don G. Tomlinson. The spent .357 Magnum revolver brass (and single live round) in Officer Alleyn's Model 19 revolver was recovered with his gun and secured at the scene by CHP Officer Jack Burniston, who put them on the floorboard of CHP Sergeant Paul Connell's vehicle. These cases were later booked into evidence, when they were delivered by CHP Sergeant Cable to the LASO Crime lab. The single round of spent .357 Magnum brass fired in Officer Gore's Colt Python revolver was recovered from the floor of the Hoag residence by Los Angeles County Sheriff's Detective Sergeant John Brady. The remaining handgun cartridge cases at the scene came from Twining's .45 ACP pistols.

The brass marked JHC #18 was later examined by the Los Angeles County Sheriff's Department Crime Lab, where Sgt. James Warner determined that the brass had been fired in Officer Pence's Colt Python revolver.

There is no mention of the spent brass in the detailed post-mortem report completed by Los Angeles County Coroner Gaston Herrera, M.D.

In summary, the only spent revolver brass that was found loose on the ground at the crime scene was the brass marked JHC #18 by Sheriff's investigators. This JHC #18 brass was found in the location where Officer Pence was completing his reload when he was murdered. It was seen there by an officer who was the first on the scene and remembers seeing it in the immediate moments after the fight. It was also seen by the lead investigator for the homicide (who was from another agency), within 50 minutes of the end of the gunfight. It is not possible that this brass came from another weapon at the crime scene, as scientific examination verified that this brass was fired in Officer Pence's revolver, and all other revolver brass at the scene was accounted for. There is no reason to believe that the brass was recovered at the Coroner's Office in Officer Pence's pocket during post-mortem examinations, then transported back to the scene of the crime to be fraudulently deposited there, as some have speculated. The timeline doesn't support such a theory, because the bodies had not been transported to the coroner yet when Sgt. Brady first arrived on scene and saw the brass on the ground. Additionally, to coordinate this kind of conspiracy, a large number of people from different agencies would have to have been compelled to lie about a very minor detail of the case, at a time when the investigation was just beginning and they were struggling to understand the very basics of what had occurred during this monumental event. It hardly seems likely that this minor detail of evidence would have been perceived as critical enough to warrant a conspiracy to lie this early in the case. Officer Pence did not pocket his spent brass.

In the wake of Newhall, the CHP made an intensive study of training practices and made many corrections to ensure that bad habits that would jeopardize officer safety on the street were not taught during training. One of these corrections was a requirement to eject brass onto the ground during training and clean it up later, rather than eject it neatly into the hand and drop it into a can or bucket, as had been the practice before. It is believed that instructors and cadets of the era may have mistakenly believed that this change in policy was due to a specific error made by Officer Pence during the fight. The myth began, and it was innocently perpetuated throughout generations of officers in the CHP and allied agencies.

Anderson states that the rumor was propagated by law enforcement trade publications of the time, which really sealed the "fact" into the collective memory of the law enforcement profession. This is certainly the case with contemporary gun and law enforcement magazines, which have continued to treat this myth as fact, some 40-plus years later.

This does not detract from the valuable training lesson embedded in the myth. It is important that negative habits that can jeopardize safety are not encouraged during training. These "training scars" must be avoided, and the "pocketed brass" story is an effective and relevant metaphor to prove this lesson. There have indeed been other documented cases of this phenomenon occurring (pocketing spent brass), but it did not occur at Newhall.

Personal interview with CHP Sgt. (ret.) Harry Ingold (2011), and Anderson, J., & Cassady, M. (1999) The Newhall Incident. Fresno, CA: Quill Driver Books. p.146 and Los Angeles County

Sheriff's Department Homicide investigation files.

39. CHP Officer Harry Ingold recalls that, after the fight was over, Officer Pence was found slumped forward with his knees and face on the deck, the brim of his uniform hat trapped between the ground and his forehead. His hands were trapped under his body near the waist and not in sight. When Officer Pence's torso was raised up, his revolver was found in his hands with the cylinder open and six rounds of live .357 Magnum ammunition in the cylinder, indicating that he had almost completed his reload before he was executed by Twining.
Anderson describes that Officer Pence had fumbled two of the six rounds during the reload and was able to recover one of them from the ground and load it in the revolver before he closed the cylinder, but it's not clear how the number of fumbled cartridges was known, and other elements (number of loaded cartridges, cylinder closed, etc.) conflict with Officer Ingold's clear recollection of an open cylinder with six cartridges. Massad Ayoob's narrative, based on the CHP's version, confirms the notion that Officer Pence was able to reload all six cartridges before he was executed.
Disturbingly, it appears Officer Pence wasted precious moments immediately before he was executed by Twining. Had he accepted a partial load of the gun and returned quickly to the fight, instead of fully loading the revolver, he might have been able to close the cylinder on his revolver and fire upon Twining before Twining could deliver the final killing shot. Of course, it must be realized that Officer Pence was horribly wounded at this point and his body and mind were under tremendous stress, both of which would make this kind of detached, analytical thinking exceptionally difficult, if not impossible. Anderson, J., & Cassady, M. (1999) The Newhall Incident. Fresno, CA: Quill Driver Books. p.146, and Ayoob, M. (1995) The Ayoob Files: The Book. Concord, NH: Police Bookshelf, p.122, and California Highway Patrol. (1975) Newhall: 1970 [Film], and personal interview with CHP Sergeant (ret.) Harry Ingold (2011)

40. Mister Kness heard Twining make the comment and saw the execution shot immediately after his unsuccessful attempt to fire a second shot at Davis with Officer Alleyn's revolver. Hearing the "105mm Howitzer" boom of Twining's pistol and seeing Officer Pence go down was the final straw that convinced him he needed to escape. Interview with Mr. Kness. Santa Clarita Valley Historical Society. (2010) The Newhall Incident: A Law Enforcement Tragedy [Film]. Santa Clarita, CA, courtesy of Santa Clarita Valley Historical Society and SCVTV, <http://www.scvtv. com/html/scvhs040510btv.html>.

41. Officer Ingold remembered the Polara's speedometer was indexed up to 130 miles per hour and the red needle of the speedometer was in the black, past this last unit of measure. The 1969 Polara was the most famous and adored of all the CHP cruisers, because it was the king of speed. During the test trials at Chrysler's track in Chelsea, Michigan, the 440 cubic-inch, 375 bhp (brake horsepower) muscle car set a track record for the highest top-end speed achieved by a factory built four-door sedan—an impressive 149.6 miles per hour! The record remained unchallenged for 25 years, and even then there are those who question whether the 1994 Chevrolet Caprice (with its specially tuned Corvette engine), honestly and fairly beat it. Huffman, J. (1994, June) Chrysler Police Cars 1956-1978. Motor Trend Magazine, 102-106, and Ellestad, S. (n.d.) The History of Chrysler, Dodge and Plymouth Police Cars-1969. [Online], <http://www.allpar.com/squads/history.html> and "Grant G." posting as "Granttt73". (n.d.) [Online], <http://www.flickr.com/photos/13411027@N00/566744694/>, and personal interview with CHP Sergeant (ret.) Harry Ingold (2012).

42. At the time, neither Officer Robinson nor Officer Holmes realized that their car had been hit by gunfire. After spending most of the morning participating in the manhunt for the felons and giving statements to investigators at the scene, the two officers took their unit back to the Newhall Area Office to do volumes of reports. While there, the day shift officers reported for work and received their beat and unit assignments. The officer who was assigned Officer Holmes and Robinson's vehicle discovered the bullet strike during his pre-shift walk around inspection, and found Officer Robinson to question him about it. Incredulous, Officer Robinson followed him outside to look at the vehicle, and realized for the very first time that one of the felon's bullets had struck above the "H" in the "Highway Patrol" rocker, dotting one of the bars "like a lower case 'i'." It was then that Officer Robinson realized how close he had come to getting shot as he bailed out the door. Personal interview with Officer (Retired) Richard Robinson.

43. In the stress of the event, Mr. Kness didn't realize he had the empty revolver in his hand until he ran into Officer Robinson. It was then he realized that he was covered in blood, holding a gun, and fleeing from a shooting scene, none of which looked good. Hiding the gun behind his thigh, Mr. Kness directed Officer Robinson towards the killers and hoped that the officer wouldn't think he was one of them. Fortunately for Mr. Kness, Officer Robinson had not consciously noticed him or the gun. Officer Robinson later recalled that in the extreme stress of the moment, he was so totally focused on the escaping Pontiac that he had no memory of running across Mr. Kness at all. Whether it was Officer Robinson's extreme focus on the Pontiac/threat (tunnel vision?) or his rapid subconscious assessment of Mr. Kness as a "friendly" who didn't bear further investigation, Mr. Kness fortunately escaped becoming the tragic victim of fratricide. After the brief encounter with Officer Robinson, Mr. Kness sat down in the ditch and waited, emotionally spent. Interview with Mr. Kness. Santa Clarita Valley Historical Society. (2010) The Newhall Incident: A Law Enforcement Tragedy [Film]. Santa Clarita, CA, courtesy of Santa Clarita Valley Historical Society and SCVTV, <http://www.scvtv.com/html/scvhs040510btv.html>, Personal interview with CHP Officer (Retired) Richard Robinson, and Los Angeles Sheriff's Department homicide investigation files.

44. The sequence of events during this part of the shooting is not entirely clear. In the CHP narrative of the shooting, Officer Holmes fires at Davis as Davis is getting into the driver's side of the vehicle, and then fires again at the Pontiac as it speeds off through the gas pump islands. However, in his report that was filed that morning, Officer Holmes wrote that, as they arrived on the scene, he observed a suspect at the rear of Unit 78-12 by Officer Pence. This suspect ran to the left rear of the Pontiac, turned, and fired once at Officers Holmes and Robinson as Officer Holmes was getting out of the door. The suspect fired with his right hand across the rear trunk deck, and then entered the vehicle on the driver's side. Officer Holmes fired at this suspect with one shot.
This suspect would have been Twining, not Davis. Twining had just executed Officer Pence and was standing near him. Additionally, Twining is the suspect that fired at Officers Holmes and Robinson as they arrived, according to the CHP narrative and witness statements.
Adding to the confusion, Officer Holmes described the suspect as wearing a yellow shirt, but it was Davis who had a yellow windbreaker on during the shooting, not Twining. Twining was wearing a green sweatshirt. Perhaps it took on a yellow tint under the neon lighting from the gas station, or perhaps Officer Holmes was just confusing the details of the fast-breaking situation. So, while it is unclear whether Officer Holmes fired at Davis or Twining, it is presumed that his memory of firing at Twining (the suspect who was near Pence when they arrived, and who shot at them), was correct.
Other witness testimony about this phase of the fight is also unclear, particularly when it comes to how Twining entered the Pontiac. Some witnesses reported that Twining entered the vehicle on the driver's side after Davis and pushed Davis out of the way. Others reported first seeing Twining entering on the driver's side, then witnessed considerable movement and hearing shouting within the vehicle before it drove away. Still others reported that Twining entered the vehicle on the passenger side, perhaps confusing the timeline for when he entered the vehicle this way earlier in the fight to obtain the 1911 handgun on Unit 78-12's arrival.
The blood inside the vehicle suggests that Twining may have crawled into the back seat before they fled, because there is a noticeable preponderance of Twining's blood in the rear of the vehicle (particularly on the driver's side) and almost none in the front. There is no noticeable blood on the front passenger seat. The few drops of blood found on the inside of the passenger side door were probably deposited as Twining rummaged through the vehicle looking for weapons and ammunition. If Twining crawled into the back seat when Davis was already at the wheel, this would explain some of the movement that was reported by witnesses.
In this scenario, Twining would have approached the driver's side with the intention of driving the vehicle away, only to realize that the driver's seat was already occupied by Davis. At this point, Twining would have climbed into the back seat of the vehicle because it would have been faster and would have allowed him to get behind cover more quickly.
This assumption is further reinforced by the fact that both felons exited the Pontiac out the driver's side of the vehicle when it came to a stop. The abandoned car was found by officers with the passenger side door closed.
California Highway Patrol. (1975) Newhall: 1970 [Film], Personal interview with CHP Officer (Retired) Richard Robinson, and Los Angeles County Sheriff's Department Homicide investigation files.

45. Officer Alleyn died enroute to Golden State Hospital. This is the format of Officer Holmes' radio call per the California Highway Patrol, but Officer Holmes' partner, Officer Richard Robinson, clearly remembers the shocking radio call differently. Officer Robinson vividly remembers Officer Holmes stating, "11-41, three, no, four possible 11-44" (ambulance required, three, no, four possible dead). Anderson, J., & Cassady, M. (1999) The Newhall Incident. Fresno, CA: Quill Driver Books. p.163, and personal interview with Officer (Retired) Richard Robinson.

46. Interview with former CHP Officer Palmer. Santa Clarita Valley Historical Society. (2010) The Newhall Incident: A Law Enforcement Tragedy [Film]. Santa Clarita, CA, courtesy of Santa Clarita Valley Historical Society and SCVTV, <http://www.scvtv.com/html/scvhs040510btv.html> and Los Angeles County Sheriff's Department Homicide investigation files.

47. Interview with CHP Sergeant (ret.) Ingold and Los Angeles County Sheriff's Department Homicide investigation files.

48. Personal interview with CHP Officer (Retired) Richard Robinson.

49. Davis encountered Daniel Joseph Schwartz during his escape and fired a single shot at him while Mr. Schwartz was inside the camper shell on his 1963 International Scout pickup. Mr. Schwartz blindly returned gunfire through the door of the camper with his Enfield No.2 Mk I* revolver, chambered for the relatively impotent .38/200 (or .38 S&W) cartridge. One of his three bullets struck Davis and slightly wounded him, according to the CHP. The weak bullets didn't have much energy after penetrating the camper, which is why Davis was not more seriously wounded.
After Davis threatened to burn him out, Mr. Schwartz exited the vehicle and fired his remaining three rounds at Davis (perhaps wounding him again—Davis had an armpit wound and a wound to the right neck/collarbone area), whereupon Davis clubbed him with the now empty revolver that he had stolen from the dead Officer Frago.
Having savagely beaten Mr. Schwartz, Davis escaped in the truck, only to be captured by Los Angeles County Sheriff's Deputies Fred Thatcher and Don Yates at a roadblock along San Francisquito Canyon Road around 04:15 on 6 Apr '70.
Twining escaped in the hills to the south on foot and attempted to steal a car at the residence of Steven G. (alternately, "Glenn") and Betty Jean Hoag around the same time that Davis was captured. When he was discovered by Mr. Hoag, he took him hostage, using the CHP shotgun. Mrs. Hoag had enough time to call the nearby CHP Newhall office (half a block away, at the bottom of the hill!) and ask for help before Twining took her hostage, as well. Responding CHP Officers and LASO Deputies rescued Mrs. Hoag and her teenage son, but Mr. Hoag remained captive until Twining released him approximately five hours later. After negotiations failed, a team of LASO Special Enforcement Bureau (SEB) Deputies launched a tear gas attack on the house, shortly retreated, then reentered the home after the gas had cleared somewhat. Twining committed suicide with Officer Frago's stolen shotgun during the ensuing gunfight. Anderson, J., & Cassady, M. (1999) The Newhall Incident. Fresno, CA: Quill Driver Books. P.155-180, and Kolman, J., Capt.. (2009) Rulers of the Night, Volume I: 1958-1988. Santa Ana, CA: Graphic Publishers, pp. 134-139 and Los Angeles County Sheriff's Department Homicide investigation files.

50. Interview with CHP Sgt. Ingold (ret.). Santa Clarita Valley Historical Society. (2010) The Newhall Incident: A Law Enforcement Tragedy [Film]. Santa Clarita, CA, courtesy of Santa Clarita Valley Historical Society and SCVTV, <http://www.scvtv.com/html/scvhs040510btv.html>.

Photo Gallery

Aerial view of the crime scene, with J's Coffee Shop in center and Standard Station at bottom left. The Pontiac was abandoned at the end of the road at middle left, but towed back to its origin during reconstruction, as shown. (Photo courtesy of California Highway Patrol)

Day breaks on a murder scene. Officer Alleyn's cap on Unit 78-8
in foreground, Officer Pence's cap on ground by Unit 78-12 in
background. Pools of blood mark the positions in which these valiant
officers were slain. The blanket near 78-12 was placed over the fallen
Officer Pence by Citizen-Hero Gary Kness when the smoke cleared.
(Photo courtesy of CHP Sergeant [Ret.] Harry Ingold).

As the sun comes up, Units 78-8 and 78-12 are visible with CHP Sergeant
Paul Connell's car in background and evidence markers in foreground.
The portable spotlights on the curb helped investigators to work the scene
throughout the night. (Photo courtesy of CHP Sergeant [Ret.] Harry Ingold).

The side windows on Unit 78-12 now lay on the ground in shattered pieces next to the vehicle. The human shadow on the left is from the photographer, CHP Officer Harry Ingold, who put the yellow chalk markings on the ground (next to the human shadow on the right) to mark Officer Gore's position. The helicopter in the background ferried CHP Commissioner Harold Sullivan to the scene. (Photo courtesy of CHP Sergeant [Ret.] Harry Ingold).

Units 78-8 and 78-12 in the driveway, with CHP Sergeant Paul Connell's car in background and evidence markers in foreground. The Pontiac had not been towed back into its original position yet at this early hour. (Photo courtesy of CHP Sergeant [Ret.] Harry Ingold).

The ground in front of Units 78-8 and 78-12 is littered with evidence markers, identifying the locations of spent brass and other significant items of evidence. (Photo courtesy of Los Angeles Sheriff's Department).

The northbound shoulder of The Old Road, with (left to right) the front nose of Unit 78-19R, Sergeant Paul Connell's car, Unit 78-12, Unit 78-8, and the felon's Pontiac visible. The ditch to the right is where Gary Kness took cover after shooting Officer Alleyn's weapons dry in the gunfight. (Photo courtesy of Los Angeles Sheriff's Department).

The rear window of Unit 78-8 is a frosty haze from Officer Alleyn's final gunshot, fired just before he fell forward onto the trunk of the car and slid off onto the ground at the right rear of the vehicle, where Gary Kness attempted to pull him back behind cover. (Photo courtesy of CHP Sergeant [Ret.] Harry Ingold).

One of the three CHP shotgun shells fired by Officer Alleyn is visible underneath Unit 78-8, by the right front tire. Another is visible near the curb. Note damage to the rear window, passenger side white spotlight and left outboard headlight. Also, note Officer Gore's blood and marked position on the asphalt in right foreground. (Photo courtesy of Los Angeles Sheriff's Department).

The windshield of Unit 78-8 was struck by a bullet or shotgun pellet during the fight, right above the ticket book that was left on the dash by Officer Gore or Officer Frago. (Photo courtesy of Los Angeles Sheriff's Department).

The left front fender of Unit 78-8 was struck by a bullet or shotgun pellet, creating an outward bulge. This may have been caused by the same projectile that damaged the left outboard headlight. (Photo courtesy of Los Angeles Sheriff's Department).

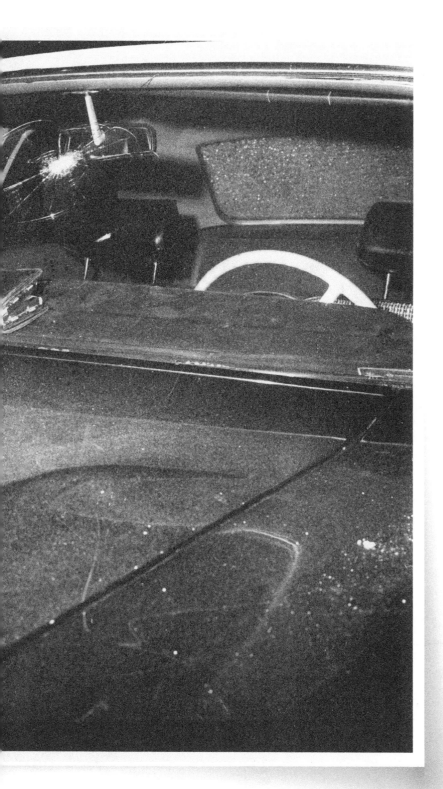

Davis' shotgun pellets left streaks along the right side of unit 78-8 as he was shooting at Officer Alleyn. (Photo courtesy of Los Angeles Sheriff's Department).

The white spotlight of Unit 78-8 took 3 hits, presumably from Davis' shotgun, during the fight. The pellets, glass and debris from the strikes probably injured Officer Alleyn as he fired from behind the door with the CHP shotgun, since witnesses reported his face was bleeding when he abandoned this position. (Photo courtesy of Los Angeles Sheriff's Department).

One of the three expended Winchester Super-X shotgun shells fired by Officer Alleyn rolled under the vehicle and was later found by investigators. (Photo courtesy of Los Angeles Sheriff's Department).

In the afternoon of 6 April, the Pontiac was towed back into the position where it initially stopped in the driveway of the Standard Station, to help reconstruct the scene. The narrow channel between Unit 78-12 and Unit 78-8 is where Davis advanced with the shotgun and killed Officer Alleyn with two shotgun blasts to the chest and face as he popped up at the left rear of Unit 78-8. During their escape, drove the Pontiac straight ahead through the gas pump islands of the Standard Station in the background. (Photo courtesy of Los Angeles Sheriff's Department).

The right side of Unit 78-12 was heavily damaged by the felon's gunfire. Two shotgun pellet strikes are visible on the right fender. Other pellets streaked across the hood from the middle of the right fender towards the windshield. The headlights had not been turned off yet by investigators at this point. (Photo courtesy of Los Angeles Sheriff's Department).

Heavy damage to the side windows and window post of Unit 78-12. (Photo courtesy of Los Angeles Sheriff's Department).

Officer Pence's initial fighting position as he battled Twining. (Photo courtesy of Los Angeles Sheriff's Department).

A myth debunked, over 40 years later. Officer Pence's spent .357 Magnum brass, photographed where it was dumped on the ground by Officer Pence during his reload, and spotted by Officer Ingold and Sergeant Brady in the immediate aftermath of the shooting. The evidence envelope reads, "#18 By Side of Vehicle #2." (Photo courtesy of Los Angeles Sheriff's Department).

Units 78-12 and 78-8 in the left foreground, with J's Coffee Shop illuminated in the background. Officer Pence's hat and postmortem blanket covering mark the spot where he was executed by Twining. Note the bright lighting of the scene, provided by the adjacent Standard Station. (Photo courtesy of Los Angeles Sheriff's Department).

Officer Pence's baton and ticket book are clearly visible through the open door of Unit 78-12, on the front seat. The radio microphone he used to transmit the "11-99" call is stretched out and hanging across the seat as well. The tan object in the front seat is a leather pad, attached to the seat belt. The left rear tire of the unit was shot out during the fight. (Photo courtesy of Los Angeles Sheriff's Department).

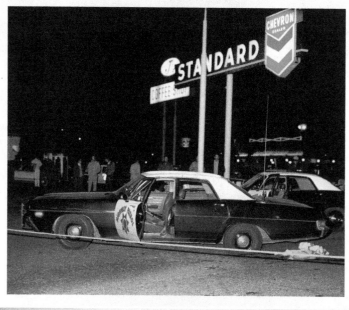

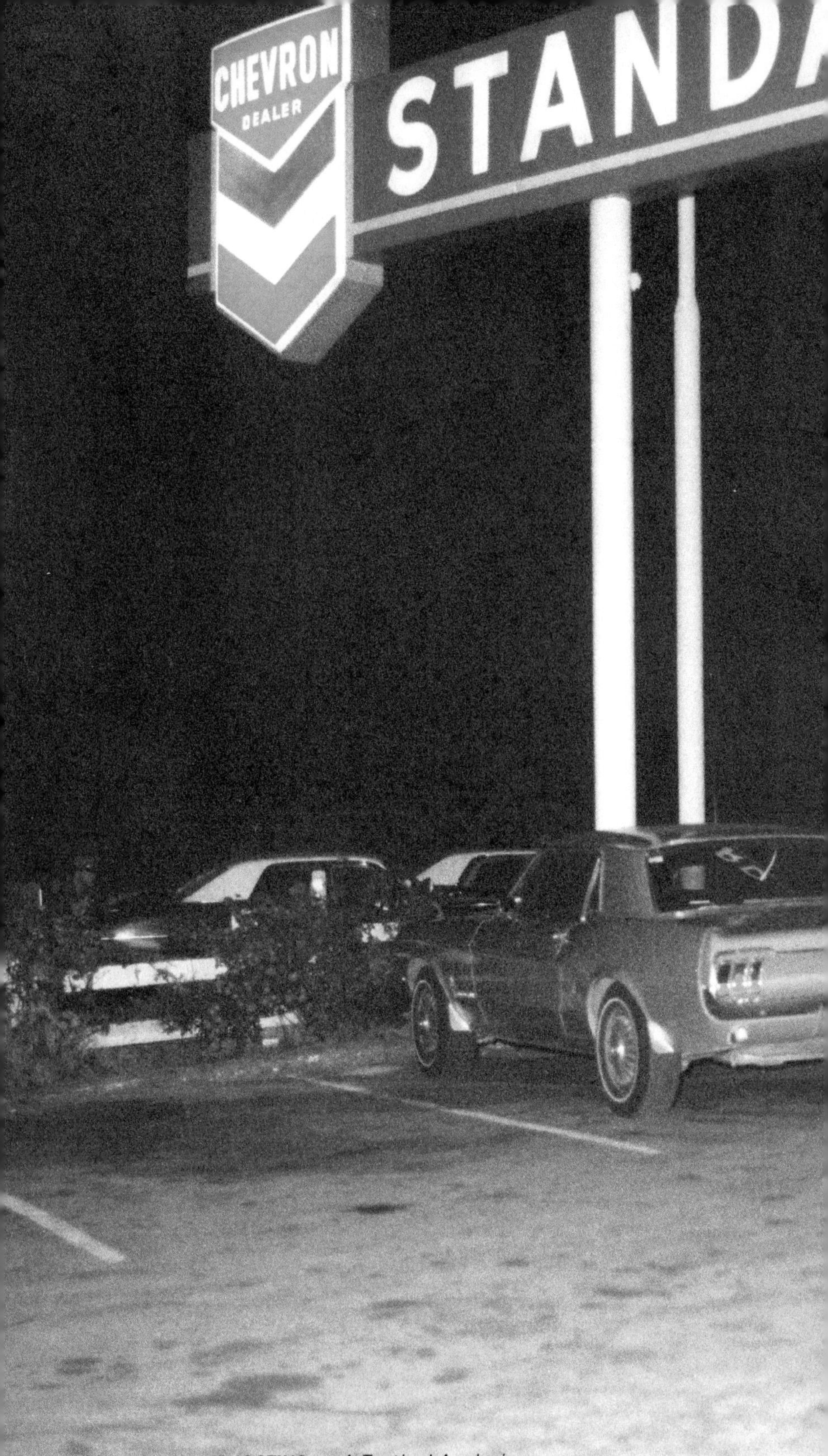
CHEVRON
DEALER
STAND

This unusual picture is from the 27 Apr 70 investigative recreation of the shooting that was done following the gunfight. Witnesses were asked to position the actors as they remembered them in an attempt to model and recreate what happened. The Mustang in the foreground represents the vehicle that was struck by Officer Gore's missed shot on Twining. The actor at the front of the Pontiac is portraying Davis. The actor on the ground is playing the deceased Officer Frago. (Photo courtesy of Los Angeles Sheriff's Department).

Officer Pence's Colt Python revolver, Officer Alleyn's Smith & Wesson Model 19 revolver, and Officer Alleyn's Remington 870 shotgun (marked "CHP 39") were placed on the floorboard of CHP Sergeant Paul Connell's car until they could be booked into evidence. The names of the officers were written on the grips of the guns ("Pence" and "Mike") in the yellow chalk used to mark accident scenes. Note the cylinder of Officer Pence's gun is loaded with ammunition and the cylinder of Officer Alleyn's bloody gun is held open with a spent case wedged under the extractor star. The red object is a plastic muzzle cap that went on the end of the shotgun's tube when it was in the patrol car's rack, to prevent debris from going down the muzzle. (Photo courtesy of Los Angeles Sheriff's Department).

Investigators examine the bullet-riddled Pontiac that morning, dusting for prints and collecting blood samples from the hood and fenders. The Pontiac would be towed back near the CHP units that afternoon, as part of crime scene reconstruction. (Photo courtesy of CHP Sergeant [Ret.] Harry Ingold).

Twining's hurried pair of shots on Officer Gore impacted the side and roof of the Pontiac, instead. (Photo courtesy of Los Angeles Sheriff's Department).

The felon's Pontiac is inventoried where it was abandoned during their flight from the scene. Twining pulled the contents out of the car to load his pockets with some of the shotgun shells from the box in the foreground and additional revolver ammunition, before he fled. The bullet strikes in the side of the car were likely fired by Officer Pence as he engaged Twining. The crystallized rear window was courtesy of Officer Alleyn's Remington 870. (Photo courtesy of Los Angeles Sheriff's Department).

Damage to the Pontiac, caused by fire from Officer Alleyn, Officer Robinson, or Mr. Gary Kness. One of these strikes—probably the one on the window trim--is where Mr. Kness' shot broke up and fragmented before striking Davis. (Photo courtesy of Los Angeles Sheriff's Department).

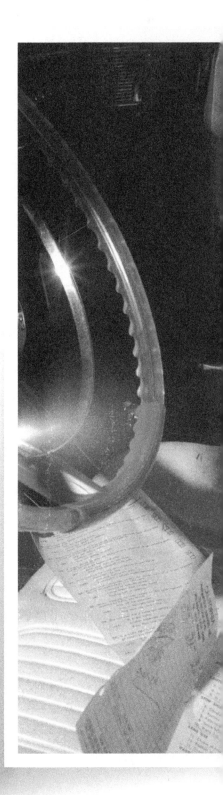

Twining's second 1911 pistol, now empty, was ditched in the front seat of the Pontiac and recovered by investigators. (Photo courtesy of Los Angeles Sheriff's Department).

The back seat of the abandoned Pontiac contained all kinds of equipment and debris, including a spotting scope and the Smith & Wesson Model 38 revolver used by Davis to threaten the Tidwell's and kill Officer Gore. Twining's blood is evident all over the back seat, spilled from the head wound caused by Officer Alleyn's buckshot blasts, which also shattered the rear window. (Photo courtesy of Los Angeles Sheriff's Department).

Another view of the interior of the abandoned Pontiac. The floor is littered with cartridge boxes, a flashlight, a pistol belt, trash, and the factory carton and instructions for the Model 38 revolver used by Davis. Note the bullet hole above the glove box and Grand Prix logo. (Photo courtesy of Los Angeles Sheriff's Department).

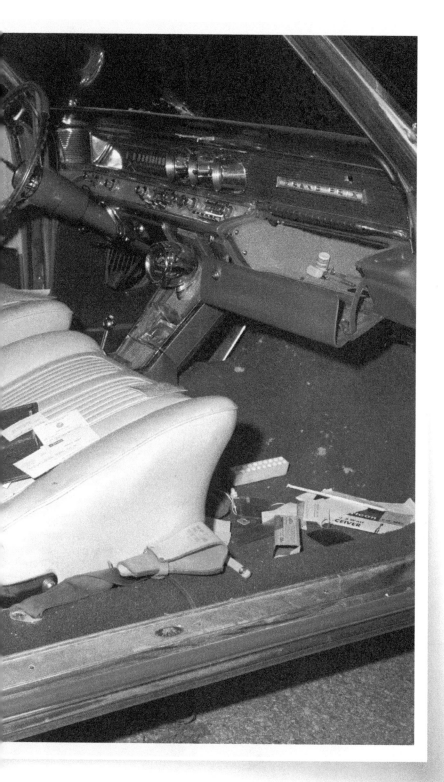

SPECIAL SECTION: Photo Gallery 93

Another view of the interior of the abandoned Pontiac. The spotting scope, Davis' Model 38 revolver and Twining's blood are all visible. Not pictured is the first 1911 pistol pulled by Twining, which malfunctioned. The jammed and loaded pistol was recovered on the floorboard behind the driver's seat, just beyond the bottom edge of this photograph. (Photo courtesy of Los Angeles Sheriff's Department).

Davis escaped under the freeway bridge on the left in the distance, following the riverbed. Sergeant Paul Connell's car, Unit 78-8, and the felon's repositioned Pontiac are visible. (Photo courtesy of Los Angeles Sheriff's Department).

Carswell Wins on Nomination Test

HERALD EXAMINER

4 CHP OFFICERS SLAIN

The Herald Examiner headline, the following day. (Photo courtesy of CHP Academy Museum).

Officer George Alleyn	Officer Walt Frago	Officer Roger Gore	Officer James Pence

The CHP Academy graduation photos of the four fallen officers. (Photos courtesy of California Highway Patrol).

The State of CHP Training in 1970

Introduction

In the wake of Newhall, as the department, the public, and the law enforcement community as a whole were grappling with the shock of losing four officers to violence, a series of newspaper reporters flocked to the CHP Academy on Meadowview Road in Sacramento, looking for answers. They found an efficient and professionally run school that was heavily engaged in the task of pumping out officers to meet the increasing demands of the public and legislature.

The reporters who visited the Meadowview academy were treated to a show that was carefully orchestrated by the CHP, and they left Meadowview suitably impressed with the state of CHP training to intimate that whatever had happened at Newhall was not the result of the training they had received.[1] Readers were regaled with detailed descriptions of the academy's 900-hour, 16-week curriculum, learned about the highly competitive screening process and the exceptional caliber of the recruits, and heard firsthand from the men responsible for training them about the low attrition rate and the superior results achieved in training.[2]

To be fair, the CHP had a lot to be proud of. At this time in American law enforcement, many agencies throughout the nation still did not have formal training academies for their officers, instead preferring to teach them the skills they needed "on the job." The state-of-the-art training facilities, rigorous training programs, and highly professional instructor staff at the CHP Academy made it a recognized standout among its peers, which is why the academy frequently hosted visits from agencies throughout the world and trained selected officers from all over the globe. Even so, the reporters' visit was heavily scripted to deliver the right message.

Significantly, the reporters were treated to a demonstration of "enforcement tactics," in which officers removed suspects from a vehicle at gunpoint, using techniques that would later form the core of what the law enforcement community generically labeled "felony stop procedures." From behind the cover of their vehicles, the officers commanded the driver to display hands, slide across the seat, open the passenger side door from the outside, and exit out through the passenger side with hands visible. The suspect was directed into a kneeling position with hands on his head and covered by one officer who remained ensconced behind the open door of the patrol car with weapon drawn as his partner approached, frisked, and cuffed the suspect, taking him into custody.

This tactics demonstration occurred a mere seven days after the Newhall shooting.

How can this be? It's an article of faith among many that the officers in Newhall were inadequately trained (even untrained) in "felony stop procedures" during their time at the Academy, and this was the principal reason for the events that followed. While it's true that the classic felony stop procedure that evolved after Newhall would greatly improve on many aspects of the demonstration described above, the drill displays a higher level of tactical innovation and competence than the CHP is typically given credit for. If this drill truly reflected the state of CHP training prior to Newhall, then the commonly accepted "truth" that the academy failed Officers Gore, Frago, Pence, and Alleyn because it didn't provide basic skills in felony stop procedures is debunked. Had they executed the procedures demonstrated in the drill, unsophisticated as they are by later standards, is it hard to believe that Davis and Twining might have been taken into custody that evening in the parking lot of J's?

The truth of the matter is that the issue of CHP training—and particularly "felony stop" training—is complex, and the simple conclusions drawn by many observers in law enforcement might work neatly in their narratives of Newhall, but they are incomplete and, in many cases, inaccurate. Further analysis is required to develop a more balanced and accurate portrait of CHP procedures and training, circa 1970.

CHAPTER 8

Internal Struggles

The newspapermen who reported so glowingly on the state of CHP Academy training in the wake of Newhall were particularly taken by CHP Sgt. Ron Von Rajcs, an influential staff instructor at the academy known colloquially by the cadets as "The Red Baron." Sgt. Von Rajcs, the lead instructor for the Academy's "Enforcement Tactics" class, dutifully explained to the reporters that the class was "the most important course at the Academy," because "it wraps up all the theory they have studied in books in the classroom. It's taken in their final month and is the course that actually teaches them to go out and do their job." [3]

While Sgt. Von Rajcs was eager to promote the benefits of the 36-hour class to the reporters and to emphasize the importance of the survival skills it taught the officers, there was much more to the story that wasn't fit for public consumption. It was important for the department, and the Academy in particular, to salvage its dignity and reputation in the wake of the Newhall disaster, and airing its dirty laundry in front of a press that was often uncomplimentary to the department was not the path to accomplishing that goal. [4] Therefore, Sgt. Von Rajcs was left to explain how there were many possible explanations for the tragic shooting that were unrelated to the quality of training received at the academy, to wit: "Sometimes an officer gets to thinking that nothing can happen to him," and, "sometimes he gets careless." [5]

What Sgt. Von Rajcs couldn't tell the press is that, while the CHP academy was indeed "one of the finest law enforcement training schools in the world," certain elements of the curriculum were suffering as a result of time budgets and internal political struggles at the Academy, including his vaunted "Enforcement Tactics" class. [6]

It's axiomatic within institutions of higher learning that every instructor believes his subject is the most important and deserves greater attention. It's also true that there is never enough time to cover all the required subjects to the desired depth. Thus, Sgt. Von Rajcs found himself in a position familiar to anybody who has been a teacher—he simply didn't have enough time to teach his busy cadets what he wanted them to know—and what he wanted them to know was critical to their survival.

In a 900-hour, 16-week schedule crowded with 70-plus subjects, Sgt. Von Rajcs was allocated just 36 hours for his Enforcement Tactics class, which, at its core, was a class devoted to the tactics of felony car stops.[7] Of those hours, 30 were classroom hours and only six were practical, hands-on "field exercises" in which the cadets had the opportunity to integrate and apply the lessons from all the subjects taught in the previous three months.[8] When asked by an incredulous reporter if six hours was enough time to devote to this critical work, Sgt. Von Rajcs could only answer that "We give them about as much as they can absorb," an answer that he surely found as unsatisfactory as the reporter did.[9]

What made this an especially bitter pill for Sgt. Von Rajcs and staff was the knowledge that they had personally been fighting an internal battle with the Federal Bureau of Investigation (FBI) for control of the curriculum for the past five years, and valuable training hours had been wasted in the process.

Under Director J. Edgar Hoover, the FBI had established a presence at the CHP Academy and installed several guest instructors on the faculty in a move that was seen as mutually beneficial to both agencies. The FBI earned as much prestige as it gave via its association with the CHP, which even at this early date had established a strong reputation among law enforcement agencies.

Unfortunately for the FBI, CHP officials were not satisfied with some of their techniques and procedures, which they felt were ineffective, and unsuitable for CHP officers and their working environment. This situation had come to a head a few years earlier, when Sgt. Von Rajcs' boss, Physical Training Supervisor Sgt. George Nuttall, had convinced the CHP Commissioner after a six-month fight to replace an FBI-developed curriculum of baton and arrest method training with a more effective one developed by an officer at a rival agency. The adoption of Los Angeles Police Officer Bob Koga's baton and "Twistlock" control methods in lieu of the FBI's baton and come-along techniques was a significant blow to the prideful FBI, which immediately recalled the lead FBI instructor at the CHP Academy who had "allowed" this to pass.

The FBI sent a replacement to the CHP Academy, and he was tasked with teaching the one remaining FBI class of "Techniques of Arrest." This instructor, nearing retirement, was clearly unmotivated and did not embrace his new

(Opposite) Academy cadets observe as Enforcement Tactics instructors (in street clothes) demonstrate 1950s-1960s era "Hot Stop" procedures, using two of their CTC I' 59 classmates (in coveralls) as "suspect" role players. In the top picture, the standing suspect has just been directed out of the vehicle and is kicking the door shut with his foot, as instructed by officers behind the doors of the patrol car to the rear. In the middle picture, the officers have left their cover positions to move forward and place the suspects in custody. In the bottom photo, the instructors and cadets have switched roles, and the instructors are now the suspects. Note the revolver in the front breast pocket of the suspect in right foreground--a dangerous surprise and valuable lesson for the young officer in training. Photos courtesy of the California Highway Patrol Museum.

job with fervor. In Sgt. Nuttall's and (soon to be Sgt.) Von Rajc's opinion, the FBI agent's poor instructional technique and lack of commitment to teaching these critical, high-risk skills for placing people in custody resulted in "nothing but a dog and pony show" that wasted valuable teaching time, encouraged sloppy techniques, and would eventually get someone hurt. After Sgt. Nuttall's tour of duty expired and Sgt. Von Rajcs took the helm as Physical Training Supervisor, he eventually completed Sgt. Nuttall's vision of eliminating the FBI's direct involvement in this area of CHP training entirely.[10]

In the short term however, Sgt. Von Rajcs and his fellow Enforcement Tactics instructors were left in the unenviable position of having to simultaneously teach their cadets lots of new material essential to their survival, and also correct the bad habits they had learned in the FBI-led Techniques of Arrest course, all in an incredibly compressed timeframe that included a mere six hours of hands-on field work.

The techniques taught in the Enforcement Tactics class compared favorably to those taught in agencies and academies throughout the world. Indeed, the CHP had a reputation for being on the leading edge of training at the time, and the skills modeled by Sgt. Von Rajcs and staff were probably state of the art for the era. Under the spotlight of evaluation that followed the Newhall shooting, deficiencies would be identified and improvements would be incorporated, but it appears that the critical limitation was not the quality of the information imparted, but rather the limited time allocated to ingrain the desired good habits.

Cadets Gore, Frago, Pence, and Alleyn managed to survive the intensity of the Red Baron's course, but under the glow of the neon lights from the Standard station at the corner of Henry Mayo Drive and The Old Road, they confirmed the fears of Sgts. Nuttall and Von Rajcs that, while the academy could afford to spend 22 hours of the curriculum on "Basic Reports" and six hours on the "History and Geography of California," a half-assed 17-hour course on arrest techniques and six hours of field work dedicated to high-risk car stops just wasn't enough.

CHAPTER 9

Firearms Training

The time budgeted for firearms training at the Academy was not so limited. In the era that Gore, Frago, Pence, and Alleyn reported to the Meadowview Academy, cadets spent 72 hours of the 900-hour program working with the revolver and the shotgun, the majority of it with the revolver.[11]

In many respects, CHP handgun training had not come very far since the department's inception, in 1929. Throughout the 1920s, 1930s, and early1940s, formal firearms training was almost nonexistent in most American law enforcement agencies, including the CHP. By the later 1940s and 1950s, the CHP had adopted more formal standards for firearms training, but the program was immature and incomplete by modern standards.

California Highway Patrol training and doctrine had centered on firing the handgun from a single-handed position at the hip for all short-range firing. Long-range firing was accomplished by bringing the gun up to eye level to see the sights (still with a single hand), while the non-shooting hand was placed on the hip or in a pocket in classic "Camp Perry" competition profile. Single-action ("thumb-cocking") fire predominated, especially at longer distances.

Very little "combat"-oriented training existed in this era. Courses of fire began with the gun in hand, not in the holster. Officers mostly fired at match-style bull's-eye targets in training, and they loaded from trays or cans of ammunition that were frequently located on a waist-level table in front of the shooter. They were expected to police their brass during the course of fire and neatly collect it for disposal later. The whole affair was a rather orchestrated and orderly process—a test of marksmanship perhaps, but bearing no resemblance to the chaotic conditions encountered in a real gunfight.

About the only real concession to "combat" training was the use of the "Drawmeter," a unit that was developed in the 1930s to time quick draws. The Drawmeter's clock started when an officer removed his hand from the unit upon a signal to draw and fire on a special target that stopped the chronograph when it was hit, providing a record of the officer's reactions and speed. The whole event had the air of a carnival attraction and probably provided more entertainment than real training, but the practice surprisingly lasted in service until well into the 1960s.

Single hand, single action firing at the Meadowview indoor range. Note the cans used to police the spent brass and the cartridge boxes used for reloading the revolvers. Cadets of the era may have learned the fundamentals of marksmanship during this training, but they certainly didn't learn how to fight with a gun. Several of the shooters aren't even wearing their Sam Browne rigs. The picture dates from early 1959 (Cadet Training Class I' 59), but with a few subtle changes, a similar scene could be viewed on some law enforcement ranges even today. Photo courtesy of the California Highway Patrol Museum.

As the late 1950s arrived, the short-range technique incorporated a deeper crouch with the gun thrust out in front at chest level (the classic "FBI crouch"), and the bull's-eye targets were largely replaced with the Colt Police Silhouette Target for a more realistic flavor. But the essentials of the technique were the same—single-handed shooting from a position below the line of sight.

An additional FBI influence was the adoption of that agency's Practical Pistol Course (PPC), which had been developed by the FBI shortly after its agents were armed by congressional act in 1934.[12] During the 1940s and 1950s, the FBI exported the course to other law enforcement agencies, which adopted it as a centerpiece in their (frequently infant) firearms training

Cadets practice their "combat" shooting in this 1957 photograph at the Meadowview Academy's outdoor range. Note that the Cadets are firing with a single hand, with the weapon below the line of sight. More effective techniques would be developed later to enhance accuracy and control. The target in use is the CHP Silhouette target. Photo courtesy of the California Highway Patrol Museum.

programs. The National Rifle Association (NRA) embraced the FBI's course as well (renaming it the "Police Pistol Combat" course), and popularized it via its influential Police Division.[13] By the 1960s, it was the mainstay of law enforcement firearms training in the United States, particularly at the state-level agencies.

The CHP adopted the PPC course, which included double- and single-action shooting on silhouette targets from fixed distances out to 25 yards.[14] The PPC course included some stages in which the officer shot from a standing position around a barricade and could brace against it with the non-shooting hand, but the use of a single hand to hold the revolver was still the standard. The non-barricade standing shooting stance was traditional "Camp Perry" or "match"-style, with the revolver held in a single hand and extended at arms length while the non-shooting hand was placed on the hip. Although the NRA standards for the course involved stages shot from prone, kneeling, and sitting positions, some reports indicate that the course was typically shot from standing only at the CHP Academy, in deference to keeping neatly pressed cadet uniforms clean and undamaged. Additionally, bull's-eye targets were

Night marksmanship training on the "indoor range" at the Meadowview CHP Academy, Circa 1950's-1960s. The single hand shooting stance used by these cadets would be familiar to CHP officers 30 years before this picture was taken. Note the large cans used for collecting fired brass, and the cartridge trays for resupplying the guns during the course of fire, both of which are located on the bench. These two relics of firearms training would disappear in the CHP as a result of Post-Newhall reforms, but they still linger in many areas of law enforcement firearms training today. Photo courtesy of the California Highway Patrol Museum.

frequently substituted for the silhouettes.[15]

Sometime between 1958 and 1965, CHP Officer (later, Sgt.) John Pedri was assigned as an Academy Firearms Instructor. A crack shot, Officer Pedri often supplemented the PPC training with "combat shooting" demonstrations on Saturdays, conducted with the aid of Smith & Wesson factory representative Chuck Cheshire. Officer Pedri and Mr. Cheshire would amaze the cadets with demonstrations of speed and accuracy, providing "pointers" on topics such as alternative firing positions (sitting, kneeling, crouching, shooting from cover, etc.), quick-draw training, shooting at night with a flashlight (held away from the body at arm's length with the non-gun hand in the "FBI" position), and even some two-handed shooting techniques (which were still "point shooting" techniques with the revolver held between waist and chest level, below the line of sight). Support or "weak" hand-only firing positions were still notably absent from the curriculum, and shooting on the move was not taught either.[16]

During this same timeframe (definitely prior to 1965), a CHP variation of the Colt Police Silhouette Target was standardized for training use, in a small concession to realism. However, officers continued to observe administrative

A cadet from Class IV-57 fires his Colt Officer's Model Match in single action mode on the Meadowview Academy's indoor range, showing the classic target shooting stance designed for the range, and not the street. Photo courtesy of the California Highway Patrol Museum.

range practices such as loading from trays or cans and policing spent brass during the course of fire.[17]

After 1964, limited familiarization training with the Remington 870 shotgun was incorporated into the curriculum, with officers training on the silhouette targets and shooting the shotguns from the hip as often as from the shoulder. Upon graduation, most cadets of this era would not receive regular follow-up or "in-service" training with the shotgun for many years, as this segment of doctrine, tactics, and training was neglected by the CHP until the post-Newhall era.[18]

By modern standards, the firearms training received by Cadets Gore, Frago, Pence, and Alleyn was rudimentary and ill suited to prepare them for a real gunfight, but by the standards of the day the training was actually rather comprehensive. The CHP cadets received more training than officers in many allied agencies, and the methods and techniques were on par with, or better than, the national law enforcement standards of the era.

The cadets also responded well to the instruction received. In a typical class, 60 percent would graduate with the top-level "Expert" rating, and 40 percent would graduate at the "Sharpshooter" level.[19] Significantly, when legendary CHP firearms instructor (and national competitor) Bill Davis was interviewed by the press just days after the Newhall shooting, he said, "Three of the four guys [who] were killed were real good shots, and one was tops in his class."[20]

Indeed, Officer Gore had achieved a perfect score on the "combat firing course" as a cadet and had fired an impressive 290/300 on the PPC targets, taking honors as the best shot in his class.21 Tragically, his prowess on the Meadowview range did not translate into a real-world hit on Twining before he was murdered at contact distance by Davis on the night of April 5, 1970. Officer Gore's shooting skills simply could not rescue him from the hole that his poor tactics had dug for him.

Nor did his counterparts fare any better. Officer Alleyn's Field Training Officer would later recall him as "the most competent officer I ever trained," whose "ability with firearms was extraordinary."[22] However, the match-style of target shooting that made up the bulk of the academy curriculum, and which he excelled in, did little to prepare this gallant young officer for fighting his way out of the violent ambush launched by Twining and Davis as he drove up on scene.

In fact, this was probably one of the most significant takeaways from the tragedy—that training must be relevant to street conditions for it to be of any use in preparing the officer to do the job.[23] Perfect scores and shiny Expert badges earned on an unrealistic course of fire are no protection when facing off against hardened killers across a cold parking lot. In 1970, the CHP and the law enforcement brotherhood still had a lot to learn in this regard.

CHAPTER 10

Growing Pains

In 1966, California was a rapidly growing state with a bright future. The road to that future was packed by an ever-increasing number of cars and trucks, and the resources of the CHP were stretched thin in an attempt to police all those golden highways and the state's rapidly expanding, adolescent freeway system.

That same year, the voters of California elected Ronald Reagan as Governor in a landslide election over Edmund G. "Pat" Brown. Reagan had campaigned as a tough "law and order" candidate who vowed to crack down on the growing trend of violent anti-war and anti-establishment protests and riots that were gripping the state in places like the University of California, Berkeley campus.[24]

Reagan found an ally in the "Father of the Freeways," state Sen. Randolph Collier, whose 1947 Collier-Burns Act gave birth to the California Highway Plan and resulted in the most significant post-war freeway construction program in the nation.[25] Together, they pushed for a rapid expansion of the CHP to meet the state's growing commitments on the highways and freeways, man a new statewide vehicle inspection program, and prepare a reaction force capable of handling "large-scale civil disobedience" like that seen in Berkeley and other places in the turbulent era.[26]

Senator Collier's S.B.317 provided for a doubling of the Highway Patrol in three short years—a phenomenal growth curve that would bring the Patrol's end strength up to about 6,000 officers between 1966 and 1970.[27]

The CHP academy on Meadowview Road, built in 1953 to house and train 80 cadets at a time, began a corresponding expansion project in 1965 to meet the demand. The cadet dorms were expanded to accommodate 360 cadets, five new classrooms, and 10 new offices were added, and a new mess hall was constructed, as well.[28] The improvements allowed the CHP to run three simultaneous classes of 120 men each on a staggered basis, so that a week after one class graduated, another began.[29] Officers Alleyn (who reported to the academy in April of 1968, Class III-68), Frago, and Gore (classmates in Class V-68, August 1968), and Pence (Class I-69, January 1969) were all products of this high-production machine.

An aerial view, Circa 1955, of the new Meadowview CHP Academy (used 1953-1976). At top left is the outdoor firing range, and at top center is the "indoor" (covered) firing range. This small facility would go through an aggressive expansion project in the mid-1960s to accommodate a surge in hiring. Photo courtesy of the California Highway Patrol Museum.

While the CHP's rapid expansion was critical to the welfare and development of the state and an impressive institutional accomplishment, it did not come without hazards. There was a concern among some veteran officers that the quality of training was slipping in the rush to grow the Patrol. Crowded facilities at the academy caused by a spike in the number of students were a concern, and so was the quality of the probationary, "on the job" training that newly minted officers received after reporting for their first assignment.[30]

Field Training Officers (FTOs) are typically mid- to senior level officers with a wealth of experience, maturity, and judgment that make them ideally suited to mentoring young officers fresh from the Academy who are full of book sense, but not street sense. The CHP, like other agencies, would pair up the young rookies with FTOs who would help them make the jump from the largely sterile, black-and-white academic environment of the Academy to the gritty, vague, and dynamic environment of the real world. Under the tutelage of a seasoned FTO, the young officer would quickly learn the path to success, efficiency, and survival in the field.[31]

The process was short-circuited by the department's rapid growth from 1966 to1970, however, because there was a critical shortage of experienced officers to serve as FTOs and stand watch over the new charges as they learned to spread their wings. The CHP found itself in the unenviable position of having its rookies negotiate their way through the break-in period under the guidance of officers who were still rookies themselves, especially in junior-manned offices that lacked seniority, like Newhall.[32] As each batch of new officers arrived fresh from the Academy, they began taking their cues from officers who were barely ahead of them on the learning curve, a process that was just as unfair to the trainers as it was to the trainees.

The logistics of the situation also dictated that the young officers fresh off of break-in training would be unlikely to get assigned to a senior partner that might further their training. The few veteran officers to be found were typically working the more desirable day and afternoon shifts, which their seniority allowed them. Day shift ("A Watch," 05:45-14:15) and afternoon shift ("B Watch," 13:45-22:15) cars were usually manned by a single officer, in contrast to the evening "graveyard" ("D Watch," 21:45-06:15) cars, which were manned by two officers. Thus, junior officers typically wound up working with each other on the graveyard shift with few experienced mentors to learn from.[33]

This pattern was certainly the rule in the junior Newhall office of 1968 to 1969. On the night of the shooting, Officers Gore and Frago were just 16 months out of the Academy, Officer Alleyn just four months senior to them, and Officer Pence had but 12 months experience. Their training officers were hardly more experienced. Officers Gore and Frago were trained by break-in officers who had less than one year of experience at the time.[34] Officer Pence was trained by Officer Harry Ingold (Unit 78-19R—the driver of the fourth car on scene at the shooting), who was only slightly more seasoned with about two years experience on the job at the time he took Officer Pence under his wing. Officer Ingold would later wryly remark, at a seminar hosted on the thirty-ninth anniversary of the shooting, that, "Back then, we [Ingold and partner Roger Palmer] … thought we knew everything there was to know."[35]

Indeed, with just three years experience on the night of the Newhall shooting, Ingold, a salty vet by comparison, hadn't even put in enough time to qualify for his first "hashmark" on his uniform sleeve (awarded upon completion of five years of service).

In contrast, Twining had been committing felonies since age 13 (21 years) and had earned a PhD in violence in nine federal prisons. He had killed at least two men and had spent only 16 months outside of prison since his adolescence.[36] Davis had entered the Marine Corps to avoid an "assault with a deadly weapon" charge and had killed his first man, a fellow Marine, at age 19. By age 21, he was in federal prison for a series of bank robberies, where he remained until a little less than nine months before the night Officers Gore and Frago pulled him over in Newhall.[37]

CHAPTER 11

Princes of the Highway

Aside from training and experience deficiencies, the four officers slain at Newhall had an additional hurdle to manage that made them less prepared to handle a violent confrontation with Twining and Davis—they'd grown up in an agency that placed its public image ahead of officer safety.

Since its inception in 1929, the Patrol had always been very conscious of its public image and went to great lengths to ensure the public saw it in positive terms. The Patrol wanted its officers to be known as helpful and friendly servants, committed to the safety of the traveling public. There's no discounting the fact that service on the Highway Patrol could be violent at times (the guns weren't just symbolic, after all), but unlike some other agencies that embraced their law enforcement status and weren't afraid to flex some muscle in the quest to curb criminal activity, the Patrol was careful to cultivate the "Officer Friendly" persona and tread lightly.

It did so in a variety of ways, to include common public outreach projects like driving simulators at the state fair, traffic safety presentations to community groups, trick motorcycle demonstration teams, and some early, progressive alliances with television and the movie industry, which established a trend that would continue well into the future.[38]

Uniform standards were strict, as a professional appearance before the public was critical. Officers found to be out of uniform (lacking the proper tie or being found outside the vehicle without a hat on), were subject to punishment. Frequent inspections ensured that the military-style khaki uniforms (more suitable for a parade ground than for crawling around in vehicle wreckage), looked crisp and sharp, with infractions swiftly dealt with by watchful sergeants.[39]

It wasn't all about uniforms, however. In addition to wanting to look good for the public, the Patrol was eager to emphasize its traffic safety mission, which was generally popular and accepted by the public, and distance itself from other, grittier law enforcement roles in which its officers were more likely to use force and perhaps draw the public's ire. Indeed, the Patrol actively discouraged its officers from getting involved in law enforcement actions that were not directly related to traffic, preferring to let other agencies handle sticky issues like robberies and homicides, even when the criminals who committed these acts fled to the highways in escape, as they invariably did in this increasingly auto-centric culture and age. The chain of command made it very clear to officers that their primary mission was to keep the traffic flowing safely, and to defer other law enforcement duties to the policemen and deputies who served the concerned municipalities and counties.[40]

All these things helped to cement the image of the California Highway Patrolman as a professional, virtuous public servant with the sole mission of traffic safety—a "Prince of the Highway," as the early officers mockingly described themselves. But there was a dark side to this practice, as the department's commitment to maintaining "the image" clashed with the tactical realities of law enforcement.

Officers who approached a vehicle with their hand on the grip of their revolver during a suspicious or risky stop were frequently subjected to unwarranted punishment by the department after unhappy citizens (some looking to "get even" for a ticket they felt they didn't deserve), complained of "excessive force," even if the bogus claims were unsubstantiated.[41] Indeed, officers felt the department's chain of command was typically quick to support these allegations and take unjustified action against the officers in order to appease the complainants. This state of affairs literally made officers gun shy about taking reasonable precautionary measures, and extremely cautious of appearing combative or aggressive, even if only to avoid a clash with superiors and the penalties that would ensue.

Whereas other law enforcement agencies in the state and throughout the nation had an established history of issuing long guns (rifles and, especially, shotguns) to their officers, the CHP was slow to follow suit, in large part because of the exceptionally martial appearance of the weapons, which might intimidate the public.[42] It took the November 15, 1963, shooting of Officer Glenn W. Carlson at the hands of parolee bank robbers in Truckee, and the resulting action of nearby California Assemblywoman Pauline Davis, before the CHP was finally provided a limited number of shotguns, in 1964 (about one per every five to 10 officers).[43] Even then, the brass was leery of the new guns and ordered them to be sealed with perforated evidence tape wrapped around the barrel and the fore-end in such a manner that it would be broken if a round was chambered (police shotguns are routinely stored with an empty chamber in the car for safety reasons). Each time an officer broke the seal, he was required to write a memo justifying the reason for charging the gun, and thereafter the gun had to be inspected by a sergeant who would ensure the gun was returned to "cruiser ready" status—hammer down on an empty chamber, loaded magazine—before reapplying a new seal.[44] As expected, the entire procedure dramatically discouraged officers from employing this important, life-saving tool, even at times when the tactical circumstances dictated such

Prior to Newhall, an adhesive paper seal was applied around the barrel and forend of all CHP shotguns, as shown in this photo from the 1965 CHP Shotgun Training Manual. The purpose of the seal was to determine if a round had been loaded into the chamber, but the net effect was to discourage use of this lifesaving tool by officers. Photo courtesy of California Highway Patrol Museum.

action.

This was the culture that Officers Gore, Frago, Pence, and Alleyn were steeped in upon graduation from the Academy. It was a culture in which the officers wryly joked that they were nothing but "Triple-A with a gun," as far as the department and the public was concerned. A culture in which aggressive policing, or even just basic precautions could get you in trouble with the brass. A culture in which the Princes of the Highway were sent forth to do battle, handicapped by a chivalrous code and flawed rules of engagement not shared by their enemies. It was a culture that left them at a significant disadvantage when their paths crossed with hardened killers like Davis and Twining that night in Newhall.

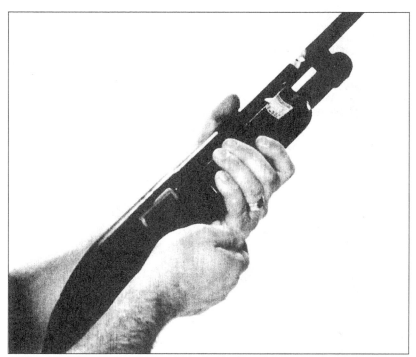

Another view of the adhesive shotgun seal required by the CHP, this one broken because the forend has been pumped. A shotgun with a seal such as this one would require inspection by a Sergeant, who would reload and reseal the weapon while the Officer was writing a Memo for Record to describe why it was necessary to chamber a round in the gun. Photo courtesy of California Highway Patrol Museum.

ENDNOTES

1. *Indeed, they were ably "assisted" to this conclusion by the academy staff itself. The lead instructor featured prominently in one of the articles was "certain the Newhall incident wasn't due to inadequate training," and postulated that the officers were merely careless because they felt "nothing could happen to [them]." McLain, J. (1970, April 12). You Could Get Shot For Missing Class Here. The Sacramento Union.*

2. *Ibid.*

3. *Ibid.*

4. *Interestingly, the tragedy of Newhall struck a nerve even at one of the newspapers traditionally adversarial with the CHP. In an 8 Apr '70 editorial, the Editor of The Newhall Signal sheepishly admitted it had been critical of the department "at intervals," but on that day it issued a heartfelt tribute to the officers of the CHP, and particularly to the four slain officers. The paper even announced it would establish a trust fund for the families and initiate the donations with a $500 contribution of its own. Unknown Editor. (1970, April 8). Editorial: In Memoriam. The Newhall Signal.*

5. *McLain, J. (1970, April 12). You Could Get Shot For Missing Class Here. The Sacramento Union.*

6. McLain, J. (1970, April 12). You Could Get Shot For Missing Class Here. The Sacramento Union, and personal interview with Von Rajc's former Academy supervisor, CHP Capt. George C. Nuttall (ret.), 6 Sep 10.

7. In the CHP parlance of the time, these stops were known as "hot stops" or "high-risk stops." The "felony stop" term, widely used and recognized by the modern law enforcement community, was adopted post-Newhall to describe the greatly improved tactics and procedures used in these situations. McLain, J. (1970, April 12). You Could Get Shot For Missing Class Here. The Sacramento Union, and unknown source newspaper article from CHP Academy museum.

8. It's worth noting that the "Hourly Distribution of Subjects" from the CHP Cadet Class I-65 syllabus (reporting January 1965) actually allocated only five hours to Introduction to Enforcement Tactics and 26 hours to Enforcement Tactics, which was even less than the figures quoted by reporter McLain in the article, making the situation even more serious. McLain, J. (1970, April 12). You Could Get Shot For Missing Class Here. The Sacramento Union.

9. Ibid.

10. Nuttal, G.C., Capt. (ret.). (2008). Cops, Crooks and Other Crazies. Chula Vista, CA: New Century Press. pp. 293-299 and personal interview with CHP Capt. George C. Nuttall (ret.), 6 Sep 10.

11. It's worth noting that the "Hourly Distribution of Subjects" from the CHP Cadet Class I-65 syllabus (reporting January 1965) actually allocated only 47 hours to Weapons Orientation and Training, which is less than two-thirds of the 72 hours quoted by reporter McLain in his article. McLain, J. (1970, April 12). You Could Get Shot For Missing Class Here. The Sacramento Union.

12. Federal Bureau of Investigation. (n.d.) The FBI Academy: A Pictorial History. [Online], <http://www.fbi.gov/about-us/training/history>.

13. The NRA's Police Division trained and certified law enforcement instructors for agencies throughout the United States and provided badly needed education and training resources to support the development of law enforcement firearms training programs. It developed distinctive qualification badges for agencies to issue to officers that proved their marksmanship abilities, and hosted the first National Police Pistol Championship, in 1962, as a means of encouraging departments to nurture the development of firearms skills amongst their officers. By 1966, more than 600 police departments had formally affiliated with NRA, the association had certified over 1,000 instructors, and thousands more individual officers had taken NRA training courses. Rodengen, J.L. (2002). NRA: An American Legend. Fort Lauderdale, FL: Write Stuff Enterprises, Inc. pp.53, 86, 138.

14. The FBI's and NRA's courses had a 50-yard stage, but it appears the CHP did not shoot over this distance, instead limiting the course to a 25-yard distance. Personal interview with CHP Officer Jay Rice (ret.), and National Rifle Association. (n.d.) NRA Police Pistol Combat Rules. [Online], <http://www.nrahq.org/compete/RuleBooks/Police/pol-index.pdf>.

15. Personal interview with CHP Officer Jay Rice (ret.), who was a cadet in 1965.

16. Ibid, and personal interview with CHP Capt. George C. Nuttall (ret.), who attended his first in-service training, in 1958, after graduating from the Academy in late 1954. He later returned as an instructor in Dec 1965. The changes occurred between his 1958 in-service training and his arrival in Dec 1965.

17. Ibid.

18. Ibid, and personal interview with CHP Officer Gil Payne (ret.).

19. McLain, J. (1970, April 12). You Could Get Shot For Missing Class Here. The Sacramento Union.

20. Ibid.

21. *The CHP's qualification test involved 30 rounds, each worth 10 points apiece. The officer was required to get an aggregate score of 210/300 to pass the test. This remained unchanged until the late 1990s to early 2000s, when the Task Oriented Qualification Course replaced it. See Appendix A for details. Anderson, J., & Cassady, M. (1999). The Newhall Incident. Fresno, CA: Quill Driver Books. p. 33.*

22. *Uelman, D. Lieutenant (ret.). (1995, April). Remembering the Newhall Murders: April 6, 1970. The California Highway Patrolman, 8-16.*

23. *An evaluation conducted by Thomas J. Aveni of the Police Policy Studies Council (PPSC) indicates no measurable correlation between training scores and actual gunfight performance. Aveni considered two separate studies conducted by the New York Police Department (NYPD, 200 cases) and the Metro-Dade Police Department (MDPD, 15 cases), which attempted to determine if there was a connection between range and street performance, and concluded that neither study provided enough evidence to establish a link. Aveni notes that "Until such time that police handgun qualifications involve naturally and randomly moving targets, and until such time we can simulate life-threatening dynamics during handgun qualification, direct comparisons [between range and street performance] are largely pointless." Additionally, Aveni notes that such comparisons are "complicated by the fact that most agencies have adopted 'pass-fail' qualification protocols," making it even more unlikely that a meaningful connection can be established. Aveni, T.J. (2003, August). Officer-Involved Shootings: What We Didn't Know Has Hurt Us. The Police Policy Studies Council. <http://www.theppsc.org/Staff_Views/Aveni/OIS. pdf>.*

24. *Kahn, J. (2004, 8 June). Ronald Reagan Launched Political Career Using the Berkeley Campus as a Target. The UC Berkely News. <http://www.berkeley.edu/news/media/ releases/2004/06/08_reagan.shtml> and Barton, B. (2000). U.S. Navy Presents Award to CHP: Governor Speaks Out on Dissidents. The California Highway Patrolman, Originally published October 1968, 54.*

25. *California Department of Transportation. (n.d.) Timeline of Notable Events of the Interstate Highway System in California. [Online] <http://www.dot.ca.gov/interstate/timeline.htm> and California Secretary of State, California State Archives, Online Archive of California. Inventory of the Senator Randolph Collier Papers, 1939-1976. [Online] <http://www.oac.cdlib.org/ data/13030/6s/tf2f59n56s/files/tf2f59n56s.pdf>.*

26. *Unknown source newspaper article from CHP Academy museum and Anderson, J., & Cassady, M. (1999). The Newhall Incident. Fresno, CA: Quill Driver Books. p. 80.*

27. *Unknown source newspaper article from CHP Academy museum.*

28. *California Highway Patrol Academy, Academy Museum Display. (2010, 1 September).*

29. *Unknown source newspaper article from CHP Academy museum.*

30. *Anderson, J., & Cassady, M. (1999). The Newhall Incident. Fresno, CA: Quill Driver Books. p. 80.*

31. *In the CHP, this break-in period was a fast 30 days. Every 10 days, the FTO completed a report on the trainee's progress and submitted it to the sergeant for review. In general, the FTO would provide a lot of assistance to the probationary officer in the first reporting period, would give him some rope to make his own mistakes, intervene as appropriate in the second reporting period, and would expect the officer to demonstrate he could work independently in the last reporting period. At the end of the 30-day stretch, an officer who was progressing slowly could have his FTO training period extended for an additional 10-day period by the sergeant. This was a fast transition for the young rookie officers, and much shorter than the break-in periods allotted to officers in other departments. In example, Los Angeles County Sheriff's deputies rode with FTOs for six months of patrol training when they first hit the streets. They were just getting warmed up about the time that CHP rookies were expected to take the ball and run with it by themselves.*

32. *Interestingly, the CHP never changed this practice after Newhall and even today continues to*

use a 30-day break-in period for new officers. Additionally, in some junior offices, the department still has a hard time finding seasoned officers to serve as FTOs, leaving junior officers to fill the role in a page right out of the 1960s' playbook. Interview with CHP Area Training Officer Craig Kuehl and Tompkins, E.W. Officer (ret.). (2008). 101 Road Patrol Tales From a Chippie of the California Highway Patrol. West Conshohocken, PA: Infinity Publishing.com. p.14.

33. The two-man car policy for the evening "D" shift ("graveyard") was a relatively new development on the Patrol, having been instituted only in February of 1960. Prior to that, the Patrol frequently required officers to work single-man cars around the clock, in an effort to stretch resources. The practice came to an end after the murder of Officer Richard D. Duvall on February 23, 1960, at the hands of an escaped convict that had just committed an armed robbery. Officer Duvall had stopped the suspect for a speeding violation on U.S. Highway 66 outside of Victorville, and as he approached the stolen vehicle, the felon opened fire with a .32-caliber handgun and killed the officer. Ironically, Officer Duvall had been working the afternoon "B" shift, and the murder occurred around 21:30, but the Patrol made no changes to the "B" shift policy. Officers on "B" watch continued to patrol solo in the wake of Officer Duvall's death, and the only watch that was required to double up was the graveyard shift. Nuttal, G.C., Capt. (ret.). (2008). Cops, Crooks and Other Crazies. Chula Vista, CA: New Century Press. p.65, and Officer Down Memorial Page. (n.d.) ODMP Remembers. [Online] <http://www.odmp.org/ officer/4420-officer-richard-d-duvall> and California Highway Patrol. (n.d.) Badges of Honor – 1960 Through 1969. [Online] <http://www.chp.ca.gov/memorial/memorial60.html> and personal interview with CHP Capt. George C. Nuttall (ret.), 6 Sep 10.

34. Anderson, J., & Cassady, M. (1999). The Newhall Incident. Fresno, CA: Quill Driver Books. P. 80.

35. Santa Clarita Valley Historical Society. (2010). The Newhall Incident: A Law Enforcement Tragedy [Film]. Santa Clarita, CA, courtesy of Santa Clarita Valley Historical Society and SCVTV, <http://www.scvtv.com/html/scvhs040510btv.html>.

36. Anderson, J., & Cassady, M. (1999). The Newhall Incident. Fresno, CA: Quill Driver Books. Pp. 9, 95.

37. Ibid. p.30.

38. The 1936 movie Crash Donovan and the hit TV series Highway Patrol, which starred Broderick Crawford and ran from 1955 to 1959, were early examples of this alliance. In later years, the drama CHiPS would become very popular during its TV run from 1977 to 1983 (lead actor Erik Estrada would receive a Golden Globe nomination for best TV actor, in 1980). From 1993 to 1999, the series Real Stories of the Highway Patrol was very popular with audiences, as well, and CHP Commissioner Maury Hannigan hosted the show for each of the six seasons.

39. This hyperactive preoccupation with stringent uniform policies sometimes bordered on the absurd and ridiculous. The Patrol traditionally had a rigid schedule in which the winter uniform of long sleeves and ties was mandated throughout the state during certain months of the year, regardless the actual weather or assignment location. In a state where it can be snowing up North on New Year's Day, while the residents of the South are grilling steaks in their T-shirts and shorts around the pool, a rigid policy like this was bound to make some officers roast in the heat, particularly during the transition months. While some of the stories have probably been embellished (in the timeless tradition of troops in any military or paramilitary outfit), there is no shortage of anecdotal evidence about the silly and overly-punitive enforcement of rigid uniform standards on the Patrol, particularly in the years prior to the early-1970s. Many former Patrolmen have described events in which officers received administrative punishments for minor uniform infractions, such as a failure to wear the issued hat when outside of the vehicle on a traffic stop. In a favorite legend, one officer came to the aid of a superior who was wrestling with a suspect, only to receive a day off for the effort when the superior noted the officer had previously unbuttoned his collar and shed his tie to be more comfortable in the extreme heat! Perhaps the real story didn't go down exactly that way, but it's certainly representative of the spirit of the CHP culture during this period, according to officers who served during the era.

40. A representative story occurred with one CHP officer who joined a police pursuit that had started on city streets and led to the highways. The police officers from the city were in jeopardy of losing the four robbery suspects, when the CHP joined the chase and terminated it, capturing the criminals. The involved CHP officer expected a much warmer reception from his sergeant than he got, however. Instead of congratulating him on the successful capture of four felony suspects, an accomplishment that any officer (and his supervisor) should rightfully be proud of, the sergeant chided the officer for exceeding his mandate, telling him that "You need to concentrate on speeding violations." Perry, M. (2011, March) My Lifetime of Firearms, Part 14. The Firing Line. California Rifle & Pistol Association, Sacramento, CA.

41. Personal interview with CHP Capt. George C. Nuttall (ret.), 6 Sep 10.

42. The CHP brass was also concerned that arming its officers with shotguns might make the agency resemble a paramilitary force more than the traffic and public safety agency it desired as its public image. As a result, when the California Association of Highway Patrolmen (CAHP), out of safety concerns, began pressing the CHP, in 1963, to issue shotguns in the patrol cars, the Commissioner demurred, explaining the legislature would not go for it at the time. A limited number of .45 ACP submachine guns had been issued during the World War II years for military-related missions, but these did not see regular use on routine patrol and spent more time in the weapons rack than on the road, especially after the war's conclusion. They remained in inventory into the 1950s, more as a curiosity than anything else. Crane, B. (1970). CAHP Golden Chronicle 1920-1970. Sacramento, CA: California Association of Highway Patrolmen. Pg.28 and personal correspondence with CHP Capt. George C. Nuttall (ret.), and California Highway Patrol Academy Museum.

43. California Highway Patrol Headquarters General Order 72.4, published 16 November 1964, stated that, "Shotguns will be distributed to commands on the basis of six guns for each ten patrol vehicles." This worked out to be about one gun for every five to 10 officers, depending on the size of the office. California Highway Patrol Shotgun Training Manual, circa January 1965, and personal correspondence with CHP Capt. George C. Nuttall (ret.).

44. California Highway Patrol Headquarters General Order 72.4, published 16 November 1964, stated that:
"Upon receipt of the weapon, respective commanders shall ... designate a uniformed member of the command who will be accountable for the following:
"... (2) Loading of weapons to be assigned with the approved load of 4 rounds of #00 buckshot in the magazine. As each gun is loaded, it will be sealed so that the chamber cannot be loaded without the seal being broken. He will be further responsible for reloading and resealing the weapons which have been returned to him with seals broken."
Furthermore, it mandated that:
"All personnel to whom guns are assigned for use are accountable for the following procedures:
"a. Each member shall immediately check to see if the seal is broken. If so, he shall report the fact immediately to his supervisor and have the weapon resealed ... .
"e. ... If during a tour of duty it becomes necessary to load a round into the chamber, the member should accomplish the following:
"ii. ... Take the necessary steps to have the weapon resealed and reloaded ... ."
California Highway Patrol Shotgun Training Manual, circa January 1965, and personal correspondence with CHP Capt. George C. Nuttall (ret.), CHP Officer Jay Rice (ret.), and CHP Sgt. Harry Ingold (ret.).

Analysis of the Newhall Gunfight

Traditionally, in such cases, we, the police, have reported only those facts acceptable to us. Under the circumstances, it is much easier to say, "Our officer was shot down in an heroic attempt to . . .", or, "Our officer died without a chance . . . ", or, "As the officer attempted to arrest (or question) the subject he was suddenly shot and killed without warning."

It is easier to avoid dwelling upon the "Why." It is easier on the families, it is easier on the department and, most of all, it is easier on ourselves. In almost every instance of a police officer murder we have subconsciously (or consciously?) blocked out any thought that the officer might have erred. That the officer committed an error is really "why" he died.

We cannot continue to disregard unpleasant facts when police officers are murdered. Difficult though it might be, we must admit that many police officers who die in the field have made mistakes. Perhaps not intentionally, but an error nevertheless. An awareness of the most commonly made errors and constant alertness will, undoubtedly, greatly increase the officer's chance of survival in the street.[1]

—Pierce R. Brooks, Officer Down, Code Three

"Indeed, he must be a very extraordinary man who, under these impressions for the first time, does not lose the power of making any instantaneous decisions."

—Karl von Clausewitz, describing a novice's introduction to the horrors and terrors of the battlefield in the book On War.

Introduction

More than 35 years ago, in 1975, Pierce R. Brooks wrote his groundbreaking book on officer survival, Officer Down, Code Three. As a Los Angeles Police Department (LAPD) Homicide Detective, and the lead investigator on the infamous "Onion Field" murder of LAPD officer Ian Campbell, Brooks was familiar with the mean streets, and he knew that unless someone was willing to break the silence and discuss the errors made by slain police officers, more of them would die as victims of those same mistakes.

Brooks wrote that, "Too often, there is a common practice of departmental secrecy designed to hide the true facts when a slain officer is found to have died through his own error." He understood that this practice was often grounded in respect for the dead and the protection of their families, but he also knew that burying the truth would pave the way to even more police funerals. Brooks knew he had to shine the light on these cases and provide his fellow officers a chance to learn from the critical mistakes made by their brothers, so they wouldn't do likewise.

It's important to note that Brooks' underlying assumption is that the officers failed to achieve the desired performance in combat because they made errors of cognition. That is, they made mistakes that were rooted in their thinking process. This is certainly the case in many instances, but, in the last 15 years or so, there has been a growing awareness of the influence of physiology on performance, with the result that we now know some officers perform poorly in combat because they are the victims of uncontrollable physiological changes in their bodies. These changes can alter or shut down some cognitive processes entirely, can make them freeze in place when they should be moving, and can also dramatically impact basic senses like sight and sound, which can corrupt or block the information an officer needs to make proper and timely decisions and take precise actions. Despite the advances of the last few years, we still don't fully understand the mechanics of these changes and the extent of their impact, but we're beginning to appreciate why the novice that Clausewitz wrote about was so likely to "lose the power" of decision making when he perceived his life was in danger.

Thus, any study of the mistakes made by law enforcement officers in combat must tread very lightly. It's in this spirit that the following analysis of the Newhall shooting is attempted. The goal is not only to identify the errors made by the officers, but also to identify the flaws in training, policies, procedures, tactics, and equipment that contributed to their performance. Additionally, the study will attempt to explore some of the involuntary human factor influences that may have inhibited their performance.

Although the analysis will be critical of the officer's actions, it is not intended to assign blame for the tragedy or to smear the personal reputations of the officers involved. The analysis is simply designed to learn the lessons of their great sacrifice, in order to give them meaning and allow them to save the lives of other good men and women. It must be presumed that the fallen officers would be supportive of this goal, were they still available to discuss it.

As students and analysts of this fight, we benefit from all the advantages that the officers did not have. We can analyze the fight from the safety of the sidelines and spend hours leisurely pondering decisions that the officers had to make in fractions of seconds under intense stress, physical punishment, and threat of death. We have extensive knowledge about the threats, their weapons, their plans, their locations, and all the other essential elements of information that the officers lacked. We know what all the other players in the fight were doing at any given time. We know how the fight would develop and how it would end. As such, we can clearly see things that they could not in the fog and friction of the fight. We can identify errors, make observations, and draw conclusions that the officers were unable to, as they struggled to adjust to the ever-changing chaos around them. It is important to be mindful of this moving forward.

Therefore, this analysis is presented with a humble admiration for the officers, their extreme courage in the face of danger, and the way they handled this extremely difficult situation. The analysis will be critical because it must be to be of any utility, but the reader should know that none of the criticisms are intended to discredit the reputations of the heroic officers involved.

CHAPTER 12

Massad Ayoob's Priorities of Survival

In order to provide some structure for the analysis, the incident will be evaluated with respect to the "Priorities of Survival" model espoused by noted law enforcement trainer and author Massad Ayoob.[2] Ayoob's model includes the following survival priorities, in order of decreasing importance:

- Mental Awareness and Preparedness
- Proper Use of Tactics
- Skill with the Safety Equipment
- Optimum Choice of Safety Rescue Equipment. [3]

The first priority, Mental Awareness and Preparedness, addresses the state of mind of the individual. The individual must be aware of his environment to detect threat cues in a timely manner and allow enough time to formulate and initiate a response. Absent this kind of awareness, the individual has a significantly reduced chance of surviving a violent attack, because his first sign of attack will be the blow of his enemy.

Similarly, if the individual has not mentally prepared himself to deal with a violent attack, he will probably fail to respond properly when under duress. An individual can be completely aware of his environment and can recognize an attack is imminent, but if he has not mentally prepared himself to deal with the attack and made the decision beforehand to use violence in self-defense, he may be frozen with fear, confusion, or indecision at the moment of truth.

Ayoob's first priority recognizes the simple truth that the primary weapon in every officer's arsenal is his brain, and if it's not kept in a state of readiness, then it doesn't matter what kind of equipment is on his belt or what kind of training he has received.

Proper Use of Tactics encompasses the methods and processes used by officers to confront and engage a threat, and it is the second priority in Ayoob's model. Officers who employ good tactics increase their advantage and quickly attain superiority over their opponents, often making the employment and selection of their equipment (the third and fourth priorities in the model, respectively), less important. The proper use of tactics may even make these latter priorities irrelevant, if the confrontation can be resolved without firing a shot.

If the situation deteriorates to the point that shooting is required, the previous use of good tactics will ensure the most advantageous shooting environment for the officer (i.e., from behind cover or as part of a group with superior firepower), and lead to the greatest opportunity for success.

The third priority, Skill with the Safety Equipment, is not to be downplayed. It is critical that officers are able to properly and expertly use the equipment they are issued to achieve maximum effect. In the present context, this means they must be able to do things such as handcuffing a suspect quickly and skillfully. Similarly they must be able to shoot quickly and accurately and must be competent in the skills necessary to keep the gun in operation (i.e., malfunction clearance and reloading).

The last priority, Optimum Choice of Safety Rescue Equipment, takes a back seat to the other three, but still remains a priority. A competent shooter with less capable equipment is sure to fare better in combat than an unskilled shooter with top-drawer gear, but that same skilled shooter will be much more effective in combat if armed with equipment suitable and optimized for the task.

There is an interesting conundrum inherent in Ayoob's model: Understanding and mastery of the priorities at the top of the ladder are the most difficult to achieve, while those at the bottom are much easier to achieve, and these bottom priorities may be more interesting and entertaining, as well. As a result, the most important priorities in Ayoob's model are the ones that are often the most neglected in training, while the less important, low-hanging fruit at the bottom of the tree gets more attention than it probably deserves.

For example, the task of mental awareness and preparation is a very difficult one for the instructor and student to tackle, because it's hard to define, teach, attain, and evaluate. Improving one's mental state requires intense concentration, hard work, and a long-term commitment to the task. It's not fun or sexy or dramatic or entertaining. For a student, it can be hard, exhausting work, and for an instructor, it can be extremely frustrating, because there is no universal method that will guarantee results, and because it's hard to measure progress and get meaningful feedback. Truly changing the mental habits of a person and training them to think and operate differently than they already do is a very individual, difficult, time-consuming, ethereal task, but it's also the most critical matter to attend to from a survival standpoint.

In contrast, and at the opposite end of the spectrum, the task of selecting equipment such as a firearm and ammunition is much less arduous and infinitely more objective. Failure rates, accuracy, and muzzle velocities are easy to define and measure. Physical, mechanical objects you can see and touch are easier to understand and evaluate than elusive concepts like awareness and preparedness. It's also a lot more entertaining—for most trainers and students, it's much more exciting, dramatic, and fun to shoot guns than it is to work on mindset. Picking the right gun for duty is certainly an important task, but having good situational awareness, mental toughness, and tactical competence is infinitely more critical to an officer's survival than whether he has a Glock or a Smith & Wesson in his holster.

Fortunately, Ayoob's Priorities of Survival model takes these considerations into account and provides a sound tool for the planning, execution, and evaluation of law enforcement training. It will also work equally well to provide structure for an evaluation of the Newhall gunfight. Using Ayoob's model, the entire incident will be viewed through this lens to identify the core lessons of this encounter, arranged by priority.

CHAPTER 13

Mental Awareness and Preparedness

"The spirit must be able to win no matter what the weapon."
—Miyamoto Musashi, The Book of Five Rings

In his seminal officer survival text, Officer Down, Code Three, Pierce Brooks discussed 10 "Deadly Errors of Law Enforcement" that were the cause of most officer deaths. Of those 10 errors, six of them fall into the Mental Awareness and Preparedness rung of Ayoob's survival ladder, dramatically showing the preeminence of this survival priority over all others.[4]

Awareness and preparedness are complementary states, with a direct connection between them. Yet, although Ayoob groups them both into a single priority in his model, they are very distinct tasks that often occur at different times. Mental Awareness is primarily an ongoing process that happens in the current moment, whereas Mental Preparedness is largely based on efforts that have occurred in the past. A person becomes prepared based on efforts he has made to develop the proper mindset, capabilities, and skills during training, but stays aware based on efforts he is currently making, in the moment, to stay in tune with their present environment and current situation. The two share a definite link, but will be examined independently in the following consideration of the Newhall shooting.

As the task of preparedness comes chronologically before the task of awareness, it will be the first to be addressed. Thoroughly discussing the broad concept of preparedness would take volumes in its own right, so the following analysis will primarily focus on a much narrower view of preparedness that centers around two key preparedness concepts for law enforcement officers, the will to survive, and the will to kill.

MENTAL PREPAREDNESS AND THE WILL TO SURVIVE

"I know I'm hit … but I've got a job to do."
—Officer Jared Reston

On January 26, 2008, Officer Jared Reston of the Jacksonville (Florida) Sheriff's Department was shot by a shoplifting suspect that he was trying to apprehend after a foot chase. That shot sent a .45-caliber bullet through the officer's jaw and out the side of his neck, and it knocked him to the ground. As Officer Reston fell, the suspect continued to fire at him, hitting him six more times before Reston's return fire killed him.[5]

Officer Reston later commented that, "When I realized he was shooting at me and was doing it, it pissed me off. It kicked me in [to thinking] this son of a bitch is not going to sit there and kill me … ."[6] As his body continued to be struck by the .45 ACP bullets fired by the suspect, Officer Reston could feel the pain but pushed it aside, saying to himself, "I know I'm hit … but I've got a job to do and I've got to end this and I've got to end it now."[7]

Officer Reston's ability to set aside the pain of horrible wounds and focus on the tasks he needed to complete to end the lethal threat he faced was the result of a superior mindset. It was a mindset that was so focused that he was able to shut out anything that did not directly relate to his survival and the means to ensure it. This mindset has been termed many things by many people (the will to win, the warrior spirit, the combat mindset), but we will simply call it the will to survive, and it is the most important thing an officer can develop if he wants to go home at the end of his shift.

It's widely taught in law enforcement and military circles that there are three ways to stop an opponent with gunfire: damage the central nervous system, cause excessive blood loss, or cause sufficient psychological trauma (pain, fear) to force the opponent to stop. If it's true that an opponent can be shut down solely via psychological means when the body has not been damaged enough to cause a physical breakdown, then this also represents fertile ground for mental preparation activities that encourage a survival response instead of surrender.

Almost every person is predisposed to value their own life and wants to continue living. This instinctive desire for self-preservation is not unique; it's part of the human condition. However, in some individuals, the desire for survival is not strong enough to prevent them from giving up when faced with lethal circumstances that are potentially survivable. In these people, the will is not strong enough to overcome the physical pain or emotional trauma of their circumstances and they lose hope in their ability to survive. In the end, these people perish because they surrender to death when they had a viable option to fight it and survive. They die not because their bodies are unable to go on, but because their minds are unable to will them to.

For a person with the will to survive, surrendering to death is not an option. The person with the will to survive recognizes that the body can endure tremendous punishment and continue to function if the mind is strong enough to command it.[8] A person with the will to survive knows that there might come a time when they want to quit due to pain or trauma, but they have programmed themselves to resist these temptations and continue fighting. They have chosen to think positively about their chances of survival, knowing that this positive mental attitude may mean the difference between life and death.

A person with the will recognizes that, while they may eventually be wounded so grievously that survival is not possible, they are committed to fighting to live until they have exhausted every last bit of life that is left in their body.

DEVELOPING THE WILL TO SURVIVE

Developing the will to survive first requires an individual to acknowledge the risks they face and to acknowledge that someday, "it" might happen to them. Recognizing and accepting the possibility will spare the individual significant confusion and stress if they ever find themselves in a lethal encounter. The denial response, which can overwhelm the unprepared and leave them mentally paralyzed, can be bypassed, freeing the mind to respond to the threat. Instead of becoming engrossed in an endless cycle of "This can't be happening to me," the individual can quickly accept—"I knew this might happen"—and then move on to "I know what to do now." The individual must program himself to believe that even if the worst does happen to him, he will not surrender or give up, but will instead fight to the very last to defeat his opponent and to stay alive.

In building the will to survive, it's helpful to create a basic, flexible plan to deal with potential scenarios—something the person can access in the moment of truth to organize his thoughts and focus his response, something that will forestall the panic of not knowing where to start, what to do. Even the most elementary of plans will help to break the "non-cognitive mental freeze" described by veteran trainer and author Rory Miller, which can prevent a person from acting when they confront a violent situation.[9]

This ability to control arousal, prioritize, and focus under extreme stress, to measure the situation for what it is, determine the priorities, and formulate an organized plan to act on those priorities, is crucial to a person's ability to survive after being wounded. Instead of losing control to blind panic, a person with the will to survive is able to table their fears, their pains, their questions and concerns about things that are out of his control, and focus on the short-term critical tasks that will guarantee survival. "All that later," as Mark Moritz observed.[10]

Training to develop this mindset is not easy, and there are no universal techniques that work for everybody, but it is undeniable that "practice is essential," and that "proper experience and training engrains a skill so that it's much harder to disrupt under any condition, including one of stress and arousal."[11]

Some techniques that might be useful in developing this ability include the "Tactical Performance Imagery" discussed by Dr. Asken and Lt. Col. Grossman, simulation or role-playing activities, and deliberate attempts to program positive habits, beliefs, and values into the brain (such as telling yourself before duty that "If someone tries to kill me today, I will defeat them and I will live."), so that they become a "default setting."[12] As with all learned skills, competence and confidence can only be achieved through dedicated work.

"Modeling" is another effective tool to develop the proper mindset. Despite what television and movies would have us believe about the lethality of gunfire, there have been many law enforcement officers and military personnel who have continued to live, fight, and achieve victory after sustaining grievous wounds. By studying these cases, officers can learn valuable lessons about the will to survive and can establish a mental expectation that they will follow suit in a similar circumstance. They can program themselves to model these successful behaviors, and this can be a powerful motivator in a time of need.

There is a physical element to developing the will to survive that should be addressed, as well. Learning to overcome physical pain, exhaustion, and other physical limitations is an inherent part of developing the will to survive. Officers who regularly engage in strenuous physical activities and sports where they push their body to the limits will gain experience in dealing with physical pain and exhaustion, and learning how to think clearly and operate in spite of it. Clearly, the pain of a muscle cramp does not equal the pain of a gunshot wound, but it doesn't need to in order to be of training value. The intensity of the pain is not the goal; the goal is to train the mind to function in spite of the pain or fatigue. The pain or fatigue itself is merely a tool, the method by which the stage is set to challenge the mind, and the experience that comes from facing this challenge and learning how to deal with it will be a critical aid when the circumstances are far more serious. The physical challenge is but a gateway to aid in developing a resilient mindset.

Perhaps nobody understands this need for a strong mindset better than officers who have been there, such as Officer Reston or FBI Agent Ed Mireles, Jr., whose heroic actions put an end to the FBI's own "Newhall," the April 11, 1986 "Miami Firefight," in which two agents were killed and five (including Mireles) received horrible and potentially life-threatening wounds. Of that fight, Agent Mireles observed:

"If it's one thing that this incident shows, it's the value of a positive mental attitude by both subject and agents. This case has shown that the human body can take tremendous punishment and still keep going if the individual wants to keep going. It has shown that the individual with a positive mental attitude, the will to survive, and good training can control the pain, fear, terror and persevere against a committed adversary."[13]

Today's officers would be wise to heed these lessons, paid for by the blood of their brothers in uniform.

MENTAL PREPAREDNESS AND THE WILL TO KILL

"Treat everyone like royalty - but have a plan to kill them."
—Unknown Source

"Have a prayer on your lips and homicide in your heart."
—Evan Marshall

While the will to survive is critical to the success of an officer on the street, the flip side of the coin, the will to kill, is equally paramount to their victory.

The use of force, and especially lethal force, by law enforcement officers is relatively rare, according to the best available information. According to a 2008 Rand Corporation study, the United States Department of Justice estimates that "Of the 43.5 million persons who had contact with police in 2005, an estimated 1.6% had force used or threatened against them during their most recent contact, a rate relatively unchanged from 2002 (1.5%)."[14] The Rand study went on to note that data obtained from the New York Police Department (NYPD) reflected the same, with officers pointing their weapons at suspects in just 0.5 percent of the half million plus contacts with suspects that were analyzed.[15]

Yet, despite the rarity of lethal force situations for law enforcement officers, perhaps the most important thing they can bring to the job is a mental preparation to use deadly force if it is needed, as this is the most critical mission that the public has entrusted to them. Author and researcher Lt. Col. Dave Grossman notes that, "You need three things to survive in combat: the weapon; the skill; and the will to kill."[16] Without the will, the weapon and the skill are not enough, for, "If at the moment of truth you cannot pull the trigger, then all your training and all your equipment are wasted, and the lives of those you are sworn to protect will be wasted, and you will be an abject failure."[17]

Evan Marshall, a streetwise veteran officer who survived scores of lethal confrontations working on the mean streets of Detroit in the 1960s, '70s, and '80s, puts a less academic twist on the subject that is sure to resonate with officers with families:

"The key is not what you're armed with but your willingness to use deadly force. The first night after graduating from the Academy I went into my son

John's room, and looked down at him sleeping in his crib and whispered to him, 'John, your dad will always come home to you.' After making that promise to him, there wasn't anything I wasn't willing to do to keep it."[18]

For Marshall and the other officers on his elite Tactical Unit (which specialized in the suppression of violent crimes and the apprehension of violent felons), that required a distinct shift in mindset when they hit the streets. It required them to be hyper-vigilant, tactically aware, and primed to use deadly force without hesitation or restraint when the circumstances dictated it. This mental preparation for duty was so complete that the transition was manifested in physical and behavioral ways that were often noted by fellow officers, one of whom said:

"None of this [tactics, equipment] is of much use if your head is not screwed on right. When I was in the Tactical Unit in the early 70's we had rookies fresh from the Academy to ride as third men. One of them observed that while we seemed casual and relaxed prior to roll call, we changed when we left the garage. People who play sports call it a 'game face,' I simply referred to it as my 'Survival Soul.'"[19]

DEVELOPING THE WILL TO KILL

Developing this mindset, this will to use deadly force against evil in defense of the innocent, can be difficult, as we are conditioned in our society to deemphasize it. Grossman quotes the noted military historian Brig. Gen. S.L.A. Marshall on this subject, who believed the average soldier generally lacked the will to kill, and we as a society:

"… must reckon with the fact that he comes from a civilization in which aggression, connected with the taking of life, is prohibited and unacceptable. The teaching and ideals of that civilization are against killing, against taking advantage. The fear of aggression has been expressed to him so strongly and absorbed by him so deeply and pervadingly—practically with his mother's milk—that it is part of the normal man's emotional make up. This is his greatest handicap when he enters combat. It stays his trigger finger even though he is hardly conscious that it is a restraint upon him."[20]

Thus, the law enforcement officer who wants to prevail in combat must take Rory Miller's advice to "Give yourself permission to quit being a nice person and start being an effective animal."[21] The officer must make a conscious effort to develop and cultivate the will to use violence in defense of the innocent, and overcome any resistance to the notion that he might have to use violent, lethal force in the execution of his duties. Setting these mental affairs in order prior to a deadly force incident is absolutely critical, as there will be no time to address these concerns once the action has begun, and any attempt to do so will distract the officer from the more important survival tasks at hand. Chic Gaylord, the legendary gun holster craftsman and student of combat, neatly summarized the issue, when he noted, "The peace officer who is psychologically unprepared for a gunfight is fighting two men when he goes into combat. He must conquer both himself and his adversary."[22]

Former law enforcement officer and noted trainer Gabe Suarez echoes this sentiment, describing four basic components to developing what he calls the "combative perspective." Specifically, Suarez believes the mental capability to win a violent fight hinges upon a desire for victory, the elimination of uncertainty (which leads to hesitation), the development of situational awareness and, most importantly, the willingness to act, all of which must be addressed prior to the fight.[23] In so doing, Suarez has added his voice to the chorus that emphasizes the power and impact of the elusive quality of will to mental preparedness for duty.

It should be emphasized that an officer who develops the combat mindset and its associated will to kill is not cultivating a desire or passion to kill. Instead, he is merely laying the mental groundwork for the possibility that he might have to kill in the course of his duty, and is preparing his mind and body to act quickly and decisively when the specific set of preconditions that justify lethal force are present. This will undoubtedly cause anxiety among the squeamish, uncommitted, and naïve elements of society who fail to understand the necessity of this preparation (which unfortunately sometimes includes civil administrators and command elements within the law enforcement organization), but the officer cannot allow outside resistance to distract him from the task if he wants to ensure his survival and his victory in combat.

EVALUATING MENTAL PREPARATION IN NEWHALL

It's impossible to accurately determine the state of mental preparedness of the officers who died in the Newhall gunfight, and any attempt to make specific judgments on their willingness to use lethal force would be unwarranted. However, there are some general observations that seem appropriate, relevant, and worthy of discussion.

It is notable that the officers were raised in a department that did not possess a strong culture of officer safety. Courtesy and confrontation avoidance were prized over aggressive enforcement, behaviors that often brought condemnation and punishment from superiors, even in some cases when the officer acted reasonably. Administrative practices, such as the sealing of shotguns, made officers hesitant to deploy tools that could save their lives. Furthermore, the department's training, particularly the firearms training (like that of virtually all law enforcement agencies at the time), did not adequately prepare the officers for the stress and confusion of real world violent encounters. As a result, the officers had many inherent obstacles to overcome on their way to achieving Ayoob's priority of being mentally prepared for the possibility of violent confrontation.

The officers also had an additional challenge, because they were good men who were not immersed in a world of violence. They were raised in good families and were busy starting families of their own. When they weren't at work, they devoted their energies to happy, positive, and productive pursuits and surrounded themselves with their loving families and friends. They fixed cars, attended barbeques, painted the baby's room, hugged their spouses, attended church, changed diapers, planned for the future, and did a million other everyday things completely unrelated to preparing for violent combat. They were raised in and lived in a culture that discouraged violence and stamped all kinds of hidden imprints on their brain that would cause hesitation to use force, even when it was justified and necessary.

As a result, they had a long walk to take in their mind each time they put on the uniform and stepped into a world that was quite unlike their off-duty lives. A tour of duty could bring them into contact with sudden violence at a moment's notice and demand them to respond in kind, so the officers had to clear their minds of everyday thoughts and concerns, compartmentalize them, and put them on hold for a while so they could focus exclusively on the demands of the job and be prepared to respond to whatever they encountered. The journey to becoming "combat ready" at the beginning of every shift required deliberate action, as Marshall described, so that the officers could divorce themselves from the life they would leave behind for a few hours and become the "effective animal" espoused by Miller. This transformation is no easy task, and it's realistic to assume that the officers, subject to the foibles of being human, could have been anywhere along that path of preparedness on the night of April 5, 1970.

In contrast, their opponents were steeped from their earliest years in a culture of violence they could never really walk away from. They didn't get the opportunity to "switch off" and let their guard down in prison, or when they were outside and on the run from the law. Life had trained them to be "switched on" all the time to ensure their safety and freedom. Their lifestyle provided ample opportunities to mentally prepare them for combat—indeed, each of them had already killed other men—and they lived in a constant state of preparation to do it again. The use of violence to achieve objectives was common and casual in their world, a world devoid of any messy ethical entanglements that might cause hesitation. For men like Davis and Twining, there was no journey to becoming "combat ready," because they lived in a constant state of wariness and readiness.

Davis and Twining were true predators, prepared at any moment to use decisive, savage violence without reservation or limitation, to achieve their objectives.

They lived. The officers died.

A LACK OF PREPAREDNESS AT NEWHALL

While the officer's readiness to use violence is difficult to determine, there are other aspects of mental preparedness that are easier to evaluate in connection with Newhall.

Witness statements indicate that, when Officers Gore and Frago first confronted the felons in the driveway of the parking lot, Officer Gore established a kneeling cover position at the left front fender of the CHP vehicle with his weapon pointed at the Pontiac, while Officer Frago assumed a standing position with the shotgun at the ready (but not pointed at the suspect vehicle) near the right fender in a position that was completely exposed.

These actions belie an element of confusion between the officers that brings to question their communication skills and perhaps their mental preparedness to confront the felons. Officer Gore's actions were consistent with a belief that the suspects in the vehicle were dangerous and, thus, preventive measures such as taking cover and aiming a weapon at the suspects were necessary. In contrast, Officer Frago's actions demonstrated a much lower level of alarm, because he did not feel it necessary to seek cover or point his weapon at the suspect vehicle. To an outside observer, it would appear that Officer Gore was using established high-risk ("hot stop") tactics, while Officer Frago was using low-risk ("routine-stop") tactics at this stage of the confrontation— an obvious conflict that would cause problems for them.

After the Newhall shooting, the CHP was quick to note that the brandishing report that precipitated the stop was a common occurrence in the rural area and, thus, it was possible that the officers who responded were predisposed to treat it as a routine, low-threat stop.[24] However, it appears from the disparate initial reactions of Officers Gore and Frago that this view was not unanimous between the pair and that they were not mentally prepared to mount a coordinated defense against the threat.

As the stop progressed, Officers Gore and Frago would prematurely initiate contact with the suspects prior to their backup arriving on scene, and Officer Frago would leave his observation position to extract the suspect passenger in contradiction to established practices (discussed later). These actions may indicate that the two officers felt they had the suspects under sufficient control and/or the suspects were going to be compliant, which in turn indicates they were probably mentally unprepared for the sudden, violent attack launched by the felons, which caught them by surprise and resulted in their deaths.

It would appear that Officers Pence and Alleyn were equally unprepared for what they encountered upon their arrival at the scene. The officers had no idea they were driving into an active gunfight and ambush, and they were taking fire before the vehicle even came to a stop. As a result, they both experienced dramatic spikes in their stress levels that affected their performance in the fight (such as Officer Alleyn ejecting the live shotgun round by mistake).

In contrast, the officers in Units 78-16R and 78-19R had more warning of what they were about to encounter (courtesy of Officer Pence's 11-99 call), and were therefore better mentally prepared. This extra time allowed them to understand, accept, and deal with their situation, which probably allowed them to operate at lower overall levels of stress and body alarm and make better decisions, such as when Officer Ingold stopped his vehicle at a distance from the scene to avoid driving directly into another hasty ambush.

The latter officers had access to better information, but it's interesting to consider whether their higher level of mental preparation could be achieved by other means, such as mental rehearsal and "war gaming" en route to the scene. Officers who consider the various possibilities of what they will encounter and the appropriate responses to these situations would seem to have a leg up on officers who arrive "cold" and without any forethought. Pattern recognition and decision making speed would probably be improved, priming these officers to make more timely and appropriate tactical decisions in the heat of the moment.

THE MENTAL AWARENESS PRIORITY AND THE OODA LOOP

The flip side of Ayoob's mental preparedness coin is mental awareness. Mental awareness is achieved when the individual is in tune with his environment and is cognizant of the changes within, to include the actions of people around him. The key task in mental awareness is to be able to detect and identify threats early, so that a proper response can be formulated and acted upon.

That process of detecting, analyzing and responding to threats was eloquently modeled by Col. John Boyd, a USAF fighter pilot, tactician, and strategic thinker, who originally created his "OODA Loop" concept to describe the means for achieving success in combat by making appropriate decisions faster than your opponent.[25]

Boyd theorized that, in air combat, a pilot must first Observe his enemy, Orient himself to the threat (analyze the available information to develop an understanding of what it means and its impact to the situation--in other words, figure out what is happening), Decide what to do, and then Act (O-O-D-A).

Boyd's contention was that the first pilot to complete the OODA loop would maintain the initiative and would overwhelm his opponent by making decisions faster than the opponent could react to them. This would place the slower reacting pilot at a severe disadvantage and always a few steps behind his opponent, who would be landing blows (acting, the last step of the cycle) as the slower pilot was stuck in the initial stages of the sequence (observing and orienting).

Boyd recognized that the OODA loop was constantly in motion—every change in a combatant's actions would start the OODA cycle all over again for each player, since they would be forced to observe the change, orient to it, make a new decision, and act upon it. Boyd felt that if a pilot could "get inside" his enemy's OODA loop and force changes upon the enemy so quickly he would not have time to adapt and react before the next change occurred, he could prevent the enemy from moving into the decision and action stages, and would short-circuit the enemy's ability to fight back effectively, therefore guaranteeing his defeat.

Law enforcement trainer and author Rory Miller notes that "The slowest parts of the OODA loop are usually orient and decide," and since "time is damage" in a violent encounter, it is of the utmost importance to accelerate these middle steps and move on to the action stage as quickly as possible.[26] He notes that an officer's ability to orient quickly is a function of training and experience (both of which reduce recognition time), while his ability to decide is largely affected by the number of options available to him and any innate tendencies to gather more information before making a critical decision (both of which increase decision time).[27]

DIFFICULTIES WITH THE OODA LOOP AT NEWHALL

These thoughts have tremendous significance to the Newhall fight and law enforcement training in general. It has been previously discussed that the officers at Newhall were rookies, without much time on the job at the time of the shooting. As such, these officers had not been given the opportunity to assemble the wealth of real world experience that would have made the task of orienting to the threat posed by Twining and Davis much easier. The officers had certainly interacted with a fair share of motorists during stops, but most of these contacts were probably non-violent and did not involve suspects who were resisting. They did not have a database of experiences in their heads that matched their current situation and that would have allowed them to quickly recognize patterns and make rapid judgments about the situation.

Unfortunately, they also did not have the training experiences necessary to make these quick assessments. The capstone Enforcement Tactics class at the academy only involved six hours of hands-on field work, and similar classes dealing with important subjects such as searching and handcuffing were likewise limited in scope. It's impossible for any basic academy to deliver enough experiences and build enough data points for an officer to thoroughly prepare them for the street, but the situation in the late 1960s was even more desperate, since the "state of the [training] art" across the industry was immature at the time (in contrast to today's standards), and left the officers unprepared for what they would encounter in the field.

These shortfalls in training and experience made the task of orienting to the threat much more difficult for Officers Gore and Frago during the initial stages of the stop. It's not inconceivable to believe that these officers really didn't sense or understand the types of characters they were dealing with until the very moment that Davis and Twining sprung their trap. The cues given by the felons were not detected and analyzed, perhaps because the officers hadn't seen their likeness before and their memory banks were blank.

The officer's ability to move on to the next stage of the cycle and make a quick decision was also compromised by factors largely beyond their control. For example, the department's lack of a strong officer safety culture (evidenced by giving officers days off for approaching a vehicle with their hand on or near their holstered gun, or by discouraging access to life-saving tools like the shotgun, for example), was almost certainly an impediment that slowed the officers as they struggled to decide on an appropriate course of action for an unfamiliar situation during the initial stages of the vehicle stop.

These things have serious ramifications for those involved in law enforcement training today. It is critical that today's trainers take every opportunity to enhance the realism and frequency of training received by their students in basic and in-service training, to improve their ability to recognize patterns of behavior, and respond with quick judgments so that they can shorten the orient stage of their OODA loops and more quickly advance into the decision stage.

As Miller observed, the decision stage is rife with troubles for officers, and their trainers, as well. In a direct application of Hick's Law, if an officer has many options to choose from (tools, techniques, tactics), then his selection process can be slowed as he evaluates the merits and applicability of each. This has serious implications for today's officers, who are provided with so many force options (control holds, baton, Taser, OC spray, firearm, etc.), that they could understandably suffer delays as they choose the right tool to respond with. These same officers are also held strictly accountable to very complex use of force policies, which could introduce harmful delays in their decision making process as officers seek additional information to build an unassailable justification for their use of force.

MENTAL AWARENESS AND THREAT ASSESSMENT
"Evil has no age or height requirement."
—Evan Marshall

The observe and orient stages of the OODA loop essentially represent the task of threat assessment, a key part of Ayoob's Mental Awareness priority and one that bears further inspection in relation to the Newhall shooting.

It's impossible to know whether the felons displayed subtle cues (such as furtive glances, hand signals, and so forth), that were undetected by Officers Gore and Frago and that might have tipped the officers off to the felons' plans. But even without such discrete giveaway signals, there were visible signs that the officers were dealing with more than a simple misdemeanor stop.

Consider the following facts, known or observed by Officers Gore and Frago:

• The suspect was reported to be armed.

• The suspect had reportedly threatened somebody with the gun.

• Only a single suspect had been reported by the complainant, but there were now two people in the car.

• The driver of the car had evidently spotted Unit 78-8 and made an early exit from the freeway at Henry Mayo Drive in an attempt to shake them off.

• The driver of the car stopped in an unusual place—right in the middle of the driveway to the Standard Station.

• The driver of the car refused to follow orders to exit the car with his hands up, despite the fact that Officer Gore had ordered him multiple times to do so.

• The passenger in the car similarly refused to exit the vehicle, even after the driver finally complied with the repeated instructions from Officer Gore.

• Even when the driver of the car finally did exit the vehicle, he did not put his hands up as directed by Officer Gore and had to be told again to do it.

In retrospect, a proper evaluation of these facts alone should have indicated that this was not a routine misdemeanor stop; the violators were not behaving appropriately for the circumstances. It should have been evident that increased caution was required and there was no reason to rush the contact with backup only a minute away.

It is difficult to explain how Officers Gore and Frago thought there was enough of a threat to draw weapons in the initial stages of the stop (and in particular, to take the elevated step of deploying the shotgun), but not enough to justify waiting for nearby backup to arrive before making contact, or to use the "high-risk" tactics they had been trained in. In part, this was a breakdown in their ability to assess the threat and understand the full meaning of the suspect's actions—a failure to properly observe and orient.

INTERPRETING NON-VERBAL CUES

A distinct part of threat assessment is the ability to perceive and interpret non-verbal cues or "body language." This is an additional skill that is a critical part of Ayoob's Mental Awareness priority, and there is evidence that the Newhall officers may have had problems in this area.

Witnesses stated that Officer Gore issued three orders to Davis and Twining to exit the car with his hands up before Davis finally complied. While it's true that a variety of factors could explain this (hearing impairment, language barriers, ambient noise), the fact is that, when an otherwise normal suspect fails to respond to an officer's commands, it is often a warning sign of something much more important.

In his book, Management of Aggressive Behavior, author Roland Ouellette describes how the human body automatically goes through physical changes during conflict without the knowledge, assent, or control of the subject. These changes are an essential part of the non-verbal communications we transmit as humans, and every officer needs to be able to correctly interpret these signals since "It is easier for people to lie with words than with their body language. Body language is much harder to control than words."[28]

Ouellette discusses other advantages to being able to read body language. He notes extensive body language studies that were conducted by Ray Birdwhistell, which indicated that "Ten percent (10%) of the message we deliver to people is verbal, ninety pecent (90%) is non-verbal."[29] This led Ouellette to conclude that "When verbal and non-verbal communications conflict, we should rely on the non-verbal signals."[30]

Ouellette identifies three stages people go through during conflict. They are anxiety, losing control verbally, and losing control physically. He notes that, in the last and most serious phase, loss of physical control, " … verbalization stops. The focus of their brains is now on what they will do, and not on what they are saying."[31] Additionally, they begin to experience auditory exclusion, making them less capable of receiving and understanding the directions an officer is giving them.

All of these facts indicate that a suspect who is non-communicative and non-responsive in the apparent absence of mitigating factors (obvious physical or mental disability, language incompatibility, environmental noise or distraction, etc.), should probably serve as a warning signal to the officer.

Therefore, Davis' reluctance to exit the car despite multiple commands while being held at gunpoint was a significant non-verbal cue laden with meaning and which should not have been dismissed. Additionally, Twining's complete disregard of the exit commands, even after his partner reluctantly complied, was another significant non-verbal cue that should have warned the officers they were not dealing with typical traffic violators, and which should have given them reason to approach the situation with greater caution and deliberation than they appeared to have done.

There are other non-verbal cues that might indicate a person is receiving the "chemical cocktail" of adrenalin and other hormones that are a natural part of the body preparing to fight or flee. Changes in posture, pallor, breathing, pulse, focus, and muscle control are all common elements of the "body alarm reaction" an officer needs to be sensitive to.

Suspects considering violence against an officer also commonly display other signs that are not automatic body reactions, but, instead, specific behaviors. Some other non-verbal "pre-assault cues" of this type might include the suspect scanning the area as they look for avenues of escape or potential witnesses to the violence they are preparing to unleash, or pushing up their sleeves and removing wristwatches as they go through administrative preparations for combat. An officer observing signs such as these should move into a heightened state of alarm or awareness, perhaps moving from Cooper's "Condition Orange" to "Condition Red," and should take appropriate measures to ensure their safety while they plan or takes their next action.[32]

CHAPTER 14

Proper Use of Tactics

"Hence to fight and conquer in all your battles is not supreme excellence; supreme excellence consists in breaking the enemy's resistance without fighting."

—Sun Tzu, The Art of War

The Chinese military strategist Sun Tzu realized that the best battles are the ones that are won without fighting, and in this sense he had a lot in common with today's law enforcement officers. It's critical to understand that the Proper Use of Tactics, Ayoob's second survival priority, may allow an officer to resolve a potentially violent situation without the use of additional force. An adversary that realizes the superiority and dominance of an officer's position may determine that the officer's advantage is too great and surrender without further resistance. This is the ultimate objective of tactics in the law enforcement environment—to end hostilities without further violence—and it prevents the officer from ever having to rely upon the skill set embodied in the third tier of Ayoob's model (Skill with the Safety Equipment).

To be effective though, the tactics themselves must be sound and appropriate for the situation, and they must be properly executed. As we're about to see, these preconditions did not exist for the CHP officers during the Newhall shooting, which opened the door for successful resistance by the felons who made good use of their own set of tactics in the fight.

SUPERIORITY OF NUMBERS

When Officers Gore and Frago first fell in behind the Pontiac at Castaic Junction, they sensibly began to coordinate with Officers Pence and Alleyn for assistance in stopping the vehicle. A plan was quickly developed in which the stop would not be initiated until Officers Pence and Alleyn could join the pursuit, which would give the officers a superiority of numbers, a significant tactical advantage. The plan, though, was short-circuited by the felon's early exit from the freeway and their self-initiated stop in the parking lot. These unforeseen actions placed the officers and felons at parity for several precious minutes before Unit 78-12 could drive the single mile that separated them from the location of the stop, thus reducing the officer's tactical advantage.

While the premature stop temporarily interrupted the plan to achieve a superiority of numbers, it did not condemn it, and the officers should have been able to salvage it if they had slowed the action for a few minutes and given time for their backup to arrive. The felons had chosen the time and place for the stop, but, after stopping, made no attempt to exit their vehicle and accelerate the contact between them and the officers. The officers were in a position of tactical advantage and had no reason to expedite this contact, no reason to do anything other than hold the felons where they were until backup could arrive.

Unfortunately, the officers did not take advantage of the felon's temporary compliance and the time on their side. Instead, they chose to proceed with extracting the felons from their vehicle and making contact with them. These premature actions guaranteed a superiority of numbers would not be available during the initial phases of the stop and needlessly sacrificed a valuable tactical advantage.

USE OF TERRAIN

Another issue with the Newhall stop was the terrain. The felons chose to stop their car in an awkward location, right in the middle of the driveway to the Standard Station. This necessarily left the CHP unit in a chokepoint at the mouth of the driveway, where there was little room to maneuver due to the ditch and railed fence on either side of the driveway entrance. In contrast, the felons retained the ability to maneuver on all sides of their vehicle, placing them in a better position than the CHP cruiser. The felons also gained another advantage, because they channeled the direction of the responding backup CHP units; due to the design of the parking lot, any backup cars approaching from The Old Road would be forced through the same narrow chokepoint, where they could be easily monitored and targeted by the felons, who were thusly relieved of the responsibility of protecting their flanks and rear as they faced the officers.

Interestingly, the felons' choice of stopping location also mitigated a key advantage of the CHP officers—control of lighting. Had the felons been stopped on the shoulder of the freeway as originally planned, their car would have been illuminated by the headlights and spotlights of the CHP cruisers from the rear, making the occupants very easy to see. This would have also placed the officers in the relative dark, hidden behind a "wall" of light, where it would be difficult for the felons to locate and target them. However, by stopping in the driveway, the felons placed both cars in a bath of light from the nearby service station and restaurant. Although it was just a few minutes before midnight, the bright lights from the service station clearly illuminated both vehicles as if in daylight and robbed the officers of a critical advantage.

This was a less than desirable position for the officers, but they had options to mitigate the disadvantages that they did not exercise. The first option for the officers was to continue driving through or past the scene so they could maneuver and approach the felons' position from another angle, or even just disengage entirely, back off, and monitor while waiting for backup and another opportunity to stop the car in a more favorable location. While it may rankle the senses of some officers to do the latter (because it looks like they are running away), this tactic of "extending the fight" is a legitimate tool used by military personnel such as fighter pilots to ensure that the fight is joined under favorable terms and not from a position of disadvantage from the start.

A second option available to the officers was to command the felons to another location via the public address (PA) system. At the time the vehicles stopped, the felons had shown no signs of resistance and appeared compliant. The felons did not exit the vehicle to flee or launch a hasty attack on the officers, rather they simply remained in their parked car. Officers Gore and Frago had no reason to believe that the felons would not comply with a command to move the vehicle forward into the parking lot or to another location of the officer's choice, but they made no attempt to resolve the situation in this manner, effectively ceding control of the terrain to the felons in the process.

SELECTION OF TACTICS

It has been previously discussed that Officers Gore and Frago displayed a bit of confusion in their approach to dealing with the felons after they had been stopped. Their initial actions of taking up positions at their cruiser with weapons drawn were indicative of a hot- or high-risk stop procedure, but Officer Frago's decision to advance forward to the Pontiac did not follow the "script" for a high-risk stop and instead mirrored more routine procedures used in situations perceived to be lower risk.

Officer Frago's decision and actions will be discussed in greater detail later, but it is significant to note that the two officers appeared to be running different "plays" at this critical juncture, and it is unlikely that any set of tactics will be successful, no matter how sound they may be, if communication between the players is not strong and their efforts uncoordinated.

HOT STOP TACTICS

As previously discussed, at the time of the Newhall shooting, CHP doctrine for hot stops held that the officer driving would move forward to search and cuff the driver after he had been extracted from the vehicle, while the passenger-side officer remained behind at the CHP cruiser in a covering position. The merits of this procedure would become the subject of intense scrutiny after the Newhall shooting, but on the night of April 5, 1970, one cannot fault Officers Gore and Frago for proceeding in the manner they had been taught as cadets at the Academy. However, the procedures themselves bear inspection for the valuable lessons that can be identified for today's officers.

Witness statements indicate that, upon stopping their vehicle, Officers Gore and Frago established positions around their cruiser to confront the felons, with Officer Gore aiming his revolver across the driver's side front fender and Officer Frago taking up a position with the CHP shotgun at the right front fender, just behind the headlight. Officer Gore's position was compatible with a hot stop procedure, but Officer Frago's high-profile, exposed position was more typical of a low-risk stop. The behind-the-headlight position was indeed part of the CHP Academy's Enforcement Tactics training and cadet manual, but it appears that cadets were taught to use the car's open door for cover when circumstances appeared to be more threatening and weapons and hot stop procedures were warranted. As such, Officer Frago's initial positioning is puzzling. [33]

Witness statements also indicate that, during the initial moments of the stop, Officer Gore directed the occupants of the Pontiac to exit their vehicle with their hands up, but they did not respond. The command had to be given a second and third time before the driver (Davis) finally exited the vehicle, and even then Officer Gore had to tell him again to get his hands up. The passenger (Twining) remained in the vehicle, against directions.

It has been previously discussed that the resistance of the passengers to follow instructions and exit the vehicle should have caused the officers to reassess the situation and the intentions of the passengers. In the context of tactics, this would have been the time for the officers to realize that the subjects were resistant and that more precautions would be necessary in dealing with them, precautions that should have included delaying an approach to the vehicle until the passenger complied with instructions and backup was available. Knowing that the suspects had a weapon and seeing that they had failed to follow the orders given to them, it would have been a good time for the officers to remain in their ensconced positions with weapons directed at the threat, rather than advancing into the threat zone and forcing the confrontation before their backup could arrive. Before backup arrived, this would have left Officers Gore and Frago in the most advantageous position at the beginning of the fight—weapons on target, the officers behind cover. [34]

Unfortunately, the officers did not recognize this and chose to press the confrontation, with Officer Gore approaching the vehicle after Davis finally exited from the driver's side of the Pontiac. The felons may not have been following the script, but Officer Gore did, executing his portion of the CHP hot stop procedure which required him to advance on the vehicle and take the suspects into custody while being covered by Officer Frago.

This action would not be prudent or directed today, using the modern felony stop procedures developed after Newhall. It is now recognized that moving an officer forward to the suspect vehicle eliminates many of his advantages, such as cover, access to radios, lighting, and weapons in the vehicle, clear and secure communication with his partner, and so on. It also places him "down range," in the same general area that his partner would be expected to shoot, should it become necessary for him to fire in support of the contact officer. Additionally, using these procedures allows the offenders to retain the advantages of cover, mutual support and communication, access to weapons, and continued access to the controls of their vehicle, which could be used as a weapon or escape vehicle.

These factors were not given the proper consideration at the time, and the hot stop tactics were therefore flawed. The old tactics negated the officer's advantages and maximized the offender's. They moved an officer into a vulnerable position inside the suspect's killing zone, a place where the suspect held all the tactical advantages. The new, post-Newhall, felony-stop tactics reverse the arrangement and allow for a greater level of officer safety, but Officers Gore and Frago would have to write those lessons in their own blood before they became commonplace in law enforcement.

SEARCH AND HANDCUFFING PROCEDURES

Another area of concern in the Newhall shooting were the procedures for searching and handcuffing suspects. As difficult as it might be to imagine it today, at the time the Newhall officers were CHP Academy cadets, there were no written materials that outlined the basic searching and handcuffing procedures to be used by CHP officers in the field. The cadets received briefings and hands-on instruction and took notes as they were able, but formal textbooks, manuals, or handouts describing and depicting the approved procedures were not available to the cadets.[35]

Perhaps this is not surprising, as the CHP Academy syllabus of the era dedicated just two hours of the 900-hour program to the complex and training intensive skill of handcuffing, yet allowed twice that amount of time, four hours, to cover topics of dubious worth such as "State Government." The hands-on "Control Techniques" class received equal time as the much more academic (frivolous?) "Enforcement Psychology" class (12 hours), and only about half the amount of time as "Reports."[36] Officers Gore and Frago could have overcome these training deficits and improved their skills with enough instruction and practical experience after the Academy, but, as previously discussed, supervised instruction was in short supply in the rapidly expanding Highway Patrol of 1970, and the officers hadn't been on the job long enough to gain much practical experience before their paths crossed with Davis and Twining. As such, when Officer Gore approached Davis on the driver's side of the Pontiac to search and cuff him, he had perhaps a day's worth, maybe two, of formal instruction on the subject, and whatever else he had managed to teach himself in 16 short months, under his belt.

Witnesses state that when Officer Gore reached the Pontiac, he ordered Davis to place his hands on top of the vehicle and spread his feet in the CHP's version of the "wall search" position.[37] He then began to frisk Davis as the pair stood at the left rear of the Pontiac. From a tactical standpoint, this left Officer Gore in a very dangerous position. To begin with, Officer Gore knew that someone in the vehicle had threatened the Tidwells with a handgun just a short while before and, thus, had to presume that one or both of the vehicle's occupants were still armed. Therefore, to approach and search Davis at the driver's side of the Pontiac while Twining remained inside the vehicle left Officer Gore at risk of a possible attack from within. It would only have taken a brief moment for Twining to shoot Officer Gore through the open door or one of the windows of the Pontiac as he searched Davis, and Officer Gore, occupied with his frisk of Davis and blind to Twining's movements inside the vehicle (because of the roof, which blocked his view), would have never seen it coming.

Although it was CHP doctrine at the time to complete the search prior to handcuffing the suspect, this provided a long window of opportunity for the suspect to initiate an attack on the officer while his hands were still free, which is exactly what Davis did when Officer Gore's attention became focused on the gunman, Twining.[38] Had Officer Gore handcuffed Davis first, then begun his search after Davis' hands were controlled behind his back, Davis would have been less dangerous to Officer Gore and may not have been able to access his hidden gun and kill Officer Gore as he traded shots with Twining across the trunk lid of the Pontiac moments later.

The standing search position used by Officer Gore also added to the hazard. It was standard CHP procedure at the time of Newhall to use this search position for almost all encounters, including suspects in a hot stop. The position relies upon placing the suspect off balance such that he needs the support of the vehicle to stay upright and cannot take his hands off the vehicle without compromising the platform and falling. This works as long as the suspect is controlled and not given the opportunity to move his feet closer to the vehicle to reestablish his balance, or push away from the vehicle to a standing position. Unfortunately, Davis was given this opportunity as Officer Gore turned to engage Twining, and because Davis' hands were still free, he was able to access the .38-caliber revolver he had threatened the Tidwells with and use it to murder Officer Gore at arm's length. An alternative search position, such as the kneeling or prone positions that would later gain favor for felony stops, would have done a better job of limiting Davis' mobility, and would have made it more difficult for him to access the weapon, turn, and engage Officer Gore before Officer Gore realized what he was doing.

CONTACT AND COVER ROLES

The hot stop tactics taught to CHP officers relied upon the foundation of "contact and cover" procedures, an essential element of all two-man patrol. In contact and cover, the contact officer approaches the suspect(s) to interrogate, search, and cuff them as necessary, while the cover officer monitors the action and the bigger picture around them from a distance, ready to come to the aid of the contact officer as necessary.

The procedure allows the contact officer to focus his attention solely on the short-range threats in front of him and relieves him of the responsibility for monitoring the larger environment surrounding him, which may include additional threats. It also allows the contact officer to shed extra responsibilities, such as communicating with dispatch and backup officers, which are better handled by an officer who is not in the immediate proximity of the suspect.

The cover officer, by maintaining distance, enhances his ability to pick up on things like pre-assault cues that might be missed by the contact officer, whose close proximity to the suspect results in a much narrower field of focus. By virtue of having greater time and distance, the cover officer can see more, process the information more efficiently, and do a better job of evaluating information in context than can the contact officer, who is busy, "heads down," and focused on a much smaller worldview.[39]

As Officer Gore, in the role of contact officer, approached the driver's side of the Pontiac to search and cuff Davis, Officer Frago initially remained at the right front of their patrol car with the shotgun at port arms, in his proper role as the cover officer. However, this contract between the two officers would quickly break down for reasons unknown, comprising one of the greater tactical errors made by the officers during the encounter.

It's unknown if Officer Gore summoned Officer Frago to the Pontiac for assistance or if Officer Frago made an independent decision to advance, but witnesses at the crime scene later told investigators that Officer Frago approached the passenger side of the Pontiac with the shotgun held in a port arms position across his chest as Officer Gore began to search Davis on the driver's side. Prior to leaving his position at the fender of Unit car 78-8, Officer Frago commanded a position of tactical dominance over both Davis and Twining that stacked the odds heavily in his and Officer Gore's favor. Even if the felons had decided to launch an attack, Officer Frago's superior position and powerful weapon would have allowed him to dominate the fight and to summon vital backup via the nearby radio in the car. However, once he moved forward to contact Twining, that advantage was completely lost. He abandoned his cover, moved forward into the felon's kill zone, and eliminated his ability to radio for assistance in those early days before on-body radio capabilities. Officer Gore's backup immediately vanished, because Officer Frago was now occupied with his own close-range business and potential threats and was not available to help Officer Gore. Both officers saw their workload spike as they were forced to simultaneously deal with their suspects and monitor each other and the environment around them. Davis and Twining would soon exploit these circumstances.[40]

THE APPROACH

Additional tactical errors were made during Officer Frago's approach that would provide opportunities for the felons. When Officer Frago approached the passenger side of the Pontiac, he rested the butt of the shotgun on his right hip, grasped the gun in his right hand to steady it with muzzle up in the air, and reached for the door handle with his left hand, to remove Twining from the vehicle.[41] As Officer Frago reached for the door, he made himself vulnerable to getting his hand smashed and/or being knocked down by a rapidly opening door as he leaned over in an awkward, unbalanced reach for the handle. Additionally, Officer Frago placed himself in a position where he would be unable to bring either of his weapons to bear quickly on Twining. The shotgun was pointing outboard, away from the vehicle and any threats within, and its muzzle was also elevated straight up, where it would take a long time to bring down and engage a threat. Before going for his revolver, Officer Frago would have had to switch the shotgun to his left hand first (which was already busy with the door handle) or drop it on the ground to free up his gun hand for the draw. Thus, Officer Frago was not only precariously off balance, his hands were tied up and he was completely incapable of deploying either of his two firearms quickly.

None of these facts escaped Twining's attention. Officer Frago's posture gave Twining the opportunity he was hoping for and he took advantage of it, rapidly opening the door and firing twice at Officer Frago, killing him instantly before he could respond with more than words. Shortly before his self-inflicted death, Twining would later tell Los Angeles County Sheriff's Deputies, with brutal honesty, "He got careless, so I wasted him."[42]

AMBUSH RESPONSE

Officers Pence and Alleyn were racing to the scene as Officers Gore and Frago made their approaches to the Pontiac and were gunned down by the felons. The officers in the second unit, driving northbound and eager to back up their friends, had no idea of the mayhem that had been unleashed in the parking lot of J's Coffee Shop. As they approached the scene along Henry Mayo Drive and The Old Road, their view of the scene was blocked by the coffee shop, parked vehicles, and the railed fence and hedges that encircled the perimeter of the parking lot. Their first clear view of the scene came as they turned from The Old Road into the driveway and came under immediate fire from the felons, who had sought refuge and cover at the front of the

Pontiac as they emptied their revolvers at the arriving CHP car.

The officers had driven straight into an ambush. As the rounds began to strike their car, they were faced with their first tactical decision of the fight—stay in the kill zone or exit immediately. They chose the former.

Officer Pence brought the car to a stop alongside the other CHP unit and put it in "Park." As he was doing so, he broadcast a call for help across the radio as they continued taking fire, giving Dispatch and backup officers their first notification that a gunfight was in progress. Next to him, Officer Alleyn retrieved the Remington shotgun from the Lektro-Lok cradle and exited the door of the vehicle to join the fight.

In approximately two minutes, they would each be dead.

Their decision to advance into the gun fight was not an easy one to make. They were suddenly thrust into a very stressful and dangerous situation and were required to make an instantaneous choice with scant information. They knew they were being fired upon, but probably did not know where the gunfire was coming from, how many people were shooting at them, what weapons were being used, what support they had, how long it would last, or any other number of important things that would have made their decision easier to make. Furthermore, they were behind the power curve, struggling with the initial stages of their own OODA loop, while their attackers were already completing their portion of the cycle and controlling the action. It is recognized that their position was not an enviable one, and they did the best they could under extremely difficult circumstances. However, they made the wrong decision.

Officers Pence and Alleyn were still mobile when they came under fire. Their vehicle was not out of commission, and they had the ability to drive away from the kill zone, which would have been the best choice.

Time spent in the ambush zone favors the attackers. Every moment that Officers Pence and Alleyn spent in the ambush zone gave their attackers another opportunity to fire at them. By flooring the accelerator and aggressively driving away from the ambush zone, Officers Pence and Alleyn would have distanced themselves from the attackers and made the felons' task of killing the officers much more difficult. Simply put, the officers' survival quotient would have rapidly increased with increasing distance from their attackers.

Such an action would also have given the officers time for many options. They would have had the opportunity to regroup and assess the situation, gathering important information about the number and location of the attackers and other critical intelligence. It would have given them time to call for assistance and pass along vital information as part of that call, which would have helped responding officers to be more effective. Rather than just asking for help, they could have provided critical details about the number of suspects, their descriptions, their location, warnings to approach from another direction, and other items that would have ensured a greater chance of stopping the criminals and greater levels of safety for responding backup units. It also would have allowed Officers Pence and Alleyn to communicate and create a hasty plan to reengage the suspects on terms that were more favorable to the officers. From a distance, the officers could have planned a new approach to the suspect vehicle—one that would position their vehicle in a more dominant location and make better use of cover, concealment, lighting, and available firepower.

Most importantly, it would have allowed them the opportunity to be the ones driving the OODA cycle. Instead of finding themselves three or four steps behind their opponents from the start, the officers could have reversed the situation with an unexpected move. Escaping the ambush would have interrupted the felon's plans and forced them back to the beginning of a new OODA cycle—a cycle in which the officers were now playing the dominant role and the felons were the ones behind, forced to respond to the officer's moves.

Some may disagree with this assertion and feel that the officers were better served by exiting their vehicle and slugging it out with the felons. They would probably refer to small unit infantry tactics that proscribe an aggressive counterattack into the ambush to break it up, rather than attempting to escape from the kill zone. They might raise the specter of the officers being wounded as they fled and might also indicate that the officers were obligated to stay in position and fight, in order to support their comrades.

These positions are not convincing, however. Small unit infantry tactics involve assumptions about unit strength, acceptable losses, lack of mobility, and volumes of firepower that are not relevant to two-man patrol cars. A more appropriate military parallel would involve modern counter-ambush procedures for military convoys, which favor maintaining mobility during an ambush and emphasize dismounting the vehicle and fighting in place only when the vehicle is disabled in the kill zone and another means of escape is unavailable.

It's possible that the officers could have been wounded during an escape from the kill zone, but the chances of being wounded if they stayed in the ambush zone were much more certain. A fast-moving and aggressively maneuvering vehicle would have made a much more difficult target to hit than dismounted officers taking cover behind a parked vehicle. The vehicle offers the same level of structural protection whether it is moving away from the ambush zone or whether the officers are taking cover behind it in the middle of the ambush zone, but hitting the moving target is much more difficult, and an accelerating vehicle that is bearing down on you like a missile tends to make avoidance a higher priority than shooting at the occupants inside.

There is no question that Officers Pence and Alleyn wanted to assist their comrades, but in order to help them they had to first survive. As many officers will recall from their time in emergency vehicle training, "You can't help anybody if you don't get to the scene safely." Fleeing the ambush zone and regrouping for a coordinated attack would have offered them a better opportunity for survival and success than dismounting in the middle of the ambush zone and beginning their fight from a position of great disadvantage.

The officers cannot be faulted for a split-second decision that, based on incomplete information, they made in a moment of extreme danger. However, this does not mean that their decision should be held up as a model for officers to follow in similar situations. While there are no absolutes, and tactics must be adjusted to fit the unique situation presented, it is generally considered that the best response for officers who drive into an ambush is to immediately drive away from the ambush if they have the capability, rather than exiting the vehicle and fighting in place.

COMMUNICATIONS AND MUTUAL SUPPORT

Communication and support between the officers was another area of difficulty for the embattled officers. When Officers Pence and Alleyn arrived on scene and came under fire from Davis and Twining, their car was stopped in a way that the right side of the vehicle was quite exposed to the gunfire and offered no protection for Officer Alleyn. As such, it was necessary for him to immediately leave that position and seek one that offered better cover. He found that position on the right side of the first CHP car on the scene, behind the open passenger door of that vehicle. This location offered better cover, but it also separated him from Officer Pence, dividing them on opposite sides of the two vehicles—Pence at far left, Alleyn at far right.

This made the task of communication and mutual support much more difficult, if not impossible for the officers. It was exceptionally difficult for them to talk to each other, share information, cover each other, and monitor each other's status. They lost the significant emotional benefit of mutual support, because they were essentially operating in two parallel, but disconnected worlds on opposite sides of the CHP cruisers, fighting their own solo battles with little idea of how the other was doing in his own fight.

This was perhaps unavoidable, given the layout of the battlefield, and neither officer could be faulted for it. However, it did make life more difficult for the two officers and provides a tactical lesson worthy of consideration. Preserving this option is always beneficial, if it can be done without sacrificing some other higher survival priority.

In contrast, Davis and Twining spent large portions of the fight in close proximity to each other, sharing the vehicle as cover and working together as a team to place effective fire on their opponents. When Twining's first 1911 pistol malfunctioned, Davis was close by and providing covering fire with the Western Field shotgun. When Twining was wounded by Officer Alleyn's gunfire, Davis was able to suppress Officer Alleyn's fire and force him to retreat from his position. Witnesses recalled the felons communicating with each other at certain periods during the fight. While it's certain that the felons also spent large portions of the fight acting independently from each other without coordination, when they had the opportunities for communication and mutual support, they appeared to make good use of them. This made them more formidable opponents.

MANEUVER AND MOBILITY

As the fight developed in Newhall, Officers Pence and Alleyn fired all their rounds from static positions near the patrol cars, while their attackers continuously maneuvered around the compact battlespace, firing on the move as they ran from position to position.[43] Their use of maneuver was an extremely effective tactic for the felons and bears further discussion.

Davis, wearing a yellow jacket that made him extremely visible in the lights from the Standard Station, began the fight against Officers Pence and Alleyn from a position near the front end of the Pontiac. He maneuvered around the passenger side and forward to the patrol cars, then down the path between them as Officer Alleyn engaged him with shotgun and revolver. After shooting Officer Alleyn, Davis made his way back to the Pontiac, maneuvered again towards Unit car 78-8 to engage Mr. Kness, then retreated back to the Pontiac to flee the scene. He was continuously shooting with his weapons while on the move.

Twining covered the greatest distance out of the shooters, starting from a position inside the Pontiac upon Unit 78-12's arrival, exiting via the driver's side, and fighting from a position near the left front of the Pontiac before he began a wide flanking movement to his right that eventually converged on Officer Pence at the left rear of Unit 78-12. After killing Officer Pence, he fled back to the Pontiac to make his escape. Like his partner Davis, Twining fired most of his shots during this phase of the battle while on the move.

While Officers Pence and Alleyn had the arguably superior positions of cover at the beginning of their fight with Davis and Twining (behind the doors of their cars, as Davis and Twining maneuvered out in the open), they were unable to place effective fire on the highly mobile suspects. The "restless" and "bobbing" suspects were just too difficult to hit under the stress of the gunfight.

Besides making themselves difficult to hit, there was an additional advantage to all the maneuvering done by the felons—it allowed them to flank their opponents and forced them to abandon cover. This is most readily seen in the wide, flanking maneuver that Twining made to get a better angle on Officer Pence. Davis also used extremely bold maneuvers to get a better angle on Officer Alleyn, as well, at the rear of Unit 78-8. Both felons used aggressive maneuvers to flush the officers out of their initial positions of cover and force them to seek less effective cover positions at the rear of their vehicles, much like a hunter would drive game out of a thicket.

It's interesting and perhaps informative to note the actions of citizen-hero Gary Kness during the shootout. Amidst all the gunfire from the three remaining participants in the battle, Mr. Kness entered the scene from the outside, attempted and then aborted a rescue of Officer Alleyn, engaged Davis with Officer Alleyn's weapon, and then exited the battle without a scratch, while Davis continuously fired on him. There are certainly many reasons why Mr. Kness avoided injury, but the fact that he was continuously moving while on the battlefield was certainly preeminent among them and constitutes a powerful lesson for today's warriors.

USE OF COVER
"All cover is temporary." -Unknown

When Officer Gore brought Unit 78-8 to a stop behind Davis and Twining's Pontiac, it was angled slightly away and to the left, such that Officer Gore was able to take a good position of cover at the left front fender of the car. Officer Frago, however, took a completely exposed position at the right front fender of the vehicle, just aft of the headlight. If Davis and Twining had decided to bail out of the vehicle shooting, Officer Frago's lack of cover could have been fatal.

In any event, Officer Gore left his position of cover to advance on the vehicle after Davis was extracted by voice commands, with Officer Frago following up shortly thereafter on the passenger's side. The errors made in contact and cover procedures have been previously addressed, but it's pertinent to note that, before he advanced, Officer Gore was actually in the better position to serve as the cover officer, while Officer Frago advanced to make contact. Officer Frago's possession of the shotgun would have made the contact officer role difficult, but if he had passed the long arm to Officer Gore and left him in place, their tactical situation would have been far superior.

When Officers Pence and Alleyn arrived on scene, they came under fire immediately and took positions of cover as soon as they bailed out of their vehicle, Officer Pence behind the open driver's door of Unit 78-12, and Officer Alleyn behind the open passenger side door of the adjacent 78-8 vehicle. These were the best and most accessible positions available to them and made good tactical sense, given their limited options. When their weapons ran dry however, each officer sought refuge at the rear of their respective vehicles— Officer Pence to the left rear of Unit 78-12 to reload his revolver, and Officer Alleyn to the left rear of Unit 78-8 to engage Twining with his revolver, now that the shotgun was empty. These fallback positions were not as defensible and created problems for the officers.

In Officer Alleyn's case, he attempted to engage Davis over the trunk of Unit 78-8 with his revolver and was immediately shot in the exposed upper chest and face with a load of buckshot. Attempting to hold himself up on the trunk of the car, Officer Alleyn was shot a second time. Officer Alleyn's choice to rise up and shoot over the top of 78-8 was probably driven by the poor visibility his position offered (he was probably having trouble locating Davis with the car blocking his view), but the choice also made him a much larger target for Davis than if he had stayed low and peered around the side or bumper of the vehicle and fired from that low barricade position.

Officer Pence's position at the left rear of 78-12 fared him no better. He took a kneeling position close to the left rear quarter panel that would have provided some protection if Twining had still been near the front of the Pontiac, but gave him no cover after Twining flanked his position. So the position left him exposed to Twining's fire, which wounded Officer Pence horribly with gunshots to both legs, including a compound fracture on one.

Then, with Officer Pence anchored by his wounds and struggling to finish his reload, Twining completed his flanking movement and shot him twice in the lower chest, then closed the distance to deliver an execution style shot to the back of the downed officer's head.

Had Officer Pence taken a position of cover that allowed him more protection and visibility (perhaps by giving himself some standoff distance from the rear of the car), it's possible he might he have frustrated Twining's flanking movement or at least recognized it in time to move to a better position. It's possible he might have avoided getting hit by Twining's shots long enough to complete his reload and get back in the fight. It's impossible to know with any certainty, but a better position of cover could only have helped him in his fight for survival, and it's a tactical lesson of great importance for modern day officers.

CHAPTER 15

Skill with the Safety Equipment

"You are no more armed because you are wearing a pistol than you are a musician because you own a guitar."
—Colonel Jeff Cooper, Principles of Personal Defense

"It's not the arrow, it's the Indian."
—Evan Marshall

Continuing with Ayoob's model, we reach the third survival priority of "Skill with the Safety Equipment," which encompasses a wide range of individual skills with vehicles, weapons, medical equipment, and other items. However, for the purposes of this analysis, the focus will remain on the officer's skill at arms.

Interestingly, much of the legend and lore that surrounds the Newhall incident inordinately focuses on this issue. For many law enforcement officers and members of the armed civilian community, their knowledge of Newhall is limited to a few quips or sound bites about the officers' inability to handle powerful .357 Magnum ammunition they did not train with and the errors made during weapons reloading. These factors are certainly significant and bear further discussion, but they must not be allowed to dominate the conversation about Newhall, lest they drown out the more significant lessons about mindset and tactics. Furthermore, they must be reckoned with the growing body of knowledge about the involuntary physiological changes associated with sympathetic nervous system activation and how these changes negatively affect performance.

It's worthwhile to remind the reader that this priority is relatively far down Ayoob's list. Mental awareness and preparedness and proper use of tactics play a more important role in the survival equation than an officer's ability to shoot, because they make it less likely that the officer will actually need to shoot to solve the problem. Most law enforcement scenarios are resolved without the need for weapons employment, but none of them are exempt from the requirements of mental preparation and the sound execution of good tactics. And when tactics fail, or when the criminal is determined to resist regardless of the superiority of the officer's tactical advantage, an officer's skill at arms is the only thing standing between him and certain injury or death.

TRAINING

The state of CHP training at the time of Newhall has been discussed in greater detail previously, but no discussion of individual skills would be complete without recognizing the criticality of proper training to develop these skills.

At the time Officers Gore, Frago, Pence, and Alleyn were cadets, the quality of instruction at the CHP Academy was equal to or better than that provided by most other law enforcement agencies, but the program still had weaknesses and deficiencies. The cadets were unable to fully integrate some of the lessons from their academy training into their skill set, because they did not get to spend enough time learning and ingraining the skills prior to graduation. Also, after graduation, the officers were deprived of a robust probationary "break-in" period that would have allowed them to fill in the blanks and establish a solid foundation for skill development.

While the CHP Academy's training compared favorably to others, the state of the art of law enforcement training at this time was still immature and inadequate across the profession. There was a large disconnect between the conditions encountered in the real world environment and the academic training environment of the Academy. Simply stated, much of the training, in particular the combat firearms training, was not realistic and was insufficient to prepare them for what they would encounter on patrol after graduation.

Realism has always been and always will be a challenging issue for any law enforcement training program, but it was an especially difficult problem for trainers and trainees in this era. Even if Cadets Gore, Frago, Pence, and Alleyn had achieved perfect scores in training, the sad truth is that the curriculum itself was deficient and did not accurately reflect the way things went down in the real world beyond Meadowview Drive. Indeed, Cadet Gore achieved distinction as the best shot in his class, and it would logically follow that, if the training program was adequate, he should have performed at a very high level during the Newhall shooting. Unfortunately, this was not the case, and Officer Gore achieved symbolic status as proof of the fact that there is often a low correlation between training proficiency and real world accomplishment.

In his study of this very issue, Thomas J. Aveni of the Police Policy Studies Council (PPSC) drew the conclusion that there is little statistical evidence right now to produce a link between performance in training and real world

hit potential in a gunfight.[44] Aveni speculates a potential cause for this disconnect is because:

"There's little resemblance between what we train officers for and what
they actually encounter on the street ... there are glaring deficiencies in the
way cops are prepared for what turn out to be fairly typical circumstances in
gunfights."[45]

While Aveni's analysis was intended as an observation on contemporary
law enforcement firearms training programs, his words are no less accurate
in describing the training program that Officer Gore encountered at the CHP
Academy, in 1968. Cadet Gore's exceptional performance in the CHP firearms
training program indicates he was fully capable of learning the required skills
and performing them to the staff's satisfaction. The only trouble is that the
CHP's program was oriented towards teaching marksmanship, while what
Cadet Gore really needed was training in how to fight with firearms, a different matter entirely.

Officer Gore's opponents did not suffer this problem. Each of them had
previously killed and were experienced at using weapons as part of their
criminal activities. They had developed excellent survival and close combat
skills during their lengthy prison terms, and were veterans of multiple assaults
in these institutions (indeed, Twining had killed a fellow inmate during one
prison fight). In this respect, their "training" occurred in the real world, and it
couldn't have been more realistic. Additionally, they frequently participated in
firearms training, and in fact were returning home from a target shooting and
firearms testing trip when they were pulled over by Officer Gore and his partner. Thus, in most respects, Davis and Twining were much better trained and
prepared for an armed confrontation than the officers who pulled them over.

ACCURACY WITH THE HANDGUN

Three of the four officers killed at Newhall fired a total of 11 shots from
their revolvers (Officer Frago fired no shots), before they were murdered by
Davis and Twining. Officer Gore fired one shot, Officer Pence fired six shots,
and Officer Alleyn fired four shots during the battle, but none of these officers
managed to hit their intended targets.[46]

In contrast, Davis fired 10 rounds from handguns and Twining fired 14
rounds from handguns during the fight. Davis struck with two of his rounds
(hitting Officer Gore at contact range), and Twining struck with seven of his
rounds (hitting Officer Frago at short range with two, and Officer Pence at
intermediate range—perhaps seven to 10 yards—with four, and at short range
with a fifth).[47]

In the aftermath of Newhall, there has been much discussion about the
reasons why the officers did not perform as well with their handguns as their
foes. We will probably never know the complete answer to this question, but

we can certainly understand some of the issues involved, and they resist simplification. To the dismay of those who are seeking for quick answers, there is no single reason why events occurred the way they did.

One consistent problem for the officers involved in the Newhall shooting is that all of them were forced into a reactionary mode from the very beginning—that is, each of the officers was already being attacked by his foe before he could understand and assimilate the information and begin to respond. In a classic case of "getting inside their OODA loop," Davis and Twining were already acting on their decisions to kill the officers before the officers even understood what was happening, which placed them at a great disadvantage from the very beginning.[48]

In example, Officer Gore's first notice that he was facing a deadly threat came when Twining killed Officer Frago, then turned his gun on Officer Gore. This placed Officer Gore several steps behind Twining, as Twining was already shooting at him before Officer Gore could even orient to the threat and decide to clear leather. Similarly, Officers Pence and Alleyn came under fire before they had even stopped their vehicle at the scene, placing them even further behind their opponents, because they had to stop the vehicle, exit it, locate their opponents, and access their weapons before they could begin to return fire on the people who were already trying to kill them.

This is more than a problem of cognitive lag time or reactionary gap, however. It's true that the time deficit is difficult to make up, and it places the officer at an immediate disadvantage as he scrambles to catch up to his foe. However, there is also a physiological element that rears its head and makes the situation even more difficult for the officer to recover from.

In circumstances where officers perceive their lives to be threatened, their sympathetic nervous system (SNS, which wrests control of bodily functions from the parasympathetic nervous system, which controls the body in normal, non-stress environments), activates and directs the body to produce a powerful mix of hormones that are designed to prepare the body for fight or flight. This is especially the case when time and distance to the threat are short, or when an officer is surprised or startled by the threat, as each of the Newhall officers were.[49] These chemicals produce beneficial results such as increased strength and resistance to pain, but they also produce some negative results, such as: loss of dexterity; muscle tremors; diminished hearing and sight capabilities (to include all forms of perceptual narrowing, such as auditory exclusion, decreased near vision acuity, loss of peripheral vision, loss of depth perception, etc.); loss of processing and decision making abilities; diminished memory; and overall decreased cognition.[50] As Bruce Siddle, the pioneering, cutting-edge researcher in the field of survival stress and combat human factors, indicates, activation of the sympathetic nervous system makes you "fast, quick and strong," but also "dumb."[51] Siddle notes that the SNS has a profound effect on "perception, processing, decision-making, motor skills, and memory" which, in the most highly stressed individuals, can initiate "a catastrophic failure of the cognitive processing capabilities, leading to fatal increases in reaction time ... ."[52]

The cognitive and motor precision necessary to fight effectively with firearms deteriorates rapidly in this state, particularly in individuals whose inexperience, lack of proper training, lack of confidence, surprise, or natural demeanor make them more likely to suffer increased levels of stress and less capable of controlling the stress response.[53] Individuals who start out behind the OODA loop of their adversary are even less fortunate, because "lost time in a survival encounter initiates a chain reaction of escalating stress" which enhances the negative effects and makes them harder to control.[54] Thus, the officers in Newhall were not only battling Twining and Davis, they were battling for control of their own bodies. The stress hormones being dumped into their bodies by the SNS made them "deaf, dumb, and blind," and their skills with their handguns plummeted as a result.[55]

Their enemies, Davis and Twining, were probably not experiencing the same levels of stress and anxiety and the corresponding decrease in performance, because they were the ones controlling the action. Davis and Twining were the hunters, not the prey. They were the ones who had completed their OODA loops and who were forcing their surprised opponents to scramble and react to their moves. Their confidence, control, and dominance of the situation allowed them better control of their body's SNS response. This increased calm allowed them to take full advantage of their sensory systems, allowed higher levels of motor coordination, and increased their processing and decision-making abilities, leading to much higher levels of overall performance compared to the officers.

Davis and Twining also doubtlessly benefited from a radically different psychological and emotional perspective than that of the officers. These men were experienced killers who had lived most of their lives immersed in a world of violence, aggression, crime, and struggle. Violence had no emotional or ethical component for them, and it would never have occurred to them to show restraint or to consider the fates of their victims. They were sociopaths who saw the killing of the officers as little more than a business transaction that had to be completed to ensure their survival and freedom. They were "in their element" during the battle and had a superior mindset for combat. The violence of the fight did not produce as strong an emotional reaction in the felons as it did in the officers who confronted them, and so they were less susceptible to the debilitating effects that such stress induces on physical performance.

Another issue that plagued the officers at Newhall was the complexity of targeting their agile opponents. As previously discussed, Davis and Twining were in a constant state of motion throughout the gunfight, making it very hard for the officers to hit them, particularly since their SNS response was robbing them of visual acuity.[56] Davis and Twining did almost all their shooting on the move. In contrast, the officers did their shooting from static positions, were not nearly as mobile, and presented less challenging targets for their opponents. Both Officer Gore and Officer Frago were shot as they stood nearby with both feet firmly planted. Officer Pence was shot as he knelt in a static position to reload his weapon at the rear of his car, and Officer Alleyn, the most mobile of the officers, was also shot as he popped up to fire his weapon from a fixed position at the rear of the other patrol car.

Davis and Twining made very effective use of cover and concealment during the fight. During much of the battle, they fired from protected positions behind their Pontiac and exposed little of themselves. The Pontiac sustained a large amount of damage from CHP bullets, but the felons were able to escape serious injury and continue fighting. During the latter stages of the fight, Twining moved into the shadows on Officer Pence's flank and launched his attack from there, a position that made it difficult for the officers to locate him in and hit with return fire.

The felons also had the advantage of distance over the officers. Both Officer Gore and Officer Frago were shot within arms length, therefore simplifying the marksmanship "problem" for Davis and Twining. In contrast, Officers Pence and Alleyn were forced to engage Davis and Twining at greater distances, near the outer edges of the battle space. During this stage of the battle, neither the officers nor the felons made hits, and it was only when the felons closed the distance with their opponents (as Officer Pence was reloading and Officer Alleyn was changing both weapons and defensive positions), that they were able to get hits on their adversaries once again.

While definitive statistics have been hard to assemble, the historical hit probabilities for law enforcement officers in the latter part of the 20th century have hovered somewhere around 15 percent, indicating a relatively low rate of success.[57] Given the fact that the officers in the Newhall shooting faced a very challenging situation—attacked by ambush, multiple attackers armed with an arsenal of powerful guns, maneuvering opponents, medium range distances—and perhaps even more challenging than many of the shootings that make up that 15-percent hit ratio, their inability to hit their opponents perhaps becomes less surprising.

It's interesting to note that the person with the greatest hit ratio in the fight was civilian Gary Kness, whose single shot struck Davis.[58] Kness specifically recalled that he used two hands on the weapon (which was notable, since throughout history to that point, most handgun doctrine—military, law enforcement, and civilian—centered on the use of only one hand; recall that much of the officer's training emphasized one handed firing) and planted his elbows on the patrol car for stability. He fired the gun in single-action and hit his target ("I knew I had him because he spun around"), then realized the revolver was empty when he attempted a second shot.[59] Mr. Kness was certainly operating in a state of significant arousal and elevated stress, but he was able to control himself sufficiently to accomplish the task at hand.[60]

Mister Kness was acting out a plan of his own creation and was momentarily in charge of the fight—he wasn't reacting to someone else's plan, he was making them react to his. He was working inside of Davis' OODA loop, which made his situation radically different than that of the slain officers. For a moment, he became the hunter and Davis the prey.

THE QUESTION OF AMMUNITION

Much has been made of the fact that the three officers who fired their handguns during the Newhall fight were all shooting powerful .357 Magnum ammunition in their revolvers, despite the fact that they had apparently trained only with milder .38 Special ammunition.[61] It has been suggested by many (to include the CHP) that the officers were unaccustomed to the increased recoil, flash, and noise of the more powerful ammunition and that this negatively affected their ability to hit their targets with their handguns. In fact, this conclusion has become widely recognized throughout law enforcement as one of the principal lessons from Newhall, and is among the first recalled whenever the subject of Newhall is discussed.

The CHP was so convinced the lack of training experience with the powerful .357 Magnum ammunition affected the officer's marksmanship, it implemented radical changes in its ammunition and training policies in the years after the shooting. Officers who purchased their own .357 Magnum ammunition were henceforth required to train and qualify with it, and the use of low-powered, .38 Special wadcutter ammunition for training was eliminated. By 1976, the use of all .357 Magnum ammunition was completely prohibited, and all officers were required to use and carry the newly standardized (and less powerful) .38 Special jacketed hollowpoint round that was issued by the state for all training and duty purposes (See Appendix A).

Satisfied that it had learned the lesson and made the appropriate corrections to policy, training and equipment, the CHP moved on to other focus areas. But were they right?

Forty years of learning and experience since the Newhall shooting indicates that, while there are good reasons for officers to train with full-power ammunition that replicates the performance of their duty loads, it is unlikely that the ammunition used in training has much influence on officer performance during a shooting.[62] Instead, it is far more likely that other factors will be the dominant influence on the officer's performance.

In the aftermath of Newhall, cutting edge researchers like Bruce Siddle and police psychologists like Dr. Alexis Artwohl identified how SNS responses such as auditory exclusion, tunnel vision, temporal distortion, dissociation, sensory exclusion, and dramatic increases in strength all make the recoil, noise, and flash of the officer's firearm less noticeable, and even sometimes unnoticeable.[63] In fact, many officers who have been interviewed following shooting incidents report that their guns sounded like small "pops" instead of the larger "boom" they were used to, and others have reported the total absence of felt recoil and blast, sometimes leading each group to fear that their weapons had somehow malfunctioned during the fight.[64] Some officers, like the legendary Jim Cirillo of the famed New York Police Department Stakeout Squad, have experienced a strange detachment from firing the gun; in Cirillo's case, he found himself asking "Who the hell is shooting my gun?" in the middle of his first gunfight.[65]

All of these experiences, combined with many others from 40 years of interviewing gunfight survivors, indicate that Evan Marshall is correct in his analysis that "recoil, noise, and flash are training issues, not gunfight issues."[66] The effects of the sympathetic nervous system work together to dull the senses to the recoil, noise, and flash generated by the firing of a weapon and diminish the possibility that these characteristics will have an effect on the officer's performance during a stressful situation, even if they appear to be significant players during a lower state of arousal (such as in training).

With respect to Newhall, it is much more likely that Officers Gore, Pence, and Alleyn failed to hit their targets with their revolvers due to the effects of survival stress on their performance and the difficulty of hitting highly mobile targets firing from cover and concealment, than due to their lack of training experience with full-power .357 Magnum ammunition. The CHP's move to formalize its ammunition policy and standardize equipment in the wake of Newhall was perhaps a beneficial step for the department in many ways, but to justify it solely on the basis of what happened in Newhall doesn't seem to pass muster today, especially in light of recent learning about human physiology and the accumulated experience of officers who are gunfight survivors.

There are still very important reasons for officers to train with ammunition that mimics the energy and performance of their duty ammunition, but habituating the officer to recoil and noise does not seem to be as important as it was once thought to be.

RELOADING SKILLS

An additional tactical concern in the Newhall fight centers on revolver reloading skills. During the course of the Newhall shooting, Officer Pence emptied his revolver and was forced to reload it from behind the cover of his patrol car while under fire from Twining. His difficulty in reloading the revolver has historically been the source of much debate, and it bears further analysis.

Officer Pence has come under scrutiny in some circles for his inability to reload his revolver quickly and reenter the fight before he was ambushed and killed by Twining. While a faster reload would have been welcomed, there were several obstacles that stood in the way of this critical goal. For example, Officer Pence, like all CHP officers at the time, was armed with a six-shot revolver and carried 12 rounds of spare ammunition in dump pouches on his Sam Browne. Each of these dump pouches was designed to deposit six rounds of loose ammunition into the hand after the snap was undone, at which point an officer would load them individually into the chambers of the revolver.[67] This action requires a fair amount of dexterity, as the shooter must juggle and manipulate all six rounds with a single hand, since the other is holding the weapon. Moving a cartridge into position where it can be controlled, oriented into the proper direction, and guided into the cylinder without dropping any of the remaining rounds can be a challenge even when there is no pressure on the shooter, but doing so under the debilitating effects of survival stress becomes even more difficult, as fine motor skills have deteriorated, cognitive processes have diminished, and massive amounts of adrenaline have induced uncontrollable shaking.

To add to Officer Pence's difficulties, he was under fire from Twining dur-

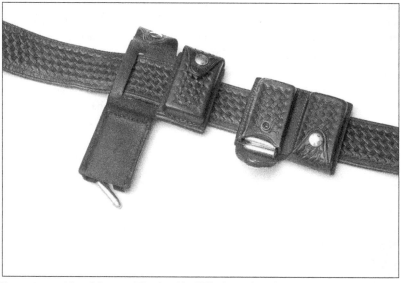

Two common styles of dump pouches used by CHP officers from the 1940s through the early 1970s. In the version on the left, each of the cells flop down to spill cartridges from the leather box when the top snap is released. In the version on the right, the cartridges fall free from the inverted pouch when the bottom flap is unsnapped. During the Newhall fight, Officer Pence reloaded from the inverted pouch design. Photo courtesy of the author.

ing the course of reloading, which induced more stress and also forced him to take a position of low cover, down on his knees and bending forward at the waist. This position crowded and pinched the area around his gunbelt between his abdomen and upper thighs, which undoubtedly interfered with the smooth operation of the already clumsy dump pouch.

During the course of reloading, Officer Pence was shot in both legs (including a serious compound fracture of the left femur), once in the hip, and once in the abdomen by Twining. Despite these serious and painful injuries, Officer Pence bravely completed his reload and was preparing to reengage Twining when he was killed at contact range by the felon, who had advanced on his position as the wounded Officer Pence struggled with the task.

It's notable that Officer Pence has frequently been accused of pocketing his spent brass in the middle of the fight in some kind of unconscious, reflexive action borne of academy firing range habits and practices. He has been criticized for this action, because it is presumed that it cost him precious moments that he needed to finish his reload and get back into the fight, and it is speculated that the action cost him his life, because it delayed his reload a moment too long.

This accusation is categorically false. The truth of the matter is that Officer Pence dumped his spent brass on the ground, roughly abeam the rear door on the driver's side of his police unit, and did not waste time pocketing the worthless cases.[68] While Officer Pence may have performed other reflexive actions under the stress of the event that would otherwise seem nonsensical (such as donning his hat as he exited the patrol car under fire, in accordance with CHP uniform policies and ingrained habits, just as Officer Alleyn had), he did not commit the infamous sin that became one of Newhall's most enduring myths.[69]

Officer Pence's reload took longer than desired, but it was the poor design and ergonomics of the dump pouch, a crouched position that interfered with the smooth operation of the pouch, a stress-induced loss of fine motor skills, and the punishing gunshot wounds inflicted by Twining that sealed his fate. There have indeed been other confirmed reports of officers engaged in battle who have senselessly retained their spent brass out of involuntary habit, but Officer Pence is not among them.[70]

Despite Officer Pence's innocence on this charge, it is important to recognize that, under stress, people will revert to the habits that have been reinforced through repetition and training, even if they are not helpful or sensible, and therefore it is critical to ensure that negative habits (such as retaining spent brass to simplify cleanup on the range), are not allowed to creep into the training process. Similarly, there is an obligation to ensure that the proper habits are deliberately programmed into training.

While Officer Pence did not waste time policing his spent brass during the fight, it is true he spent precious moments filling the cylinder of his revolver to full capacity, instead of accepting a partial load of three or four rounds and returning to the fight much more quickly. Given the fact that Twining was closing on him and wounding him with gunfire, Officer Pence would probably have been better off accepting the partial load and shooting back at Twining with a reduced number of rounds in the gun, than waiting to return fire until the gun was loaded to full capacity.[71]

Interviews conducted with officers who served at the time indicate that this situation was not specifically addressed in training at the academy.[72] It can be safely assumed that most reloads in the field would be conducted under stress, loose rounds would be fumbled, and that there would be a pressing need to finish their reloads quickly so the officer could get back in the fight and maintain continuity of fire. Under these circumstances, it would seem a reasonable tradeoff to sacrifice a full-capacity reload for the speed of getting back on target, especially with an opponent advancing on the officer's position. Had Officer Pence been trained to deal with this entirely foreseeable problem, it's possible that he might have recognized his situation and employed the tactic with enough time to shoot Twining as he made his final run at the rear of Unit 78-12.[73]

Additionally, it appears that Officer Pence reloaded his weapon at waist level and brought his head down to see what he was doing, where his posture and the bill of his cap robbed him of the ability to monitor his environment and detect Twining's approach. The nature and construction of a revolver makes it more natural, comfortable, and efficient to hold the revolver at waist level during reloading, so it's not surprising that he gravitated to this position, but it does make it much more difficult to monitor the surrounding environment.[74] This is especially critical, because it is likely that Officer Pence's SNS reaction was robbing him of his peripheral vision capabilities anyhow, turning his normal field of view into a narrow tunnel. It's unlikely that his physiology would have allowed him to pick up Twining in his peripheral vision, but if Officer Pence had been taught to load the revolver up in the center of his field of view and with his head erect, he might have been able to see Twining's advance within that central cone of vision. This might have provided the cue he needed to discontinue loading, accept what he had already loaded into the gun, and get back into the fight.

To the CHP's everlasting credit, immediate changes were incorporated into training processes and equipment was rapidly upgraded following the Newhall shooting. Administrative practices on the range that encouraged bad habits (such as policing brass during a course of fire or loading from trays or boxes instead of the ammunition carriers on the officer's Sam Browne), were eliminated, and firearms instructors emphasized improvements in tactics and procedures that increased officer safety.[75] In late 1971 through early 1972, the department began to issue newly developed speedloaders to officers in lieu of the problematic dump pouches, making them the first in the nation to do so. The speedloaders were much easier to use and significantly enhanced the reliability and speed of the reloading operation. The department obviously recognized the lessons that were written in Officer Pence's blood and did what they could to correct the conditions that led to his fate.

SKILL WITH THE SHOTGUN

As noted previously, shotguns were relatively new additions to the CHP at the time of Newhall, having only been added to each patrol car a few years before the shootout.[76] As a result, CHP shotgun training and doctrine was still in its infancy when Officer Frago grabbed the Remington 870 from the Lektro-Lok and exited Unit 78-8 into the cold night air to confront Davis and Twining.[77]

Earlier sections have addressed Officer Frago's approach to the Pontiac with the shotgun held in an unusable position. Despite the fact that this stance was one of two approved methods for carrying the shotgun in the California Highway Patrol Shotgun Training Manual at the time, this action was tactically unsound for several reasons.[78]

Aside from his inability to employ the weapon with its butt resting on his hip and the barrel in the air (as previously discussed), the position was completely untenable from a weapon retention perspective. With only one hand on the weapon and placed at a distance roughly one third of the way up the gun, Officer Frago had no strength or leverage to withstand an attack. An offender who got his hands on the barrel or forearm of the shotgun could easily lever it backwards, using Officer Frago's hand as a pivot point, and strip it from his grasp. Even if Officer Frago had attempted to hold onto the gun, his wrist would have been bent painfully backwards and his grip on the gun would have been broken, perhaps along with the wrist itself. Even a less sophisticated attack, like a simple snatch with one hand on the barrel and another on the buttstock could still overpower the officer, who had only one hand on the gun to resist it. Regardless of how it was accomplished, the fact is that if Twining had simply attacked Officer Frago with his hands, the loaded shotgun probably would have been his in moments.

Officer Frago was not the only officer to experience difficulty with his shotgun. Officer Alleyn also encountered problems with the long gun. Upon exiting the patrol car, Officer Alleyn chambered a round in his shotgun and immediately made his way around the rear of Unit 78-8, taking up a defensive position at the open passenger door. In the stress of the fight, it appears he cycled the slide an additional time and ejected an unfired round onto the ground, where it was later recovered by investigators. It is presumed that Officer Alleyn had forgotten that he had already loaded the shotgun's chamber and cycled the gun an additional time to ensure it was ready to fire.[79] This action deprived him of several precious seconds in the middle of the fight and, more importantly, it also deprived him of 25 percent of his ammunition capacity.[80]

This latter point is especially critical considering the fact that Officer Alleyn ran the shotgun empty in the fight. The shotgun was the most powerful weapon available to Officer Alleyn, and it was also the easiest to hit with, not only because of the nine-pellet pattern triggered with each shot, but because long guns have superior handling qualities that generally make them easier to use. In fact, Officer Alleyn was the only officer to hit either Davis or Twining with his weapon, and he did this with the shotgun.[81] If he had been given the opportunity to fire one more round before the shotgun ran dry, it's possible he could have scored an additional and more devastating hit on one or both of his opponents, thus turning the tide of the battle.

Alas, it was not to be. In the end, the officers were unable to rise above the level of their limited training and make effective use of the most powerful weapons in their arsenal. This was not the case with their opponents, however, as both Davis and Twining were very experienced in the use of long arms.[82] Although Twining did not access a long gun during the confrontation, Davis made effective use of his own shotgun to kill Officer Alleyn in a charge on his position late in the fight.

Optimum Choice of Safety Rescue Equipment

"Amateurs talk equipment. Professionals talk tactics."
—Unknown Source

The fourth and final column that supports Ayoob's "Priorities of Survival" is the "Optimum Choice of Safety Rescue Equipment." As it pertains to the discussion of the Newhall shooting, this particularly references the selection of firearms and ammunition.

There have been hints in previous sections about the issues surrounding this priority and how they were evident at Newhall. Indeed, there is a certain amount of overlap and interplay between Ayoob's priorities that makes it quite difficult to address one without feeling the influence of another.

For example, in the previous section, which discussed skills priority, Officer Pence's difficulty in using his ammunition dump pouches during reloading was mentioned. Although this analysis focused on the skill aspect (the software), there is no denying that the poor design of the equipment (the hardware) was a contributing factor in Officer Pence's performance. Therefore, a review of the equipment priority will necessarily tread on some familiar territory to the reader.

It is important that the CHP's selection of equipment should be considered in the proper context of the era. It would probably be accurate to point out that the CHP officers in the Newhall fight would have been better armed with semi-automatic pistols that offered a higher capacity and the ability to rapidly reload (as their opponents were—recall Twining's use of two 1911A1 pistols during the fight), but such a move would have been quite extraordinary in the law enforcement culture that prevailed at the time. Indeed, aside from the Illinois State Police (which took the extraordinary and groundbreaking step of issuing the Smith & Wesson M39 semi-automatic pistol as early as 1967), every single state police or highway patrol force in the nation issued revolvers to its officers. This trend was also followed by the vast majority of county and

168 NEWHALL SHOOTING — *A Tactical Analysis*

municipal agencies, with occasional rare exceptions (such as the El Monte, California, Police Department, which approved 1911-pattern pistols for duty in 1966). Indeed, nationwide acceptance of the semi-automatic pistol for law enforcement would not come for more than a decade after the Newhall fight. Thus, it makes little sense to argue that the CHP made a poor choice in arming its officers with revolvers when a superior choice was available. That recognition would come in time, largely as a result of incidents like Newhall, but to argue the point in 1970 would have been largely premature.

Despite this, there are still areas involving equipment selection that are worthy of analysis.

AMMUNITION POLICY

The CHP's policy of issuing .38 Special ammunition in lieu of the more powerful .357 Magnum ammunition carried by three of the four officers at Newhall has come under criticism, as described previously. But, in the Newhall shooting, it appears that this policy probably had little to no effect on the outcome of the incident. It is doubtful that the event would have turned out any differently if the officers had trained extensively with the more powerful ammunition, or had been supplied the ammunition by the department in lieu of purchasing it themselves. Issues of mindset and tactics trumped issues of equipment at Newhall.

Considering the .357 Magnum's superior penetration capabilities, it seems that it would be the preferred choice to the .38 Special for officers like highway patrolmen, who spend a lot of time working around cars and who would potentially need to penetrate thick layers of glass and steel with their weapons. However, this ammunition also places greater stress on handguns than the milder .38 Special, and it accelerates gun wear. Additionally, the greater recoil of the cartridge makes it more difficult for many officers to control during training and qualification, as many agencies would later discover during the heyday of the cartridge in law enforcement, in the 1970s. From these perspectives, a fairly good case can be made for the retention of the lesser round, which is why the Magnum never came close to replacing the Special in police service throughout the nation. Training issues aside, the CHP probably had the best possible policy in place at the time of Newhall—one that standardized the .38 Special but also permitted the optional use of .357 Magnum ammunition by those who desired to carry it. In any event, lack of handgun ammunition power or penetration was not an issue at Newhall.

This may not have been the case with the shotgun ammunition fired by Officer Alleyn. One of Officer Alleyn's pellets struck Twining in the head after it penetrated the vehicle, causing a minor wound. Some reporting indicates that the pellet had spent most of its energy penetrating into the car and didn't have much left by the time it struck Twining.83 Had this single .33-caliber

53.8-grain pellet been a one-ounce (438-grain) shotgun slug instead, it is likely that it would have delivered a much more powerful blow to the felon, possibly a fatal one. Of course, devil's advocates will note that it is also likely a slug might have missed him entirely and that Twining was only hit due to the expanding pattern thrown by the 00 Buckshot round fired by Officer Alleyn.

Interestingly, the CHP has never issued shotgun slugs for use in patrol shotguns, preferring to issue the nine-pellet 00 Buckshot load exclusively. Considering the fact that most of the CHP's potential shooting scenarios involve the use of vehicles, it would seem reasonable for the CHP to issue at least a few rounds of the better penetrating slug ammunition with each of the department's shotguns. It's impossible to say with any certainty that it would have made a difference at Newhall, but it remains an interesting academic exercise to ponder the "what ifs," and it's also conceivable that the penetrating capabilities of shotgun slugs could be useful in a future scenario.

In the present-day context, the same thought extends to the rapid proliferation of patrol rifles in the relatively light 5.56x45mm caliber. Agencies equipping their officers with these important lifesaving tools should ensure that the ammunition chosen for these firearms is capable of adequate penetration through vehicles and other objects that are likely to be used as cover by threats, and that the performance of such ammunition is suitable after defeating intermediate barriers.

SPARE AMMUNITION

It has been previously discussed that the officers at Newhall were handicapped by the dump pouches used to carry their spare revolver ammunition. The pouches were famous for being rather clumsy to use, since the officer was required to pop open the flap on the bottom side of the pouch and catch the six loose rounds as they fell out into his hand. This operation was quite error prone, especially under stress or while the officer was moving. Once the officer got the ammunition out of the pouch and into his hand, he was required to juggle the cartridges, grab a single one, turn it around so that it was properly aligned, and feed it into the narrow chamber in the cylinder. He had to do this with the same hand that was cupping and retaining the remaining cartridges, since the opposite hand would be occupied holding the revolver. The complexity and required dexterity of the task just about guaranteed that the officer would have to abandon his scan of the surrounding environment and focus on the hand holding the ammunition supply and the revolver itself.

Even in the best of environments, this is a difficult and complex motor task that requires great amounts of dexterity to perform. However, with hands that are clumsy and shaking uncontrollably as a result of SNS activation, the task becomes even more difficult. If other factors are present, such as injuries, hands wet with blood or sweat, hands numb from the cold, a requirement to load while moving, or reduced vision in dark environments, the process becomes exceedingly problematic and prone to error. The alternative method available to the CHP involved the use of ammunition loops on the gunbelt. These loops typically held six rounds on a leather slide that was threaded onto the gunbelt. In use, the officer would pluck rounds from the loops and insert them into the revolver one or two at a time. This method was probably more positive and less prone to fumbling than the dump pouch method, because the officer could control how many rounds were being handled at any given time. However, it was still sometimes difficult to extract rounds from the loops, and the process was only marginally better at withstanding the effects of negative influences like stress, cold, injuries, and wet hands. Additionally, the loops left the ammunition more exposed to the elements and to physical damage. A highway patrolman (and especially a motor officer) makes his living outside in the elements and frequently finds himself digging through car wreckage and banging around the insides of tight spaces and on the ground as he provides aid to injured passengers. The gasoline, transmission fluid, oil, and water he is regularly exposed to would quickly corrode the brass cartridges in the leather loops if they weren't regularly maintained, and the cartridges themselves are more subject to falling out or being dented when carried in exposed loops versus the fully enclosed dump pouches. These risks would have been unappealing to an agency that issued its officers only 30 rounds of duty ammunition each year and expected them to last the entire period.[84]

While the loops offered a nominal two- to four-second advantage over the dump pouch system in speed of reloading under ideal conditions, the additional risk of ammunition damage and loss probably swayed the CHP to choose the latter option. It also didn't hurt that the dump pouches provided a much more uniform look for a department that was especially conscious of appearance. Thus, the loops chosen by early highway patrolmen in the 1920s and 1930s had disappeared from use by the late 1940s, as the Department advanced towards standardization and uniformity among the officers.

The development of speedloaders, which proved far superior to either the dump pouches or the loops, was proceeding quickly around the time of Newhall. Early designs had found their way into the catalogs of law enforcement supply vendors such as F. Morton Pitt Co. by 1964, and these items were just being introduced into competitive shooting circles by the early 1970s and gaining widespread acceptance there. In the wake of Newhall, the department rapidly adopted them for law enforcement use, but it appears that these products were just in their infancy at the time of the Newhall shooting, and it's not surprising that the CHP hadn't considered them beforehand.

The CHP does deserve criticism for its hesitance to issue spare ammunition with the shotgun. The precedent for carrying spare ammunition on the long gun dated back to at least World War II, when G.I.s routinely carried spare eight-round en-bloc clips for their M-1 Garand rifles clipped to their slings, or a pair of extra 15-round magazines in pouches attached to the buttstocks of their M-1 Carbines.85 Applying the idea to an ammunition-restricted gun like the Remington 870 shotgun seems like it would have been obvious, yet it took the negative experience of Newhall before the CHP began to add canvas ammunition pouches to the stocks of their patrol shotguns. If Officer Alleyn's shotgun had been equipped with a system of carrying spare ammunition, he might have been able to keep it in the fight long enough to exact another, more damaging hit on Davis or Twining. Alternatively, the brave citizen-hero Gary Kness might have been able to get the gun into action against Davis after he picked it up and clicked on an empty chamber.

BACKUP GUNS

It has been suggested that the Newhall officers should have had access to backup guns during the fight and that such equipment might have saved some lives. While there is great merit to this observation, particularly for Officer Pence who died while reloading his empty revolver, it should be noted that the absence of backup guns at Newhall was not unusual for the period.

The use of backup guns was relatively uncommon in U.S. law enforcement at the time of the Newhall shooting. There certainly were individual officers who made great use of them, but the concept was not readily embraced by the vast majority of officers on patrol throughout the nation—and many thought such preparations were unnecessary.[86]

Officers who served in high-crime areas, or on high-risk, specialized teams (such as "stakeout squads," "tactical teams," or "felony cars"), were more prone to use backups, as were officers who worked for agencies (such as Chicago or Detroit), that dictated the use of underpowered primary weapons but had liberal policies on the carriage of more powerful secondary weapons. But the use of backup guns was simply uncommon amongst most patrol officers circa 1970. Additionally, most agencies at the time did not have policies that authorized or actively encouraged the use of backup weapons by officers. The CHP itself didn't officially authorize the use of backup weapons until sometime in the mid '70s, at which time they approved the use of Colt or Smith & Wesson .38-caliber revolvers exclusively in this role.[87] Prior to this time, some officers carried backups in contradiction to the department's intentions, but the lack of official departmental approval certainly stopped many officers from considering these lifesaving tools. In light of this specific situation in the CHP, it is not surprising that none of the Newhall officers were equipped with backup guns.

The resistance to backup guns in law enforcement eroded over time, due to a combination of factors. Increasingly violent criminals and anti-establishment figures began to attack officers with increasing frequency throughout the late 1960s and 1970s, making the use of backups more necessary. Additionally, the publicity surrounding high-profile events like the 1963 Onion Field incident, in which two Los Angeles policemen were held hostage with their own guns and one of them was killed, and the 1978 killing of CHP Officers Blecher and Freeman in similar circumstances, made officers and their chains of command more aware of their vulnerability. So, too, did the growing "officer survival" movement that gained hold in the 1970s.[88] However, these developments occurred long after the Newhall shooting, and it would be several decades before the presence of backup guns was more commonplace than their absence.

In the end analysis, the possession of a backup gun by Officers Gore, Frago and Alleyn would have made no difference, since each of these officers died while in possession of primary guns that were still loaded. Only Officer Pence, whose primary arm had been shot empty, could have benefited from having a backup gun at the ready. If he had been able to put a secondary gun into action against Twining, instead of having to reload his primary gun, he might have been able to put effective fire on his opponent and the outcome of the fight might have been different, especially if he could have held them off until the arrival of Units 78-19R and 78-16R moments later.

It should be noted that both Davis and Twining used backup guns to good effect during the fight. Davis shot at least three different guns during the fight (a snub revolver, a sawed-off pump shotgun, and Officer Frago's revolver), and Twining shot three, as well (a four-inch S&W Highway Patrolman revolver and two 1911A1 semi-automatic pistols). Neither of the felons took the time to reload an empty gun in the middle of the fight, instead opting to choose another already loaded firearm to continue the battle. Twining was especially fortunate to have access to multiple weapons, as one of his weapons (the first 1911A1 he fired) malfunctioned. Instead of fixing the gun, he simply procured another from their ample supply and eventually used it to kill Officer Pence as he struggled to reload his empty primary weapon. As fate would have it, the felons not only had the advantage of superior mindset, tactics, and skill, they were also armed with better and more plentiful equipment.

ENDNOTES

1. Brooks, P.R. (1975). Officer Down, Code Three. Schiller Park, IL: Motorola Teleprograms, Inc. p.4.

2. Massad F. Ayoob is an internationally known firearms and self-defense instructor. He was the Director of the Lethal Force Institute in Concord, New Hampshire, for 28 years and is currently the director of the Massad Ayoob Group. Ayoob has taught police techniques and civilian self-defense to both law enforcement officers and private citizens in numerous venues since 1974, and has appeared as an expert witness in several trials. He has served as a part-time police

officer in New Hampshire, since 1972, and currently holds the rank of Captain in the Grantham, New Hampshire, police department. He was the former Vice Chairman of the Forensic Evidence Committee of the National Association of Criminal Defense Lawyers (NACDL) and is believed to be the only non-attorney to ever hold this position. He has served as Chair of Firearms Committee of the American Society of Law Enforcement Trainers (ASLET), serves on the Advisory Board of the International Law Enforcement Educators and Trainers Association, and is an instructor at the National Law Enforcement Training Center. Ayoob has authored several books and over one thousand articles on firearms, combat techniques, self-defense, and legal issues, and has served in an editorial capacity for Guns Magazine, American Handgunner, Gun Week, and Combat Handguns. Since 1995, he has written self-defense- and firearms-related articles for Backwoods Home Magazine. He also has a featured segment on the television show Personal Defense TV, which airs on The Outdoor Channel in the United States, and is a regular contributor to the ProArms Podcast. For more information, go to <http://massadayoobgroup.com/>.

3. Ayoob, M.F. (1990). Lethal Force Institute, Priorities of Survival. [Film] and Izumi, M.T. (1993). In Self Defense. Concord, NH: Police Bookshelf. p.7.

4. Six of the 10 were related to Mental Awareness and Preparation (Sleepy or Asleep, Relaxing too Soon, Missing the Danger Signs, Tombstone Courage, Preoccupation, and Apathy), two were related to Tactics (Taking a Bad Position, Failure to Watch Their Hands), two were related to Skill with the Rescue Equipment (Improper Search and Use of Handcuffs, Failure to Maintain Proficiency and Care of Weapon, Vehicle and Equipment), and none were related to the Optimum Choice of Safety Equipment, all of which proves the validity of Ayoob's model. Brooks, P.R. (1975). Officer Down, Code Three. Schiller Park, IL: Motorola Teleprograms, Inc. pp.6-7.

5. Ayoob, M.F. (2010, July/August). The Ayoob Files. American Handgunner Magazine, Volume 34, Number 4, Issue 206, and Police One TV. (2011, April 26). Will to Win: Jared Reston. [Film]. <http://www.policeone.com/policeonetv/videos/3592582-will-to-win-jared-reston/>.

6. Police One TV. (2011, April 26). Will to Win: Jared Reston. [Film]. <http://www.policeone.com/policeonetv/videos/3592582-will-to-win-jared-reston/>.

7. Ibid.

8. Indeed, many medical studies indicate that the survival rate for gunshot wounds in the United States is quite high. In one study, the average survival rate for persons shot during an assault in the United States was around 80%, with the survival rate spiking as high as 84% for persons who were not shot in the head during an assault. Beaman, V., MS, and Annest, J.L., PhD, and Mercy, J.A., PhD, and Kresnow, M., MS, and Pollock, D.A., MD. (March 2000). Lethality of Firearm-Related Injuries in the United States Population. Annals of Emergency Medicine, Volume 35, Issue 3. http://www.annemergmed.com/article/S0196-0644%2800%2970077-1/abstract.

9. Miller's books are among the most insightful studies of violence and how to prepare for it ever penned. His observations are founded in real world experience as a corrections officer and law enforcement trainer, and the books are must-reads for law enforcement officers and armed citizens who want to understand the psychology of violence and how to prepare themselves for potential combat.
Miller's concept of "freezes" is vitally important and beyond the scope of this work, but the important issue here is that the person might need to force himself to act when his mind is frozen. One method that Miller discusses is talking one's self through the problem with the aid of a simple, pre-established plan of action. The plan need not be elaborate. Instead, a simple framework is what is desired.
For instance, in the aviation world, pilots are taught that, in times of stress, their priorities (in order) are to "aviate, navigate, communicate." That is, they need to keep the aircraft flying and under control first, then worry about where the aircraft is pointed, and then, finally, worry about communicating with crew, passengers, and air traffic control. When a pilot encounters an emergency, this framework doesn't provide all the answers, but it does provide a structure for organizing and executing his response appropriately and might provide an anchor point for a temporarily frozen mind.
In a similar, more relevant vein, officer survival instructor and author Rich Grassi provides a

model for what officers should do in the immediate moments after shooting stops. In Grassi's model, the officer is advised to consider the following priorities: "Cover, reload, scan, check for wounds (leak check), communicate." Again, the plan is basic, but provides some structure for an efficient response that covers the most important priorities and might help to break a freeze. Miller, R.A. (2011). Facing Violence.Wolfeboro, NH: YMAA Publication Center, pp. 126-127, and Grassi, R. (2009, May 26). Skill Set. Post Shooting Procedures. The Tactical Wire. [Online]. http://www.thetacticalwire.com/archives/2009-05-26.

10. Author Mark Moritz wrote an outstanding article on the necessity to separate the extraneous from the important during crisis. The reader is highly encouraged to read his article on the subject. Moritz, M. (n.d.). All That Later. The Gun Zone. [Online] <http://www.thegunzone.com/allthatlater.html>.

11. Asken, M.J., Dr., and Grossman, D.A., Lt. Col. (2010) Warrior Mindset. United States: Warrior Science Publications, p. XVI and p.38.

12. For an outstanding treatment of tactical performance imagery, arousal control, and the training techniques to enhance the "mental toughness skills" required by modern warriors, the reader is encouraged to read Dr. Michael Asken's and Lieutenant Colonel Dave Grossman's Warrior Mindset. Their expertise is first rate and their treatment of these critical areas is infinitely better than anything the author can propose. Asken, M.J., Dr., and Grossman, D.A., Lt. Col. (2010) Warrior Mindset. United States: Warrior Science Publications.

13. Mireles, Ed. Jr., quoted in Anderson, W.F., M.D. (1996). Forensic Analysis of the April 11, 1986 FBI Firefight. Boulder, CO: Paladin Press, p.127

14. Rand Corporation. (2008). Evaluation of the New York City Police Department Firearm Training and Firearm Discharge Review Process. Santa Monica, CA: Rand Corporation. p. 8.

15. Ibid.

16. Grossman, D.A. Lt Col. (2004). On Combat. Belleville, IL: PPCT Research Publications. p.155.

17. Ibid.

18. To be clear, Marshall knows that police officers are ethically and legally bound to use reasonable and proportional force in their duties, and is not advocating unbridled and unnecessary aggression. As an honorable, spiritual warrior, Marshall knows that the awesome power entrusted to law enforcement officers is also accompanied by an equally awesome responsibility to control it and use it prudently. His thoughts should not be construed to mean that anything goes on the street, but rather to mean that, when the specific conditions exist which justify the use of force by an officer, he must fully commit to that path, without restraint of any kind, to ensure his survival and the protection of the innocent. Marshall, E. (n.d.) Stopping Power Forums. [Online]. <www.stoppingpower.net>.

19. Marshall, E. (2009, 14 December). Stopping Power Forums. [Online]. <http://www.stoppingpower.net/forum/topic.asp?TOPIC_ID=17928>.

20. Grossman, D.A. Lt Col. (2004). On Combat. Belleville, IL: PPCT Research Publications. p.159.

21. Miller, R.A. (2011). Facing Violence.Wolfeboro, NH: YMAA Publication Center, p . 23.

22. Gaylord, C. (1960, 1997). Handgunner's Guide. Boulder CO: Paladin Press. p.147.

23. Suarez, G. (2003). The Combative Perspective. Boulder, CO: Paladin Press. p.2.

24. Newhall was a rural area frequented by large numbers of hunters and target shooters in April of 1970, and gun-related infractions were apparently common, especially misdemeanors like the one in question. It is felt in some quarters that Officers Gore and Frago had no reason to be at an especially heightened state of alert when they stopped the Pontiac containing Davis and Twining. While this conclusion may seem cavalier and reckless by today's standards, it seems that it

appeared more reasonable at the time.
However, CHP Chief John Anderson relates that, while gun-related complaints were common in the area, it was not beyond imagination that they could turn violent. According to Chief Anderson, only a few months previous a pair of motorists had engaged in a shootout in the nearby Fresno area over an argument involving the dimming of high-beam headlights. More ominously, Officer Warren Loftus had recently been shot in the Newhall area during a routine stop for speeding—an incident that, while not a "gun" call, showed that even the most mundane activity could quickly turn deadly.

25. Boyd developed the model and refined it over decades. He gave it life in a series of evolving lectures, such as the *"Patterns of Conflict"* seminar that continuously matured over time. Boyd, J. (1986). *Patterns of Conflict. [Online]. http://www.slideshare.net/noobgank/patterns-of-conflict and Wikipedia. (n.d.) OODA Loop. [Online]. <http://en.wikipedia.org/wiki/OODA_loop> and Wikipedia (n.d.) John Boyd. [Online]. <http://en.wikipedia.org/wiki/John_Boyd_%28military_strategist%29> .*

26. Actually, Miller advocates using *"Operant Conditioning"* principles to eliminate the middle steps entirely. Miller, R.A. (2011). *Facing Violence.Wolfeboro, NH: YMAA Publication Center, p . 95 and P. 137.*

27. Ibid.

28. Ouellette, R. (1993). *Management of Aggressive Behavior. Powers Lake, WI: Performance Dimensions Publishing. p.3.*

29. Ibid., p.2.

30. Ibid., p.3

31. Ibid. pp.51-53.

32. Lieutenant Colonel John Dean *"Jeff"* Cooper (ret.) popularized the use of the color code, adapted from the USMC, as a model to describe a person's mindset as they oriented themselves towards a threat. As a person progressed through the various stages of the color code, they were becoming more mentally prepared to use force against a specific threat. In the third stage of the code, Orange, a person has recognized that something is not right and has gone from a condition of relaxed alertness where there was no particular threat (Yellow) to a condition where a particular threat has caused the escalation in alert status. The person shifts focus to the particular threat and in the final step, Red, the person is prepared to fight that threat immediately when warranted. Cooper, J. (2005) *Jeff Cooper's Commentaries. Volume 13, Number 7. [Online]. http://dvc.org.uk/jeff/jeff13_7.html.*

33. The CHP Enforcement Tactics Manual of the time advised:
"When two officers are working together, both should get out of the patrol unit upon stopping a violator, one going up to the violator's car and the other standing to the right front of the patrol vehicle. At night, it is a good practice for the officer covering to stand just behind the right front headlight of the patrol car."
From the context of the manual, it is understood that this instruction is intended for "routine" operations in which there is no specific threat, but only the general threat that accompanies stopping any vehicle with unknown occupants—in other words, a low-risk or routine stop. In CHP Academy training exercises of the period involving "hot stop" procedures, the passenger-side officer is described as taking cover behind the door of the CHP cruiser with the CHP shotgun while the driver's-side officer makes the approach to the suspect vehicle, which makes much greater sense when facing opponents who are suspected to be armed and dangerous. It would seem that Officer Frago's position behind the headlight was not compatible with hot stop tactics of the time, and it is presumed that he either took this position out of routine habit or because there was a lack of coordination between him and Officer Gore and it was unclear which tactics they were going to employ. In Officer Frago's defense, it has been observed by many, including the CHP itself, that the brandishing event that prompted the stop was a routine occurrence in this area and would have been only a misdemeanor offense at the time. Such a crime would be treated differently in today's environment, but, at the time and in this rural area,

it would not have been unusual to view this as a rather routine stop. However, in a routine stop, the officers usually don't draw and aim their weapons at the suspect vehicle, and they also don't grab the shotgun from the car, which is reserved for more serious confrontations. Thus, this hybrid mix of tactics used by the officers is difficult to understand in retrospect, and perhaps indicative of some level of confusion (perhaps due to inexperience), as to how to deal with the situation.

34. Indeed, taking cover would have been essential to ensure their protection, since it is an established fact that "action beats reaction," and even if the CHP officers had the felons at gunpoint, the felons still could have drawn and fired before the CHP officers had mentally processed the action and stopped them with gunfire of their own.
This point was amply demonstrated in the research conducted by Officers Thomas A. Hontz and Raymond P. Rheingans, whose 1997 study of 76 officers indicated that criminals could draw and fire a handgun in as little as 0.78 seconds, while the average officer response time from recognition of a visual cue to the first shot fired was 1.15 seconds, a deadly 47% increase. Notably, this 1.15-second average was developed with officers starting the exercise with their weapon already in hand at a "low ready" position, similar to how they would hold a criminal at gunpoint. If the officers were required to draw their weapon from the holster as part of the response, the total reaction time to first shot fired increased to 1.90 seconds on average, a 144% increase that dramatically increased the risk of the officer being shot before he could even respond. Hontz, T.A., and Rheingans, R.P. (1997). Firearms Response Time. PPCT Research Publications, Millstadt, IL.

35. Personal interview with CHP Officer Jay Rice (ret.), whose decision to retain all his cadet materials and notes from the era was exceptionally fortuitous and a true gift to a researcher such as the author. His extensive and detailed handwritten notes provide critical and detailed insight to the instruction received by CHP cadets of the era.

36. McLain, J. (1970, April 12). You Could Get Shot For Missing Class Here. The Sacramento Union and CHP Class I-65 "Hourly Distribution of Subjects," courtesy of CHP Officer Jay Rice (ret.).

37. Although the FBI agents at the CHP Academy mentioned in class a standing search (with the suspect standing freely—the least used), and a kneeling search (a "new" position that was a "good holding position"), the greatest emphasis was placed on using a modified wall search position, with the suspect leaning forward onto the vehicle. It was presumed that the vast majority of CHP contacts would involve this search position, and it formed the core of the exceptionally short instructional periods at the Academy to the exclusion of any other techniques. Today, the CHP's PMA instruction provides for four different arrest methods—two standing, one kneeling, and one prone, with the prone method being used in all felony vehicle stops. Personal interview with CHP Officer (Retired) Jay Rice, and CHP Officer (Retired) Gil Payne, and personal papers of CHP Officer (Retired) Jay Rice.
There is conflicting testimony from witnesses regarding whether or not Officer Gore had actually begun his search of Davis when Twining's first shots rang out. Some witness statements place him at a distance from Davis, and others right next to him. The pattern and angle of Twining's shots into the side of the Pontiac indicate Officer Gore was directly next to Davis at the left rear of the car. Therefore, it is presumed Officer Gore was within arm's reach of Davis and was either actively searching Davis or a search was imminent when Twining began shooting.

38. After the Newhall shooting, the CHP would instruct officers to cuff dangerous suspects first, then search them later as part of the renewed emphasis on improving Physical Methods of Arrest (PMA) procedures. However, in the pre-Newhall era, officers were instructed to search first, then cuff. Personal interviews with CHP Officer Jay Rice (ret.) and CHP Officer Gil Payne (ret.).

39. By staying removed and monitoring the bigger picture when his immediate assistance is not required by the contact officer, the cover officer performs a very important safety function. If the cover officer allows his attention to be unnecessarily drawn into the actions of the contact officer, then the situation becomes very similar to the crew of Eastern Airlines Flight #401, who allowed all three members in the cockpit to become so engrossed with fixing a suspected landing gear malfunction (which later turned out to be nothing but a burned out light bulb), that

nobody was flying or monitoring the aircraft anymore. Unfortunately, this meant that nobody recognized the aural warning that the autopilot had disengaged, nor the subsequent gentle descent of the aircraft into the Everglades, until it was too late. A total of 101 people aboard the flight were killed in the December 29, 1972, crash.

40. Officer Frago's decision to leave the cover position was tactically unsound and the subject of much criticism in some circles, but it's interesting to consider whether a mix of armament and flaws in the standard tactics influenced his decision.
Officer Frago was armed with a shotgun, which has crude sights and fires multiple pellets in a pattern and is therefore less precise than a rifle or pistol, which shoot a single bullet and have precision sights. Although the shot pattern from Officer Frago's Cylinder-bore shotgun would probably have opened up only to a 12-inch pattern or so at the short distance to the Pontiac, it's unlikely his limited CHP shotgun training would have prepared him to understand this advanced user concept. Indeed, the layman's understanding of shotguns would have reinforced the opposite. Ever since World War I, shotguns had been known as "trench brooms" and "alley sweepers," due to their supposed ability to throw a wide pattern of devastating shot. These misconceptions had been imprinted in the collective psyche of the public by legions of returning Doughboys and scores of Hollywood films depicting cowboys and gangsters, and so were not easily ignored.
Even the CHP as a whole was somewhat taken with the mystique of the shotgun. An April 1965 article in the San Diego Evening Tribune which triumphed the "Psychological Value of Shotguns," reprinted in the California Association of Highway Patrolmen (CAHP) magazine, quipped that, "The short barrels [of the CHP's new "sawed off" shotguns] cause a quicker and wider pattern of the shot range, which makes a target within 50 yards almost impossible to miss … you just aim and fire." The CHP Shotgun Training Manual in use at the time encouraged this line of thinking, with pictures of CHP silhouette targets that had been shot at various distances displaying widely spread patterns.
It's possible that Officer Frago, like most shotgun novices and the author of that misleading Tribune piece, could have believed that his shotgun would fire a pattern so large that it would have endangered Officer Gore, who was approaching the suspect vehicle. This may have encouraged him to move forward, thereby reducing any risk of fratricide.
The other alternative would have been to abandon the shotgun and switch to his less-powerful revolver, which would have had its own tactical consequences. Additionally, Officer Frago would have had to make the tough choice between merely setting the shotgun aside (a security and safety risk), or putting it back in the cradle in the patrol car (a delay and distraction that would have been unacceptable as his partner moved forward into danger).
By this logic, did the CHP hot stop procedure that required Officer Gore to advance forward inadvertently force Officer Frago's hand? Did Officer Gore's advance leave Officer Frago no choice but to follow and move forward with shotgun in hand, lest he risk shooting his fellow officer? CHP Shotgun Training Manual, (1965), Page 2.

41. This was called the "hip rest" carry position in CHP parlance, and it was proscribed for "conditions where an officer may be holding a shotgun for an extended period of time or its immediate use is not anticipated." It was not a position that allowed the officer to quickly get the gun into action. CHP Shotgun Training Manual, (1965), Page 9.

42. California Highway Patrol. (1975). Newhall: 1970 [Film]. Sacramento, CA, courtesy of Santa Clarita Valley Historical Society and SCVTV, http://www.scvtv.com/html/newhall1970-chp1975btv.html.

43. This does not mean that Officers Pence and Alleyn failed to maneuver during the fight. They did indeed abandon their initial positions after their weapons ran dry, to assume a new fallback position at the rear of their respective vehicles, where they again began shooting. The key distinction between the officers and their opponents is that the officers did all their shooting and fighting from fixed positions, never moving and shooting at the same time, while the felons did their shooting on the move. This made the felons especially difficult to target and gave them the initiative in the fight, as they forced the officers to react to their movements, thus interrupting their OODA cycle and getting "inside their loop."

44. Aveni is intellectually honest enough to note that, while he can't disprove the link, he also cannot positively establish one either, because it is so difficult to obtain meaningful data from

law enforcement agencies. Many agencies don't collect the requisite data, and of those who do, even fewer will share it out of liability or political concerns. The lack of a standardized reporting format across the profession, which asks specific questions about important details such as lighting conditions, distances, and other critical factors, is another impediment to gaining meaningful data for analysis. Aveni, T.J. (2003, August). Officer-Involved Shootings: What We Didn't Know Has Hurt Us. The Police Policy Studies Council. <http://www.theppsc.org/Staff_Views/Aveni/OIS.pdf>.

45. Surefire Institute. (n.d.) Lowlight and Tactical Training. Study Reveals Important Truths Hidden in the Details of Officer-Involved Shootings, Reprinted from Los Angeles County Sheriff's Department, Operation Safe Streets. [Online]. <http://www.surefireinstitute.com/images/pdfs/Officer-Involved_Shooting_Study.pdf>. Aveni's conclusion is supported by a number of notable law enforcement trainers and writers, to include Richard Fairburn, Tom Marx, Gregory Morrison, and Dave Spaulding, all of whom have discussed the complexities of making law enforcement firearms training realistic and relevant to actual gunfight conditions. See Marx, T. (2010, March 1). Five Ways to Blend Marksmanship and Reality-based Training, PoliceOne.com. [Online] <http://www.policeone.com/police-products/firearms/articles/2009465-Five-ways-to-blend-marksmanship-and-reality-based-training/> and Fairburn, R. (2008, December 12). Where Did All the Bullets Go? PoliceOne.com. [Online] <http://www.policeone.com/police-products/firearm-accessories/gun-cleaning/articles/1764925-Where-did-all-the-bullets-go/> and Spaulding, D. (2004, January 21). How to Improve Marksmanship. PoliceOne.com. [Online]. <http://www.policeone.com/columnists/PoliceMagazine/articles/77176-How-to-improve-marksmanship/>.

46. Officer Alleyn's involuntary final shot into Unit 78-8 was obviously not targeted at Davis. California Highway Patrol. (1970). Information Bulletin (July 1, 1970): Shooting Incident—Newhall Area. Sacramento, CA and California Highway Patrol. (1975). Newhall: 1970 [Film]. Sacramento, CA, courtesy of Santa Clarita Valley Historical Society and SCVTV, <http://www.scvtv.com/html/newhall1970-chp1975btv.html>.

47. Ibid, and Los Angeles County Sheriffs Department Homicide investigation files.

48. Further discussions of Boyd's OODA loop concept and its application to personal combat can be found in the excellent books from Lou Chiodo, Dave Spaulding, and Gabe Suarez. Chiodo, L. (2009). Winning A High-Speed, Close-Distance Gunfight. Boulder, CO: Paladin Press, and Spaulding, D. (2003). Handgun Combatives. Flushing, NY: Looseleaf Law Publications, Inc., and Suarez, G. (2003). The Combative Perspective. Boulder, CO: Paladin Press.

49. Siddle, B.K. (2012). High Risk Human Factors [Briefing]. Human Factor Research Group, Millstadt, IL.

50. Ibid.

51. Ibid.

52. Ibid, and Siddle, B.K. (1995). Sharpening the Warrior's Edge. Belleville, IL: PPCT Research Publications, p.7-8.

53. Ibid, and Siddle, B.K. (1995). Sharpening the Warrior's Edge. Belleville, IL: PPCT Research Publications, p.91-101.

54. Siddle, B.K. (1995). Sharpening the Warrior's Edge. Belleville, IL: PPCT Research Publications, p.61.

55. Rory Miller neatly summarizes the negative effects of SNS activation on performance and trained skills when he makes the incredibly insightful observation that:
"Under attack, you will not have either the mind or the body that you have trained. You will have an impaired, partially deaf and blind, clumsy beginner who isn't that bright. You will be like a rank beginner because, surprise, you are a rank beginner."
Miller, R.A. (2011). Facing Violence.Wolfeboro, NH: YMAA Publication Center, p . 142.

56. Siddle notes that SNS-caused decreases in peripheral vision, depth perception, and the

ability to focus on close objects not only rob the individual of the ability to see things in the general environment around them, but also prevent the individual from clearly seeing their gun sights. Per Siddle, "the ability to focus on the front sight of a handgun is not possible when the SNS is activated," which complicates the marksmanship problem dramatically when engaging targets beyond "close quarters" distances, like the officers in Newhall were required to do. Siddle, B.K. (1998). Scientific and Test Data Validating the Isosceles and Single-Hand Point Shooting Techniques. Belleville, IL: PPCT Management Systems, p.3.

57. Statistics gleaned from the NYPD SOP-9 reporting system and from Metro-Dade Police data support the 15% average across the board. Of course, many variables affect the hit probabilities. Shootings that occur in low light typically have a lower hit probability than those in daylight (perhaps as much as 24 to 30 percent), while shootings that occur at close distances have higher hit probabilities than those which occur at farther distances (between two and 10 times as much, depending on distance). Aveni, T.J. (2003, August). Officer-Involved Shootings: What We Didn't Know Has Hurt Us. The Police Policy Studies Council. <http://www.theppsc.org/Staff_Views/Aveni/OIS.pdf>.

58. Mister Kness' shot struck an intervening object first, probably the car, which caused the bullet to fragment. The CHP report on the incident noted that, "two copper-jacketed fragments were found imbedded in the suspect's chest after his capture." California Highway Patrol. (1970). Information Bulletin (July 1, 1970): Shooting Incident—Newhall Area. Sacramento, CA.

59. Santa Clarita Valley Historical Society. (2010). The Newhall Incident: A Law Enforcement Tragedy [Film]. Santa Clarita, CA, courtesy of Santa Clarita Valley Historical Society and SCVTV, <http://www.scvtv.com/html/scvhs040510btv.html>.

60. Gabe Suarez notes that, "Man has the capability, based on his perspectives in prehistoric times, to engage in combat in either an emotionally aroused state with the resulting stress effects and inhibitions against killing, or in a cool predatory state, which may not have a stress response in evidence and is similar in nature to the hunting behavior [which lacks emotionally based reactions and inhibitions against killing]." It appears that Mr. Kness, like Davis and Twining, was able to function in this latter realm and capitalize on the performance benefits of this lower state of arousal. Suarez, G. (2003). The Combative Perspective. Boulder, CO: Paladin Press, p.93.

61. This situation was possible because of lax ammunition policies in the CHP, which allowed officers to provide their own ammunition for duty. The CHP issued standard pressure .38 Special 148-grain wadcutter ammunition for training and 158-grain RNL ammunition for duty, but allowed its officers to purchase .357 Magnum ammunition on their own and load it in their revolvers for duty. The officers who elected to do this were not required to train or qualify with the more powerful Magnum ammunition. In the aftermath of Newhall, the CHP adopted a .38 Special 110-grain JHP loaded to +P+ pressure levels and required its use for all training and duty purposes, prohibiting the use of privately purchased ammunition. The use of .357 Magnum ammunition would not resurface in the CHP until the late 1980s (just prior to the adoption of the .40 Smith & Wesson caliber, in 1990), when the CHP began to issue limited quantities of Remington 125-grain JHP .357 Magnum ammunition to those officers who owned privately purchased .357 Magnum revolvers (the CHP still issued .38 Special revolvers at the time). Officers who elected to carry the .357 Magnum ammunition were required to train and qualify with it under the supervision of agency training officers.

62. There are many good reasons for officers to train with full-power ammunition that replicates the recoil of their duty load. Training with such ammunition allows the officer to work on shooting skills such as recoil control (especially with the off, or "weak" hand), trigger reset, and rapid fire cadence in a realistic fashion, and helps to increase the officer's confidence and ability with his weapon.
The point of impact for a bullet relative to the point of aim can be greatly affected by the weight and velocity of the bullet. Training with duty analogue ammunition allows the officer to learn this relationship for his weapon, which enhances his ability to place his shots where they need to go in a critical situation.
There are legal precedents that encourage the use of full-power training ammunition, as well. In Popow vs. City of Margate, 476 F SUPP. 1237 (D.N.J. 1979), the law enforcement establishment

was put on notice that they had a responsibility to train officers in realistic conditions that would prepare them for their duty environment. This would seem to include training with ammunition that matches the operating characteristics of the duty ammunition.

However, the most critical justification is to validate the reliability of the firearm. The widespread adoption of semi-automatic pistols in police service led to increased capability at the price of increased complexity and maintenance requirements. While revolvers are not immune to malfunctions caused by incompatible ammunition, they are typically less sensitive to ammunition selection than semiautomatic pistols and readily function with a wide range of ammunition power levels. Furthermore, their proper function does not rely upon the shooter providing a firm resistance to the gun during recoil. In contrast, a semi-automatic pistol's reliability depends on a complex interaction between the energy of the cartridge, the properties of the recoil and magazine springs, the mass of the slide, and the support provided by the shooter's stance. If any one of these components is altered, the proper functioning of the pistol may be affected. Shooting a service pistol with full-power ammunition that mimics the energy level of the duty ammunition allows the officer to ensure all the mechanical components in his pistol (most notably, recoil and magazine springs, which have a limited service life), are in the proper working order and that his shooting stance and grip provide the proper resistance to allow reliable functioning. It also validates the officer's shooting grip, since a poor grip may cause hands to come apart during recoil or digits to interfere with the operation of the slide during recoil and induce a malfunction. Any of these latent weaknesses could go undetected if the officer only fired low-power ammunition through the pistol in training. Additionally, low-powered ammunition may not possess the energy required to ensure proper functioning of the pistol, leading to a series of malfunctions in training that detract from the training experience and decrease the officer's faith and confidence in his equipment, which could have disastrous effects on his mental readiness for combat.

63. Artwohl, A., Dr., & Christensen, L.W. (1997). Deadly Force Encounters. Boulder, CO: Paladin Press, and Grossman, D.A. Lt Col. (2004). On Combat. Belleville, IL: PPCT Research Publications.

64. In one survey conducted by police psychologist Dr. Alexis Artwohl, 88% of the 72 respondents reported diminished sound—almost nine out of every 10 officers! Some 60% reported memory loss for some of their actions, and 50% experienced dissociation, the sensation of watching the event from a detached state, perhaps even from "outside the body." Artwohl, A., Dr., & Christensen, L.W. (1997). Deadly Force Encounters. Boulder, CO: Paladin Press pp.41-2, 49 and Grossman, D.A. Lt Col. (2004). On Combat. Belleville, IL: PPCT Research Publications. pp.54-59, 94-95.

65. Cirillo, J. (1996). Guns, Bullets, and Gunfights. Boulder, CO: Paladin Press, p.73.

66. Marshall, E. (n.d.) Stopping Power Forums. [Online]. <www.stoppingpower.net>.

67. Some experienced wags would refute the statement, claiming that the pouches were specifically designed to deposit two to three rounds into the hand (all facing different directions) and scatter the rest onto the ground, in a cynical (but realistic) recognition that they were exceptionally difficult to operate. It's interesting to note that Charles Remsberg's groundbreaking and widely acclaimed officer survival "bible" of the early 1980s, Street Survival, indicated that the dump pouch system was the slowest of the available reloading methods at the time, requiring about 12 to 14 seconds to complete a reload, in comparison to the 10 seconds required to load from belt loops. The newly introduced speedloaders, adopted by the CHP after Newhall in 1972, require only three seconds by comparison, according to Remsberg. Remsberg, C., & Adams, J., & McTernan, T.M. (1980). Street Survival. Northbrook, IL: Calibre Press. pp.224-5.

68. See Section One, Endnote 38, for a discussion of the evidence that proves this assertion.

69. The bloodied hats are clearly evident in the crime scene photos, resting where the officers fell. California Highway Patrol. (1975). Newhall: 1970 [Film]. Sacramento, CA, courtesy of Santa Clarita Valley Historical Society and SCVTV, <http://www.scvtv.com/html/newhall1970-chp1975btv.html> and Anderson, J., & Cassady, M. (1999). The Newhall Incident. Fresno, CA: Quill Driver Books. p.144.

70. In his book Guns, Bullets, and Gunfights, legendary NYPD gunfighter Jim Cirillo described an officer who encountered a similar situation when he shot his revolver empty during a gunfight. According to Cirillo, "He opened his cylinder, poured the empty cases into his strong hand, and looked at his feet for the brass can before he realized there was none and that he had better dump the brass and reload quickly. Luckily by this time his opponent had taken off." Cirillo also describes another officer whose agency required trainees to fill their pockets with 100 rounds of spare ammunition during training in the interest of saving time. When one of those officers had his weapon run dry in a gunfight, "He quickly reached into his pocket, came up with a dime, a quarter and his car keys, and attempted to stuff them into his open revolver cylinder. He stated that he wondered what happened to his ammo. Who took his ammo? Why wasn't the ammo in the right pants pocket?" Fortunately for this officer, he realized his mistake and was able to complete a reload of his gun in enough time to shoot the offender. Cirillo, J. (1996). Guns, Bullets, and Gunfights. Boulder, CO: Paladin Press, pp. 62-63.

71. In his book on the Newhall incident, Chief John Anderson describes that Officer Pence dropped two of the six rounds he was attempting to load into his revolver. According to Anderson, he searched for and located one of the two and managed to load it and close the cylinder at the very moment Twining leaned over the fender to deliver his execution-style shot to Officer Pence's head. This author has been unable to confirm Anderson's account, and the available evidence actually contradicts it (eyewitness accounts from officers on scene report that when Officer Alleyn's body was moved, his revolver was found with the cylinder open and six cartridges loaded in the cylinder). However, if it is true, then it further illustrates the point that loading the gun to full capacity may have fatally delayed Officer Pence from getting back into the fight quickly enough. Anderson, J., & Cassady, M. (1999). The Newhall Incident. Fresno, CA: Quill Driver Books. p.146.

72. Per interviews with CHP Officer Jay Rice (ret.), during some timed courses of fire, CHP cadets and officers would shoot 10 rounds at each stage, loading four and six rounds. With the partial load, officers would have to pay attention to how they closed the cylinder and where the first cartridge was lined up, otherwise they might waste time clicking on empty chambers before they got to the first live round. This required officers to understand which way the cylinder turned on their particular make of revolver—on Smith & Wesson revolvers the cylinder rotates counterclockwise, while on Colt's revolvers the cylinder rotates clockwise—and position the first round accordingly. Unfortunately, this kind of exposure to the partial load was not addressed as a gunfight tactic, but as an administrative action pursuant to a marksmanship exercise. It appears that Officer Pence had no training experience that would have prompted him to consider cutting the loading process short and accepting a partially loaded gun so that he could get back into the fight more quickly.

73. Officer Pence displayed some very common traits of people who are task-saturated and trying to solve a problem under stress. When an individual becomes task-saturated, they are overwhelmed by the presence of other inputs, stimuli, and requirements that distract them from solving a particular problem. As such, these individuals shut off their sensors and ignore inputs from the environment around them in order to focus all their mental energy on completing a single action. When a person who is task-saturated identifies a solution to the problem, it is very difficult to get them to alter course after they have begun to implement it. The individual remains fully committed to the original solution, even after additional information and evidence (often unnoticed by the individual), indicates that the problem or situation around them has changed and their plan needs to be reconsidered. When the problem changes, difficulties arise, or the plan fails to work, they get stuck in a mental loop and simply redouble their efforts and try harder to make it work, rather than making corrections and changes to the plan. Additionally, people who are task-saturated lose the perspective of time, often failing to realize how much time has passed while they have been busy trying to solve the problem.
In Officer Pence's case, he was so fixated on loading six cartridges into his revolver that it probably never occurred to him to curtail the process and accept a partial load. It is likely that he was also experiencing sympathetic nervous system-induced time distortions that made him incapable of understanding how much time had elapsed while he was struggling to complete the full reload. There was nothing in his memory banks (from training) to short-circuit the mental loop that he'd gotten himself stuck in, and it was only after he finally finished the task of loading six rounds that his brain released him to move on to the next task of locating Twining and engaging him. Unfortunately, by that time, it was too late.

This is not meant as a criticism of Officer Pence, merely an observation. That Officer Pence displayed these inherently human characteristics is entirely understandable, given the intensity of his situation and the fact that he was grievously wounded.

Interestingly, lawman Jim Cirillo describes a similar situation that involved an officer reloading under fire. In the case described by Cirillo, the aggressor saw the officer fumble and drop his rounds onto the ground during reloading and recognized an opportunity to press the attack. He rushed the officer, who was able to load one round and dry-fire on two empty chambers before the live round fired, stopping the opponent when he was only eight feet away. Had Officer Pence's training or good fortune allowed him to make a similar decision, it's possible that there would have been one less dead officer on the ground at Newhall. Cirillo, J. (1996). Guns, Bullets, and Gunfights. Boulder, CO: Paladin Press, pp. 63.

74. Fortunately, the design of the semi-automatic pistols carried by most police officers today makes it very easy to load the gun up in the lower edge of the officer's field of view. Furthermore, the action is a simple gross motor skill that really doesn't depend on the officer looking at the pistol at all, which allows the officer to complete the task without taking his eyes off the adversary. This gives the semi-automatic pistol an advantage, as reloading the revolver is a more complex task and is more dependent upon fine motor skills that erode with stress. These factors sometimes demand the officer to look at the revolver during reloading.

75. CHP Officer Jay Rice (ret.) remembered many of these initiatives, pioneered by enthusiastic instructors like CHP Sgt. John Mahe. Sergeant Mahe and his fellow instructors taught officers to seek and use cover, ignore spent brass after it was ejected, keep their heads up while reloading and look for the adversary, and always keep a round ready in the chamber of the shotgun for immediate firing when they were topping off the magazine. The instructors would occasionally test officers by loading spent hulls into the shotgun to induce malfunctions and encourage the diagnosis and correction of these life-threatening stoppages. They taught an offensive, fighting mindset that made their trainees much better prepared to dominate a fight than the four officers who tragically perished at Newhall.

76. It took the November 15, 1963, shooting of Officer Glenn W. Carlson at the hands of parolee bank robbers in Truckee, and the resulting action of nearby California Assemblywoman Pauline Davis, before the CHP was finally provided with a limited number of shotguns, in 1964 (about one for every five to 10 officers). The shotguns proved invaluable during the August 1965 Watts Riot, and the CHP soon began to outfit every patrol car with one. Personal interview with CHP Captain George Nuttall (ret.).

77. The CHP's policy of sealing the shotgun has been discussed elsewhere in the book, as has the lack of focused and continued training with the shotgun. The Newhall officers, like every other CHP officer at the time, simply didn't have the right training, support, and encouragement from the department to make them fully competent and comfortable with the shotgun, which doubtlessly affected their performance on the killing field.

78. The California Highway Patrol Shotgun Training Manual that served as the textbook for all CHP shotgun training specified only two approved carry methods for the shotgun, "high port" and "hip rest." Officer Frago reportedly took the high port position while he was covering Officer Gore's approach, but later moved to the hip rest position described in the text as he reached to open the passenger door of the Pontiac. While it may have been an approved procedure, the hip rest position was tactically inappropriate for the situation and prevented Officer Frago from quickly employing this lifesaving tool when he came under fire from Twining. The California Highway Patrol Shotgun Training Manual, circa January 1965.

79. It was the CHP's conclusion that Officer Alleyn had mistakenly ejected the additional round. Presumably, this was an error prompted by the effects of survival stress. To eject the live round, Officer Alleyn would have had to unlock the fore-end of the gun with the button located forward of the triggerguard. This action is not normally required and it should have given him pause, but his thinking was probably clouded by the effects of severe stress. Some have suggested that the paper seal on the shotgun could have fouled the action and forced Officer Alleyn to eject the live round as part of a malfunction clearance. The placement and construction of the flimsy band make this unlikely, however. It's simply much more feasible that the live round was purposefully ejected by Officer Alleyn, who could not remember whether or not he had previously charged

the weapon during a moment of intense stress. California Highway Patrol. (1970). Information Bulletin (July 1, 1970): Shooting Incident—Newhall Area. Sacramento, CA.

80. The CHP initially issued shotguns without a ready supply of spare ammunition on the gun itself. The canvas pouches (later, leather loops) attached to the shotgun's buttstock to hold an extra five rounds of ammunition did not appear in CHP service until after the Newhall shooting, roughly late 1971 to early 1972. Therefore, Officer Alleyn began the fight with a sum total of four rounds of ammunition in the gun, which allowed the gun to be stored in the dashboard-mounted Lektro-Lok rack with a fully loaded magazine and an empty chamber (so-called "cruiser ready"). By ejecting one of those four rounds, Officer Alleyn significantly handicapped his ability to fight back with the most powerful weapon in his arsenal.

81. The CHP's official report on the Newhall shooting credited Officer Alleyn with striking Twining with one shotgun pellet (after it penetrated through the rear window), as Twining dove into the rear seat of the Pontiac to obtain additional weapons. The spent pellet creased Twining's scalp, creating a "minor wound" that an enraged Twining later said "hurt like hell." However, the lead investigator on the shooting, Los Angeles County Sheriff's Office Homicide Bureau Detective Sergeant John Brady, recounted that Officer Alleyn actually hit both Twining and Davis with pellets. According to Brady's testimony:
"A pellet from Alleyn's shotgun streaked across the top of Twining's scalp, ripping an angry red gash. If it had been just a little lower, it could have opened the top of his skull, or at least knocked him down. Davis was turned sideways to Alleyn. A shotgun pellet tore right over the bridge of his nose. If he had been looking directly back at the officer, the pellet would have hit him right between the eyes."
Thus, Officer Alleyn came awfully close to ending the fight with his shotgun and might have succeeded if he hadn't lost the fourth shell from his inventory. Kolman, J., Captain. (2009). Rulers of the Night, Volume I: 1958-1988. Santa Ana, CA: Graphic Publishers, pp 132-3.

82. Indeed, the felons were in the process of returning from a shooting session that involved long guns, when they were pulled over by Officers Gore and Frago. Davis was a former Marine and had received extensive rifle marksmanship training during his military service. Los Angeles County Homicide investigators also determined that, when he lived in Houston, he was a frequent visitor to Carter's Rifle Range, where he befriended some shooters and was allowed to borrow and shoot their rifles.
When the Pontiac was inventoried after the fight, officers found a Ruger .44 Magnum carbine in the trunk that had a spent cartridge jammed in the action from the day's shooting session. Davis fought part of the engagement with a sawed-off pump-action shotgun that was kept in the back seat of the car along with the two Colt 1911A1 semi-automatic pistols used by Twining during the fight. A further search of their rented apartment in Long Beach, California, turned up a 1903 Springfield rifle in .30-06 and a Remington Model 572 rifle in .22-caliber. There is no question the pair was experienced and competent with long arms. Anderson, J., & Cassady, M. (1999). The Newhall Incident. Fresno, CA: Quill Driver Books. p.137 and Ayoob, M. (1995). The Ayoob Files: The Book. Concord, NH: Police Bookshelf, p.116.

83. Ayoob, M. (1995). The Ayoob Files: The Book. Concord, NH: Police Bookshelf, p.119.

84. At the time of Newhall, the CHP issued 30 rounds of 158-grain RNL ammunition to its officers each year—six for the weapon, 12 for the dump pouches, and 12 for spares. The agency would likely have been unwilling to adopt a spare ammunition carrier that would have required it to issue more ammunition to replace damaged or lost equipment. Personal interviews with CHP Officer Jay Rice (ret.).

85. Actually, the concept dated back much farther than World War II. The frontiersmen and Indians of the late nineteenth century frequently carried spare ammunition in loops that were laced to the buttstocks of their rifles.

86. In the most important law enforcement book of the era (No Second Place Winner, published 1965), the legendary Bill Jordan, an Assistant Chief Patrol Inspector with the U.S. Border Patrol, fast draw champion, survival instructor and all-around gunfighting expert, completely ignored the concept of a backup gun. Jordan's treatment of compact handguns centered around off-duty or plain clothes use, but he never once suggested carrying one as a backup or addressed

this vital officer safety concern. Indeed, as late as the mid-1970s, officers who carried backup guns were often chided by their fellow officers as being paranoid or foolish. One officer who served in the Laguna Hills/San Juan Capistrano office of the CHP circa 1977 was jokingly nicknamed "Two Gun" in recognition of his propensity to carry a backup weapon on duty. This kind of attitude was pervasive throughout law enforcement, not just the CHP. It would take the birth of the "officer survival" movement in the mid-'70s and its eventual embrace by officers and agencies before the tide would finally turn in the 1980s and '90s. In a complete reversal, by today's standards, an officer is now considered foolish if he doesn't carry a backup gun. Jordan, B. (1989). No Second Place Winner (12th Edition). Concord, NH: Police Bookshelf.

87. The newly approved backup revolvers had to be inspected by the office rangemaster and were required to be carried in a holster with a safety strap, according to department policy. Personal interview with CHP Captain George Nuttall (ret.).

88. The "Onion Field" event received national attention with the 1973 publication of best-selling author Joseph Wambaugh's book on the subject, and the subsequent 1979 movie adaptation, but within the CHP itself, the similar murders of Officer Roy P. Blecher (a 21-year veteran), and Officer William M. Freeman (a 12-year veteran), were even more stirring and traumatic, perhaps as much as the Newhall murders themselves. During a traffic enforcement stop on December 22, 1978, the killer took Officer Blecher at gunpoint and forced him to surrender his weapon. Officer Blecher was found handcuffed and shot once in the back of the head, and Officer Freeman was shot five times by the killer. California Highway Patrol. (n.d.) Badges of Honor – 1970 Through 1979. [Online]. <http://www.chp.ca.gov/memorial/memorial70.html>.

Where Are We Now?

"... In the weeks immediately after the four deaths, the emotionally charged follow-up investigation sometimes lingered on fault-finding, but ultimately achieved the desired catharsis - a completely revamped set of procedures to be followed during high-risk and felony stops, with emphasis at every step on officer safety. If there can be such a thing as a silver lining in a cloud this dark, it would be the renewed focus on officer safety - a concern still uppermost even thirty years later.

"Firearms procedures have changed fundamentally, physical methods of arrest have been perfected, the police baton has become a more integral element of enforcement tactics, and new protective tools (such as pepper spray) have become part of the officers' standard equipment. Along with these have come far more comprehensive training - all combining to make uniformed personnel more alert and better prepared for the inevitable dangers faced by CHP officers ..."

—"The Newhall Incident," California Highway Patrol website

"Police Shootouts: How Soon We Forget."
—Police Magazine article title, 2007

Introduction

In March 2011, deep into the process of researching and writing this book, I visited the site of the Newhall shooting and walked the ground, imagining the terrible events that transpired there almost 41 years earlier. When I was done, I traveled two and a half miles north, up The Old Road, to the location of the present-day Newhall Area Office of the CHP.

Four cypress trees stand vigil over the entrance to the parking lot and a simple brick memorial with a plaque that recognizes the fallen officers of the Newhall shooting. It's the second such memorial (the first having been erected at the second Newhall Area Office—now a Caltrans building—where the original four cypress trees remain standing). While the Memorial Fountain at the CHP Academy in Sacramento lists the names of the officers and recognizes their sacrifices, the spiritual home for those who wish to remember these special four is tucked into the corner of this little parking lot.

The simple bronze plaque at the heart of the memorial bears the names of the four officers slain at Newhall, along with their dates of birth, a seven-pointed CHP star, and the inscription 'Killed in the Line of Duty.' I was moved by this memorial to these fallen officers, and in an act of respect, borne of my military background, I began to reverently polish the names and the star with some supplies from the trunk of my vehicle.

As I worked on the memorial that Saturday afternoon with nobody around, I wondered if the department and the greater law enforcement community truly understood and remembered the lessons from this long-ago shooting, or had they somehow been misunderstood and forgotten? Over two decades of military experience had taught me that the profession of arms often has to "rediscover" painful lessons from the past—lessons already paid for with the blood of our forefathers, which we should have never forgotten--and I suspected that the law enforcement profession was no different in this regard.

In one month exactly, it would be the forty-first anniversary of the Newhall Shooting, and I couldn't help but wonder if a new generation of officers would have to learn the blood lessons of Newhall all over again, the hard way? What had the law enforcement profession really learned from Newhall? Which of its lessons had they incorporated into their training and operations, and which had been forgotten over time? Could another "Newhall" happen today, because the law enforcement community had ignored or forgotten its own history? These questions and others haunted me as I polished the cold bronze.

CHAPTER 17

The Immediate Aftermath

In the immediate aftermath of the Newhall shooting, the CHP was desperate to understand how it could lose four officers in as many minutes and launched a thorough investigation into the details of the shooting. The homicide investigation was actually handled by the Los Angeles County Sheriff's Office (LASO), but the CHP actively analyzed the shooting in an attempt to discover what had gone wrong and what needed to be fixed.[1]

By July 1, 1970, the shooting investigation had provided enough details to allow the CHP to release to all uniformed personnel an information bulletin that chronicled the events of the shooting. In the weeks and months to come, the analysis would continue, as would the preparations for the trial of Bobby Davis, in October 1970. Some officers of the period would later comment that, under the stress of the situation, the comprehensive effort sometimes devolved into blame fixing and finger pointing in which the fallen officers themselves were mostly forgotten amid the criticisms and accusations, but in the end the net effect was positive.[2]

As a result of this intense scrutiny, the department identified deficiencies in training, policies, tactics, and equipment that it wanted to correct, and work began almost immediately on making the required changes. A brief look at those changes, by category, is in order.[3]

TACTICS

The most obvious development of the Newhall shooting was the creation of a new high-risk traffic stop procedure that became known throughout the law enforcement community simply as the "felony-stop" procedure. While numerous improvements were made to the CHP's former high-risk or hot stop procedure, the principal advantage to the new procedure is that it kept the officers in a solid defensive position at the patrol car to allow them to maintain tactical dominance while they commanded the suspects out of their car and back towards the officers. Prior to Newhall, the CHP's standard procedure was to send an officer forward to the suspect vehicle to affect an arrest, but, after Newhall, officers no longer had to give up their advantage and security to move forward into the suspect's killing zone. Instead, the suspects were removed from their defensive position in a controlled manner and were brought back to the ensconced officers, where they could be searched and placed into custody in an environment that was more favorable to the lawmen.

This new procedure was not strictly a CHP creation, but rather the result of a combined effort of multiple law enforcement agencies that all contributed to the process. Elements were borrowed from the operating procedures of different agencies, and the final product offered such an enhanced level of officer safety that it was quickly adopted as a standard within law enforcement.

Other changes in CHP tactics resulted from Newhall, as well. Officers were taught the importance of waiting for backup before committing themselves when the circumstances warranted it. They were also taught to appropriately match their tactics to the situation. For instance, the crime of brandishing, which had once been treated as a minor offense in some areas of the state, was now recognized as a much more serious situation that demanded a higher level of alertness and more sophisticated tactics to deal with it.

There were significant changes in CHP search and handcuffing procedures ("Physical Methods of Arrest," or PMA, in CHP parlance), after Newhall. Instead of relying upon a one-size-fits-all approach, a variety of search positions were developed and taught to officers so as to accommodate the different tactical situations that a CHP officer might encounter in the field. Additionally, there was an increased emphasis on cuffing potentially violent or armed suspects prior to searching them.

TRAINING

Immediate in-service and Academy training in the new felony stop and PMA procedures were initiated in the wake of Newhall, before the ink had even dried on the syllabus. Throughout all phases of this training, the officers were taught to approach situations with more caution, a greater state of awareness, and an appreciation for not overcommitting themselves prior to the arrival of backup. The great lesson of the Newhall shooting was that "Time is your friend," and the CHP's new training emphasized that officers should take advantage of this critical asset to maximize their safety.

The CHP's new emphasis on officer safety and increased situational awareness was perhaps best symbolized by a training tool, developed by the staff at the Academy, to promote a new kind of tactical thinking amongst the officers. The tool was an acronym that condensed many of the critical learning lessons from the Newhall fight into a memorable format:[4]

N = Never approach a felony or high-risk vehicle until all suspects are out of the car.

E = Evaluate the offense for what it is, not for what it appears to be.

W = Wait for backup before leaving yourself unprotected.

H = Have a plan of action.
A = Always maintain the advantage.
L = Look for the unusual before you go into a loaded situation.
L = Leave the scene—drive by, through, or around if in doubt about your safety.

Another significant development in CHP training was the adoption of a more realistic firearms training program. The new program became less of an academic exercise in marksmanship and more of a training program with combat utility. Administrative practices that could create negative habits, such as policing brass during the course of fire or loading from ammo buckets, were gradually eliminated. Silhouette targets completely replaced bull's-eye targets over time, and officers began to shoot courses of fire that emphasized skills such as weak-hand firing, single-hand firing, reloading from duty gear, night shooting, malfunction drills, and other relevant skills. Many of these courses of fire were fired in dynamic scenarios that involved movement and time pressure. Additionally, the CHP training began to formalize and mandate instruction in shotgun skills, to increase competence and confidence in this important weapon. Furthermore, firearms training policies were changed to mandate the use of duty ammunition during training, leaving the use of low-powered training ammunition a thing of the past.

The decentralized nature of CHP firearms training left a lot of discretion to the area training officers and rangemasters, so the adoption of many of these improvements was spotty at first, but over time they became the core of a new firearms training program that advanced CHP training far beyond the pre-Newhall level.[5]

POLICIES

Accompanying the changes in tactics and training were adjustments in associated agency policies. Most significantly, the CHP issued a new order entitled "High Risk and Felony Stops" which gave officers more latitude to draw their weapons if they believed they were dealing with a dangerous suspect. The image-conscious CHP, which had previously punished officers for their "offensive behavior" when they placed their hand on their holstered weapon during a tense stop, was growing up.[6] The restrictions on use of non-duty ammunition during training required changes not only to training policies, but to contracting and budgeting policies as well.

Staffing policies for junior officers were analyzed to see if there was a way to avoid assigning rookie officers to dangerous beats before they were fully ready to operate on their own, but, in truth, the demographics of the rapidly expanding agency worked against such changes being put into statewide practice. There were just too many rookies on the force to pair all of them with more veteran officers.

One of the most influential policy changes centered on the use of shotguns by patrolmen. After Newhall, the taped seals on the shotguns disappeared overnight, along with the requirement to write a memorandum when the shotguns were deployed from the vehicle. The culture that had made officers reluctant to use this lifesaving tool out of administrative concerns gradually began to disappear.

EQUIPMENT

Perhaps the easiest of the post-Newhall fixes came in the form of new and enhanced equipment adopted by the CHP.

The CHP became the first major agency in the nation to issue speedloaders to their officers, in recognition of the blood lesson taught by Officer Pence. Various designs of speedloaders had been available from companies like Bucheimer and others as early as 1964, but they had not been standard issue prior to this time. This situation was corrected immediately, with the CHP issuing a pair of speedloader units to every officer in order to enhance their ability to reload quickly under fire.

By 1976, the newly adopted speedloaders contained the new standardized load of the Highway Patrol, a .38 Special jacketed hollowpoint loaded to +P+ pressures. This load was required for all duty and training use. The lax ammunition policies of the past that had allowed officers to purchase and carry their own .357 Magnum ammunition (but failed to mandate training with it), were a thing of the past, and the Highway Patrol would not see the use of .357 Magnum ammunition again for almost 20 years.[7]

The shotguns lost their taped seals, and they gained spare ammunition pouches that were attached to the buttstocks of the weapons, providing officers with a reserve of ammunition to top off the weapon as necessary.

Car radios were upgraded and modified to allow them to monitor both car-to-dispatch and car-to-car transmissions, instead of just the latter.[8] This enhanced communications and officer safety.

Other equipment developments would soon come, including the issuance of chemical mace for non-lethal threats and soft body armor to enhance survivability.

CHAPTER 18

Mid-Life Crisis

CULTURE

As important as all these developments were, none of them were as significant as the overall change in CHP culture, from the brass on down to the street.

Prior to Newhall, the department desperately wanted to be seen as the premiere traffic enforcement agency in the world, and jealously protected its positive reputation with the public. These things did not change after Newhall, but there was a new level of maturity about the dangers of law enforcement and the risks to officer safety. It was as if the blinders were finally off, and the agency finally awoke to the very real (and increasing) threat of violence that officers faced when they hit the streets of the turbulent 1970s.[9] The administration slowly began to shift the focus from protecting the public image to protecting their officers. Officer safety issues gained more attention, and greater resources were committed to training and equipping the officers to handle the threats they were likely to face on patrol.

The CHP also began to embrace the idea that it was more than just a traffic safety organization. It began to view itself less as a traffic enforcement agency and more as a law enforcement organization with a specialty in traffic enforcement. The distinction is slight, but it was critical to the mindset of the agency and the officers themselves, since it forced each of them to realize that the growing threat of violence directed towards law enforcement applied as equally to them as it did to their brothers in blue and green. It was clear that the public, and especially the criminal class, made no distinction between highway patrolmen, deputies, and police officers—they were all cops, and therefore they were all subject to the same risks and threats. This understanding alone was crucial to the development of a true officer safety mindset and culture within the CHP. It was also crucial to ensure the success of the CHP's ever broadening law enforcement mission in the years to come.[10]

EVANGELISM

By 1975, the CHP had completed a full-length training film that dissected the Newhall shooting and identified some of the mistakes made by the officers. The principal message of the film was that the officers in the Newhall shooting prematurely rushed into contact with the suspects when backup was just moments away, and they paid for the mistake with their lives and the lives of their brother officers. This was a notable learning lesson from the incident, but as the foregoing analysis indicates, it was not the only one. The film was used to train and educate both veteran CHP officers and cadets alike, but it was also distributed to allied agencies as part of the CHP's effort to share the critical lessons of this incident with other law enforcement officers; perhaps not surprisingly, the training and tactics deficiencies that contributed to the problem were not addressed in the film.

It was recognized early on that the Newhall Shooting was more than a tragedy for the California Highway Patrol. It was also a watershed event within the greater law enforcement community, one of those rare moments that change the way an entire industry looks at a problem and adjusts their methods. The shooting was championed as a wake-up call for law enforcement, and many of the changes instituted within the CHP were also put into effect in agencies around the nation. Just about every agency and law enforcement training academy throughout the nation saw its training, tactics, equipment, and procedures affected by the shooting in some way.

The shooting encouraged the development of an "officer survival" movement within law enforcement agencies, and in the commercial sector, as well. Previously, there had been little interest in private-sector training in law enforcement subjects, but the shooting helped to create a new market of officers and agencies that were hungry for the training. Professional journals began to seriously address training and tactics, and a host of authors, many officers themselves, began to write some of the classic books of this genre.[11] Workshops and seminars (such as the popular Calibre Press "Street Survival" series), sprang up throughout the country, imparting life saving lessons to officers who wanted to go beyond the minimal training provided by their agency. Privately run firearms academies, such as the acclaimed Gunsite (1976), Chapman Academy (1979), and Lethal Force Institute (1981), began to offer firearms training superior in content and quality to that offered by the majority of agencies and law enforcement academies, and their classes were filled with officers and armed citizens seeking to improve their defensive skills.

LOSS OF INERTIA

As with all movements that have their birth in crisis, the intensity of the officer survival movement eventually began to fade a little. That's not to say that advances in tactics, training, and equipment came to a halt, because progress was still being made (especially in the most professional departments), but that progress came at a more measured pace.

After pushing hard to learn and incorporate the lessons of Newhall, many agencies fell into a mindset that the job was done and the problems that had existed before had been "fixed" and so needed no further attention. In these agencies, the push to evaluate doctrine, tactics, training, and equipment was relatively short-lived. They were content as long as their programs met the mandates of the certification authority within their state, and didn't feel it necessary or desirable to spend additional time, effort, and money in this area, especially during the economic downturn of the latter 1970s and early 1980s.

CHAPTER 19

The Long Haul

In the more professional departments, there was a greater long-term commitment to evaluating tactics, procedures, training, and equipment. These agencies kept the fire burning and the movement alive. They developed agency cultures that placed officer safety in the forefront and served as catalysts for progress throughout the profession.

Quite naturally, one of these agencies that refused to rest on its laurels was the CHP, which continued to make improvements in the training and equipping of its officers long after the echoes of Newhall gunfire had faded away. Like any bureaucratic institution, the CHP had its share of stumbles and missteps along the way, but there is no doubt the tragedy of Newhall promoted long-term improvements in the officer safety culture of this organization.

The comprehensive review of the felony stop, Physical Methods of Arrest, and other tactics in the wake of Newhall was not the end of the road. As noted previously, all tactics, training, and equipment fell under the spotlight, and many changes were made by the middle of the 1970s, but the improvements continued beyond that.

The 1980s saw the maturation of the CHP firearms training program and the adoption of such new equipment as radio extenders (1981), PR-24 side-handle batons (1982) and .223-caliber Ruger Mini-14 patrol rifles (1989), all of which increased the officer's capabilities and safety. The CHP also conducted a second (post-Newhall) comprehensive overhaul of its search and handcuffing (PMA) tactics, requiring all officers to be trained and evaluated in the enhanced procedures. New technologies such as video simulators, which pitted officers in shoot/don't shoot scenarios were incorporated into Academy and in-service training regimens.

In the 1990s, the CHP converted to semi-automatic pistols. It also added another non-lethal tool to the arsenal, when it began to issue pepper spray (Oleoresin Capsicum, or O.C.). In the wake of the Rodney King arrest, a serious evaluation of the department's use-of-force training was conducted, and it became apparent that improvements were needed, so the department created and fielded a "Force Option Training Simulator" (FOTS), which brought use-of-force training to a new level for the agency. The key improvement with FOTS compared to earlier shooting simulators was that it included non-lethal force options as part of the simulation—the officer had to identify the threat level and respond with an appropriate level of force, which might include an option other than the firearm. System capabilities allowed the training officer who ran the program to alter the suspect's actions, based on the response of the officer being tested. This enhanced realism and improved the training experience. The FOTS system was a mobile system that could be transported to each of the area offices in the state, ensuring all officers had access to this critical training.[12]

The 1990s also saw one of the most critical developments in law enforcement firearms training, when the CHP adopted a new framework that changed how skills were selected, taught, and evaluated. This groundbreaking effort, steered by Training Officer Lou Chiodo, implemented a reality-based training program in which officers were taught techniques that took into account the physiological effects of survival stress and the dynamics of real life confrontations. Techniques that could withstand the negative effects of these influences were identified and taught, providing the officers with a superior skill set compared to earlier training programs that neglected these important factors and so often fell short of teaching them valid survival habits. Additionally, the new firearms training program identified particular tasks in which the officers had to demonstrate competency during qualifications, and identified minimum standards of proficiency for each of the skills. In the past, officers could attain a passing score during firearms qualifications even if they hadn't performed well in a particular area, as long as their aggregate score was high enough to meet the minimum. However, under the new Task Oriented Qualification Course (TOQC) championed by Officer Chiodo, a minimum level of competency was required for each of the evaluated skills, ensuring that an officer would not go out on duty self-possessed of a dangerous vulnerability.[13]

In the first decade of the twenty-first century, the CHP's patrol rifle program expanded, and an AR-15-pattern rifle was soon in each patrol car, riding alongside the shotgun. The department adopted electronic control devices (Tasers, or "Conductive Energy Weapon," in CHP parlance), to expand its non-lethal force options. Advanced Officer Safety Training courses expanded to reinforce essential officer survival skills and included new and exciting training aids such as non-lethal training ammunition ("Simunitions," or marking projectiles that can be fired from modified weapons).

The CHP's training programs have continuously improved since Newhall, and they have become more comprehensive, as well. The old 16-week, 900-hour Academy that Cadets Gore, Frago, Pence, and Alleyn attended has grown to 27 weeks and 1,285 instructional hours in the years since. Recurrent in-service training for officers has likewise expanded in breadth and depth.

This is not to say that the CHPs performance has been perfect. It has demonstrated leadership in many facets of development, but it has also found itself catching up to other agencies that outpaced them. For example, while the CHP was the first major agency to issue speedloaders to its officers, in 1971, it was relatively late to transition to semi-automatic pistols, in 1990, falling far behind other state agencies such as the Illinois State Police (1968), Connecticut State Police (1981), and New Jersey State Police (1983).

The CHP didn't take this long walk without its share of problems, either. In 2006, the CHP lost eight officers to suicide in as many months, and a total of 13 officers between 2003 and 2006. This prompted a comprehensive review, in 2007, and the institution of several initiatives aimed at this growing and unique threat to officer safety.[14] More recently, in 2010, the CHP lost five officers to vehicular accidents in the course of two months, prompting another thorough review of CHP policies, procedures, and training.[15]

Despite these problems, the point to this discussion is that the Newhall shooting gave birth to a strong officer safety culture that has continued to get stronger within the organization as it has matured. This culture has allowed the CHP to aggressively tackle challenges such as the clusters of suicides and the string of line-of-duty deaths, and to take positive actions to fix the problems and improve officer safety.

This culture has paid dividends. Once a weakness, the CHP's felony stop tactics are now recognized as among the best in the law enforcement community. These tactics were put to the test in the most severe manner during a 17-minute shootout in July 2010, with a heavily armed suspect in Oakland, California. That incident had begun as a routine traffic stop. Hundreds of rounds were fired by the suspect and the officers during this shootout, which resulted in the wounding and capture of the gunman. Despite being fired upon with a pistol, rifle and shotgun by the armor-clad gunman, no CHP officers were killed during the shooting, and only two received minor wounds from flying glass. While the details of that shooting have not been shared with the public or the CHP's officers due to pending trials as of the date of this book's publication, initial reports indicate that the officers retreated and called for backup shortly after approaching the vehicle, which had been stopped for speeding and erratic driving. At the initial contact, the officers noted the presence of multiple weapons and apparently saw the suspect starting to don his body armor. Heeding the lessons of the Newhall shooting, the officers retreated to a tactically superior position and called for backup, both of which allowed them to survive and prevail.[16]

CHAPTER 20

State of the Industry

As encouraging as that last example may be, there are still indications that the general law enforcement community, including frontrunners such as the CHP, still has a long way to go.

Law enforcement trainers and researchers from across the industry continuously question the efficacy of today's firearms training, especially in light of statistics that indicate persistently low hit ratios (roughly 30% at best, and most probably lower on average), for officer-involved shootings.[17] Some industry leading trainers like Dave Spaulding ask challenging and troubling questions about whether officers are being trained in street relevant skills, or merely being qualified in accordance with useless, irrelevant protocols.[18]

Some industry leading departments, such as the New York City Police Department (NYPD), have contracted with research groups like the Rand Corporation (sometimes under direction from the courts or the Department of Justice), to analyze their use-of-force policies and training, as well as their actual use-of-force events. Invariably, these reports indicate there are deficiencies in the training programs that would be familiar to the Newhall investigators of a generation or two ago.[19]

Some of the policies would be familiar as well. One would think that the discredited pre-Newhall practice of sealing shotguns with evidence tape would have completely disappeared from the scene, but rumors persist that some departments have continued the practice with a modern twist by moving the seal to the rack in the car instead of placing it on the gun itself. In one major California agency, officers are required to document, via Use of Force Memorandum, every time they draw and point their sidearm at an offender in this high-crime city. Is this a "virtual seal?" Perhaps these pre-Newhall demons haven't been fully exorcised from the law enforcement culture after all?

Some of the industry's most influential trainers and publications openly editorialize and fret that officers have either completely forgotten the lessons of Newhall or were never properly taught them to begin with.[20] Others decry the organizational mindset they fear has become pervasive in law enforcement, which places "a greater emphasis on making everyone happy and avoiding complaints at all costs, than [on] the safety of the officers."[21]

The new technology of the ages, the Internet, has allowed officers from diverse backgrounds and agencies to compare notes on the "state of the industry," and even the most casual search through some of these forums will indicate a high level of anxiety from officers whose mental preparation for duty—their survival sense—is negatively impacted by fears of administrative punishment from unsupportive departments, criminal punishment from politically motivated district attorneys, or of getting sued by litigious citizens armed with video cameras that don't tell the entire story.

Then there are the failures. The information technology era has allowed us to capture many police actions and fatalities on video, where they can be analyzed in horrible detail. It's heartbreaking and baffling to law enforcement trainers to see these officers making mistakes in judgment and tactics that wind up costing them their lives, especially when the mistakes occur at the most basic level.

Who can explain the mindset of an officer who is unable to bring himself to shoot a violent and aberrant suspect who's openly loading a gun so he can use it against the officer? Why would that officer take no defensive measures (other than warning the suspect to stop over and over), right up to the point of the fatal gunshot that was clearly forthcoming? What does this incident say about the mental preparedness of the slain officer, the culture of officer safety at that department, or the state of training, if anything?

Who can explain why an ad hoc S.W.A.T. team rushes in prematurely after an armed suspect who has just killed two officers, instead of using the time they have to negotiate and wait the suspect out, or at least develop a coordinated attack plan with the proper assets prior to entry?

Who can explain how a veteran officer fails to find a 9mm handgun in a suspect's waistband during his search—the same gun that the handcuffed suspect would soon use to murder the officer from the back seat of the patrol car?

Who can explain why officers are dying from the same mistakes in preparedness, judgment, and tactics that were being made when their fathers and grandfathers walked the beat? Can we really say the lessons of an event like Newhall have been learned and ingrained in the fabric of the law enforcement culture in the face of examples such as these?

Where are we? What have we truly learned? Where do we need to be going?

A TRAINING TIMELINE MODEL

Perhaps it's instructive to step back and take a more historical look at firearms training, to see where we have been, in order so that we can determine where we are going.

Law enforcement firearms training changed relatively little from the start of the twentieth century up through approximately World War II, in that there was almost no formal training conducted in the vast majority of agencies.

In the few places where instruction was provided, it was essentially general instruction in basic marksmanship skills.

Post-war, this changed very little. Instruction became more common throughout the law enforcement community, but the curriculum still involved little more than basic marksmanship taught in a sterile, competitive target-shooting environment on a square range. Officers were primarily taught to fire from stances with little real world application and were not forced to demonstrate anything beyond basic gun handling skills. In the spirit of today's computer-driven culture, this could easily be termed as "Version 1.0" of firearms training, and it lasted roughly up to the Newhall shooting in most corners of law enforcement.

Version 1.0 = Limited Square Range Marksmanship Training

As the CHP example indicates, there was a significant change in most law enforcement firearms training programs, post-Newhall. Instruction moved beyond basic marksmanship to incorporate more dynamic and realistic skills. Shooting stances became more practical, reloads were accomplished from duty gear, full-power ammunition was used for training, use of cover was emphasized, targets became more realistic, time pressures were introduced to increase stress, and a whole host of other improvements were made. The shooting was still done on square ranges and at paper targets, but enhanced realism was stressed in all facets. This period, "Version 2" to continue the model, lasted from Newhall to approximately sometime in the 1980s for most departments, although some agencies are still using programs today that have never advanced beyond this stage, primarily because they allow them to meet the training standards mandated by most state certification authorities.

Version 2.0 = Advanced Square Range Marksmanship Training

Beginning sometime in the 1980s, law enforcement firearms training increasingly tried to link the use-of-force policies established by agencies with their firearms training. This trend really accelerated with the 1984 introduction of the Firearms Training Systems ("FATS") simulator, which provided computer-based, interactive, live-fire training scenarios for officers to navigate. "Version 3.0" of firearms training had been launched, character-ized by the dual use of advanced square range training to teach gun handling skills, and limited interactive computer simulations to teach and test decision making skills. This is the state of the art for many firearms training programs today.

Version 3.0 = Advanced Square Range Marksmanship Training + Limited Computer Simulation Training

There is no doubt that Version 3.0 is vastly superior to preceding genera-tions of firearms training, but the costs associated with computer simulation have prevented many smaller agencies from reaping the benefits of this tech-nology. Additionally, because the equipment is expensive to acquire and operate, very few agencies can purchase a large number of systems. The limited availability of these systems means they typically only make up a very small fraction of the overall firearms training program. It's valuable training, but the average officer is unlikely to experience it on a frequent basis due to logistical and budgetary issues.

Furthermore, while the simulators allow instructors to teach and evaluate candidates in conditions that cannot be replicated on the square range with live weapons and ammunition, there are limitations to the tool. The "firearm" used by the trainee frequently does not match the type of firearm, in weight, function or feel, used for duty by the officer. In some systems it cannot be holstered, so the officer must start the scenario with weapon in hand, even if that is not tactically desirable. The firearm frequently does not function or recoil like a real weapon, has a different trigger pull, cannot be "reloaded," and cannot be cleared using traditional techniques when it malfunctions, causing some trainers to wonder whether or not there might be an element of "negative training" that occurs with systems like these.

The simulator frequently cannot accommodate the introduction of props that add fidelity to the scenario, such as the addition of a police car in the projection room. Furthermore, the officer has a limited area in which he can maneuver before images on the screen are no longer viewable and before the computer system fails to register hits from the weapon. The officer cannot take cover behind objects that are clearly visible on the screen, as we would want him to do in a real situation.

Some simulator systems do not allow for non-lethal force options and are strictly designed around firearms training. The scenarios are designed to be interactive, such that the actions of the suspect can branch off into variable paths dependent upon the actions of the officer, but the character on the screen will never be able to interact as naturally with the officer as a live person and will never be as responsive to the officer's actions and commands as a real person.

Significantly, there is no pain stimulus associated with failure, either. An officer who is "shot" using computer simulation receives no blow, other than to his ego, and feels no pain, which limits the impact, literally and figuratively, of the lesson.

In Version 3.0 training, the officer gets good hands on training with the firearm in one venue and good decision making training in another, but there is little to no integration of both types of training simultaneously. So, while Version 3.0 training is a large advance, what it lacks is the ability to synthesize the advantages of training in real world and simulated environments. Agencies can and will continue to make improvements in their square range training environments and their simulation training environments, but until these two processes are truly integrated, it's unlikely that training will become any more realistic or valuable to the officer.

This is perhaps one of the most important reasons why modern law enforcement agencies have been unable to significantly improve upon a 30% or less hit probability in real gunfights. There are, of course, many other factors besides training that can affect this number, but it would seem that training is among the most, if not the most, important variable. If so, this makes it even more critical for a firearms program to focus on realism, the first of Artwohl's "Four R's of Deadly Force Training." [22]

Forward-thinking trainers have identified this issue and have addressed it by suggesting training methods that mark the beginning of a new phase, "Version 4.0" if you will.

Version 4.0 = Advanced Square Range Marksmanship Training + Computer Simulation Training + Force-on-Force Simulation:

In Version 4.0 training, square range and simulation training are combined into a new, "reality based" training where the officers train directly against other persons in simulation, using functional but non-lethal weapons. This "force-on-force" training represents the highest level of lethal force training to date, and the law enforcement community is just now starting to really get on board with the concept.

Officers have certainly dabbled in elements of force-on-force training in the past, practicing unarmed combatives or handcuffing with each other in the gym, or perhaps even limited exercises with modified weapons, but the thorough integration of realistic firearms skills, tactics, and equipment against a live actor in simulation reached its genesis only in the mid-1990s, and it didn't enjoy much popularity until well into the next decade.[23] Part of the reason for this was that technology limited the options of trainers who would have been interested in this style of training. The guns and training munitions that make this kind of training possible ("Simunitions," which, by the way, is another one of those trademarked labels that has become so common in use that it's now generically applied to the genre, much like "Kleenex" is used to describe facial tissues), simply weren't readily available or affordable prior to this time. To a large extent, the protective gear wasn't either.[24]

However, with the creation and adoption of these technologies, the door is now open for creative trainers to take advantage of the tremendous training opportunities afforded. This force-on-force training allows the students to test ther decision making skills, communication skills, tactics, and their armed and unarmed combat skills against a thinking and moving opponent in extremely realistic scenarios and environments. The training:

"… is based upon teaching students to fire at a human opponent who is exhibiting a life threatening stimulus. Without this type of stimulus, trainers cannot expect their students to respond automatically and accurately in their first combat experience."[25]

Perhaps significantly, the small sting that accompanies being struck by a Simunition round or an Airsoft pellet, even through protective garments, is likely to have a profound effect on the learning process. Even the toughest of officers doesn't want to be stung by one of these projectiles, and this motivation is likely to aid in the learning process. It's an undeniable aspect of the human condition and learning process that the lessons associated with pain are rarely forgotten—touching a hot stove is much more likely to leave a lasting impression than simply being told that it is dangerous to do so. One of the greatest utilities of a tool like force-on-force is that a pain stimulus that is sufficient to enhance learning but not enough to jeopardize the health of the student is part of the process.

The famous World War I flying ace Manfred Von Richtofen, aka the "Red Baron," once surmised that a fighter pilot's chances of survival in combat increased dramatically once he had survived his first 10 combat engagements. In this vein, force-on-force training allows an officer to experience the stress of those 10 formative engagements in a safe training environment and dramatically increase his survival quotient. As Siddle notes:

"The primary advantage of dynamic training exercises is the experience of interacting with an open environment. Each exposure to a threat stimulus allows the student a chance to identify the subtle cues, which can only be gained through experience. Each exposure allows students an opportunity to work out solutions and program the correct survival response."[26]

A firearms training program that makes well-planned and -executed force-on-force training a principal component (not the only component, but a significant one—some square range training will always be necessary and desirable), is guaranteed to prepare an officer much better for an armed confrontation than even the most sophisticated "Version 3.0" program. There is simply no substitute for dynamic role-playing with live actors and functional, yet non-lethal, training weapons to better prepare an officer for the street. Learning to think and function under extreme stress, programming good survival habits into the brain, and allowing a person to build experience that allows him to more quickly recognize and react to a threat is more critical to gunfight survival than raw marksmanship skills.

That last statement needs to be emphasized and, perhaps, explained. Most law enforcement officers who are killed in gunfights are killed at very short distances, where the marksmanship problem or task is not particularly difficult in itself. New York Police Department statistics (collected 1854 to 1979) indicate that 82 percent of their slain officers were killed within six feet of their assailants, and similar FBI data (from 2001 to 2010) indicates that nationally, 67 percent of the slain officers from those years were killed within 10 feet of their assailants (and 49 percent within five feet).[27] Further analysis of FBI data indicates that some 92 percent of FBI agent-involved shootings between 1989 and 1994 occurred within six to 10 feet.[28] From a standpoint of pure marksmanship alone, it is not particularly difficult to shoot a human-sized target from six or even 10 feet, and the training required to impart competency in this level of skill is minimal. It's a far more difficult task to teach someone how to identify and anticipate threat cues, then think clearly and function smoothly while facing lethal attack from a real person at this distance.

RESISTANCE TO CHANGE

The CHP, like many progressive agencies, is starting to integrate some force-on-force training into their program. They are in a transitional stage between Version 3.0 and Version 4.0, where the force-on-force training is not yet a significant core component of their initial and in-service training programs. For now, the CHP still spends a disproportionate share of its firearm training resources on what is essentially Version 2.0 level training—advanced, square range training.[29]

This is common throughout law enforcement, largely because agencies "teach to the test." The certification authorities that draft police training and qualification standards in the states have directed that officers must meet certain minimum standards before they are allowed to work. These standards typically specify courses of fire and minimum passing scores to be attained, and they are almost always rooted in a Version 2.0, square range mindset. In fact, many of these criteria have remained largely unchanged since their creation in the 1920s through the1940s.[30] It should come as no surprise that law enforcement agencies, whose training programs are always short on time and money, largely plan their training to optimize employee performance on these mandated tests. Force-on-force training may enhance an officer's skills and readiness, but to a bureaucrat who is more concerned with protecting and guaranteeing the size of the department's labor pool, experimenting with new teaching methods is less important than meeting the mandates that are the gateway to employment.

Budgetary trends have been a significant factor in driving agencies to cling to these outdated firearms training standards, as well. Many states, counties, and cities have drastically cut police funding in recent years, due to economic pressures (including potential bankruptcy for some municipalities), leaving very little in the budget for training of any sort. Because firearms training can be expensive (due to ammunition costs, in particular), many agencies have cut back their firearms training programs to the bare minimum required to meet state standards. Officers who once found themselves at the range four times a year when their agencies could afford it, are now qualifying once only every two years, because that is all the state requires.[31] Interestingly, the extreme affordability of force-on-force training is one of its greatest virtues and offers a potential solution for not only preserving the amount of training time, but increasing its productivity for agencies that are bold enough to embrace it as a core component of their program.

Liability concerns are yet another reason why some departments have been slow to adopt promising new methods like force-on-force training and stray beyond the qualification mandates of the certification authorities. The agencies and departments are hesitant to divert training resources into areas that are not specifically required by the state, because they don't want to appear as if they are neglecting the mandates. In this increasingly litigious age, no agency wants to look as if it short-changed the training specified by the state so that it could divert time and resources into other areas. Additionally, a program that strictly adheres to the state mandates is easily defensible in court, while an innovative program that uses methods not specifically recommended by the state, and for which the state has not developed evaluation criteria, subjects the agency's program to greater scrutiny by opposing counsel in the wake of a line-of-duty shooting.

Unfortunately, these factors appear to have a perverse effect on the quality of training received. Instead of utilizing the most promising, cost-effective methods and focusing on the areas of greatest concern, agencies find themselves preoccupied with standards that often have little to do with real world needs. Researcher Thomas Aveni puts it this way:

"Good risk management would suggest that resources should be allocated to problems that are seen frequently and to infrequent problems that are very severe when they do arise. We don't allocate resources that way in firearms training. In fact, training by and large has been part of the problem, not part of the solution."[32]

To put a finer point on it, veteran officer and survival instructor Evan Marshall observes, "Remember, qualification is simply a program to monetize liability. It is rarely training, and tragically all the 'training' some coppers get."[33]

THE WAY FORWARD

The critical task at hand, then, is to revise these standards in a way that frees agencies to implement more effective training programs with their scarce training resources. It is unlikely that law enforcement agencies will ever find themselves with enough money or time to conduct "extra" training, so we have to ensure they are allowed to maximize their efforts. Arcane courses of fire with aggregate minimum passing scores that allow an officer to fail an entire stage/skill set yet still pass the test, need to be eliminated. Qualification tests that are based on early twentieth-century training standards need to be updated to account for advances in education and learning. New standards that emphasize task-oriented qualification requirements and encourage reality based, force-on-force simulation training as a key component of a firearms training program are a necessary prerequisite to advance the state of law enforcement firearms training.

If this can be accomplished, if law enforcement firearms training can truly advance where agencies are free to use the most effective training techniques and tools to prepare their officers for duty instead of being shackled by outdated state training mandates, then the lessons written in blood in the J's Coffee Shop parking lot one dark night in April of 1970 will have finally been learned.

ENDNOTES

1. *The Los Angeles County Sheriff's Office (later, Department) was eager to collate the lessons of this incident as well, and later released their own training film that reenacted the shooting. The film identified tactical errors and suggested alternatives that would enhance officer safety, and it was widely circulated within the law enforcement community alongside the earlier 1975 CHP training film on Newhall.*

2. *Uelman, D. Lieutenant (ret.). (1995, April). Remembering the Newhall Murders: April 6, 1970. The California Highway Patrolman, 8-16.*

3. *Multiple sources contributed to elements of this discussion. Interviews with CHP Officers Jay Rice (ret.) and Gil Payne (ret.) were foundational, as well as written material from Anderson, J. (1999). Newhall Incident Prompted Police Nationwide to Make Changes in Procedures. The California Highway Patrolman.*

4. *California Highway Patrol. (1975). Newhall: 1970 [Film]. Sacramento, CA, courtesy of Santa Clarita Valley Historical Society and SCVTV, <http://www.scvtv.com/html/newhall1970-chp1975btv.html>.*

5. *Even today, the CHP's firearms training program is largely decentralized. Training and qualification standards are centrally directed, but the area training officers and rangemasters are given wide latitude, for the most part, in how they run the programs within their areas. This is mostly a matter of practicality in many respects, because the training facilities available to each area office vary widely throughout the state and prevent a more standardized approach. An office with access to a private outdoor range is capable of providing certain training opportunities that are unavailable to an office that is restricted to using a portion of an indoor public range, for example.*

6. *Nuttal, G.C., Captain (ret.). (2008). Cops, Crooks and Other Crazies. Chula Vista, CA: New Century Press. p.300.*

7. *See Appendix A for a more detailed discussion of historical ammunition and firearm developments in the CHP.*

8. *Prior to Newhall, each car was capable of monitoring Channel 2 (car-to-car) transmissions if they were in range of the relatively weak vehicle-based transmitter, but when individual officers radioed dispatch on Channel 1 (car-to-station), the officer's part of the transmission could not be heard by other officers—only the response from dispatch could be monitored. Dispatch could monitor both Channel 1 and 2 transmissions if they were within range.*
On the night of the Newhall Shooting, the embattled Officer Pence broadcast his "11-99" distress call on Channel 2 (car-to-car) and the vital transmission was picked up by Units 78-16R and 78-19R because they were within suitable range. Fortunately, because the scene of the shooting was close to the Newhall Area Office, the transmission was also received by heroine Dispatcher Jo Ann Tidley, who rebroadcast the urgent call to all CHP units in the area, including

those beyond reception of the original car-to-car transmission. If the shooting had occurred farther away from the Newhall Office, and if Units 78-16R and 78-19R had been beyond range (due to distance or terrain), it's possible that nobody would have heard the urgent plea for help on Channel 2. Post-Newhall improvements to CHP radio equipment would help to fix this potentially dangerous gap in capability and greatly improve communications, officer and dispatcher situational awareness, and officer safety.

California Highway Patrol Museum, and Anderson, J. (1999). Newhall Incident Prompted Police Nationwide to Make Changes in Procedures. The California Highway Patrolman and interviews with CHP Sergeant (Retired) Harry Ingold and CHP Officer (Retired) Richard Robinson.

9. The 1970s were the deadliest decade in law enforcement history up to the present. According to the National Law Enforcement Officers Memorial Fund, a total of 2,286 officers died in the 1970s (due to accidents and assaults), an average of almost 229 each year. Research quoted by Morrison and Vila indicates that the felonious killings of law officers peaked in 1973 at 134 officers, while the Officer Down Memorial Page statistics indicate a slightly higher average of 144 officers killed each year in the 1970s due to gunfire, stabbings, vehicular assaults, and assaults by other means. While the statistics may vary a bit, there is consistent agreement that more officers were feloniously assaulted in the 1970s than in any other decade. The reasons for this are varied, but the widespread civil disorder of the time, the mounting breakdown in societal structures (family, church, school) and values, the increasing use of powerful illegal drugs, and the rapidly growing class of violent criminal actors are among the principal causes. Officer Down Memorial Page. (n.d.) [Online] <http://www.odmp.org/search/year> and National Law Enforcement Officer Memorial Fund. (n.d.) Research Bulletins. [Online] <http://www.nleomf.org/facts/research-bulletins/> and Morrison, G.B.& Vila, B.J. (1998). Police Handgun Qualification: Practical Measure or Aimless Activity? Policing: An International Journal of Police Strategies and Management. MCB University Press. Vol 21, No. 3, pp 510-533 <http://spokane.wsu.edu/academics/crimj/vila/1996Policing,PoliceHandgunQualMorrisonVila.pdf>.

10. The CHP had already established a history of involvement with civil disturbances by the time of Newhall (such as the agricultural labor riots in the 1930s and the infamous Watts Riot of 1965, the latter of which began as a CHP traffic stop), but the decade would see an expansion of that role in the Isla Vista Riots (II and III) in April and June of 1970 (right on the heels of Newhall), and it would become one of the principal law enforcement missions for the department. The CHP would be deeply involved in other riots of the decade and later, such as the San Francisco Gulf War Protests in 1991, the 1992 Rodney King Riot in Los Angeles, and the 2010 Oscar Grant Riot in Oakland, to name but a few.

The CHP expanded into other areas of law enforcement throughout the decades to come. The "War on Drugs" saw the CHP involved in counter-trafficking efforts in the 1980s, and the 1984 Los Angeles Olympics brought a new counterterrorism mission to the agency. In the 1990s, some cash-strapped municipalities contracted with the CHP for basic law enforcement services, and, in 1995, the California State Police was absorbed into the CHP, giving the department a new security, executive protection, and S.W.A.T. mission it didn't previously have. After the September 11, 2001, terrorist attacks on the United States, the CHP also gained a new role in the "War on Terror," adding new responsibilities such as site protection for certain high-value targets, explosives detection, and other anti-terrorism missions. CHP officers now participate in an increasing number of task forces with county and city agencies, taking on non-traditional missions such as crime suppression and narcotics and anti-gang efforts, in addition to combating more traditional vehicle theft and smuggling crimes. All of this "mission creep" represents a distinct change from the original traffic safety and enforcement mission the department exclusively focused on in the early days.

11. Including such classics as Pierce R. Brooks' Officer Down, Code Three and Street Survival, by Ronald J. Adams, Thomas M. McTernan, and Charles Remsberg. The latter book actually spurred the development of a very popular traveling seminar series (co-founded by Remsberg and sponsored by the publisher, Calibre Press), which became the industry standard for this type of training. Incidentally, Remsberg is still very much a key player in the officer survival training movement.

12. California Highway Patrol. (n.d.) Force Option Training Simulator. [Online]. <http://www.chp.ca.gov/programs/fots.html>.

13. For more information regarding this reality-based training program and the TOQC concept, see Chiodo, L. (2009). Winning A High-Speed, Close-Distance Gunfight. Boulder, CO: Paladin Press or Mr. Chiodo's website at <http://www.gunfightersltd.com/>.

14. Ritter, J. (2007, February 8). Suicide Rates Jolt Police Culture. USA Today. [Online]. <http://www.usatoday.com/news/nation/2007-02-08-police-suicides_x.htm> and Lee, V. (2007, March 5). High CHP Suicide Rate Worries Officials. ABC7 News, KGO-TV, San Francisco. [Online] <http://abclocal.go.com/kgo/story?section=news/state&id=5093384> and Hill, B. CHP's New Danger: Officer Suicides. LA Daily News. [Online]. <http://www.theppsc.org/forums/showthread. php?t=1657>.

15. Watkins, T. (2010, June 28). 2010 is CHP's Deadliest Year in More Than a Decade. Associated Press. [Online]. <http://www.bakersfieldnow.com/news/97316749.html>.

16. Jabali-Nash, N. (2010, July 21). California Highway Gunman Byron Williams Aimed for "Revolution" Say Cops. CBS News. [Online]. <http://www.cbsnews.com/8301-504083_162-20011219-504083.html> and Courtney, J. (2010, July 18). Wild Morning Shootout Between Gunman, CHP Hospitalizes Three. California Beat. [Online]. <http://www.californiabeat. org/2010/07/18/wild-oakland-freeway-shootout-between-chp-gunman-sunday-morning> and Francis, M. & Greene, J. (2010, July 19). CHP Shootout Suspect Was Upset With "Left Wing Politics." NBC Bay Area.com. [Online]. <http://www.nbcbayarea.com/news/local/CHP-Shootout-Suspect-Was-Upset-With-Left-Wing-Politics-98740324.html>.

17. The reader is particularly directed to the excellent work conducted by researchers at the Police Policy Studies Council <http://www.theppsc.org/> and the Force Science Institute <http://www.forcescience.org/>, as well as the outstanding work of Morrison and Vila, whose collective research indicates that modern police firearms training might not be having any significant positive effect on gunfight performance. Morrison, G.B.& Vila, B.J. (1998). Police Handgun Qualification: Practical Measure or Aimless Activity? Policing: An International Journal of Police Strategies and Management. MCB University Press. Vol 21, No. 3, pp 510-533. <http://spokane. wsu.edu/academics/crimj/vila/1996Policing,PoliceHandgunQualMorrisonVila.pdf>.

18. Spaulding has been amongst the most vocal of trainers who have challenged establishment practices in law enforcement firearms training and questioned their utility to developing combat appropriate skills, but there appears to be rather widespread support for his position. In a 2012 survey of 411 law enforcement officers in the United States, almost 52 percent of the respondents indicated that the firearms qualification course in their agency was "primarily a marksmanship course" and not a "course designed to enhance [their] combat skills." Only 34 percent felt that the course actually focused on street-relevant skills that improved their combat capabilities. Team One Network. (2012) Basic Marksmanship Vs. Combat Skills Training Survey. http://survey.constantcontact.com/survey/a07e5sljqgwh0ojm1rk/results and http://teamonenetwork.com/index.html.

19. In example, the reports of Rand Corporation researchers who observed felony car stop training exercises at the NYPD Academy in 2007 were chillingly reminiscent of the CHP Academy's training prior to Newhall.
The NYPD academy cadets were given two hours of classroom instruction on how to accomplish felony car stops, and then were given four hours of hands-on application to cement the training. For the hands-on training, the student teacher ratio was so lopsided that over half the cadets had no direct participation in the role-playing exercises, and no cadet was able to participate in an exercise more than once. The various elements of the car stop were modeled by instructors in a disjointed, nonlinear fashion, and the cadets never once got to see the execution of a model car stop by the instructors en toto, in a complete, chronological sequence.
The cadets were neither formally nor informally tested on their understanding of the classroom material and were not individually evaluated or scored during the exercises. The instructors made no attempt to ensure each student on the roster was observed and did not take any notes on individual student performance. Students who completed the exercise incorrectly were not given the opportunity to repeat the exercise and demonstrate they could accomplish the objectives. How the staff could certify that the cadets were properly trained and could apply the lessons in the real world with any veracity remains unclear.
In retrospect, the CHP Academy's pre-Newhall felony car stop training was arguably superior,

because even though the cadets didn't receive enough hands-on training and their tactics weren't as sophisticated, at least all of the CHP cadets got their hands dirty as a participants. Rand Corporation. (2008). Evaluation of the New York City Police Department Firearm Training and Firearm Discharge Review Process. Rand Center on Quality Policing. Santa Monica, CA: Rand Corporation. [Online]. <http://www.rand.org/content/dam/rand/pubs/monographs/2008/ RAND_MG717.pdf >.

20. For example, see O'Brien, R. (2007, July 25). Police Shootouts: How Soon We Forget. Police Magazine. [Online] <http://www.policemag.com/Blog/SWAT/Story/2007/07/Police-Shootouts-How-Soon-We-Forget.aspx> and Grassi, R. (2011, May 19). Skill Set: Patrol Tactics. The Tactical Wire. [Online] <http://www.thetacticalwire.com/features/224448> and Haggard, C. (2011, April 20). He Who Ignores History. Police Magazine. [Online]. <http://www.policemag.com/Blog/Patrol-Tactics/Print/Story/2011/04/He-Who-Ignores-History.aspx> and Smith, C. (2010, September/ October). Reality Check. American Handgunner Magazine. Vol 34, Number 5, Issue 207, p.32.

21. Boyd, J. (2011 March/April). Organizational Mindset. American Cop Magazine. Vol 7, Number 2, Issue 34, p.48.

22. Artwohl, A., Dr., & Christensen, L.W. (1997). Deadly Force Encounters. Boulder, CO: Paladin Press, pp.69-75.

23. Bruce K. Siddle, one of the early advocates of this "Dynamic Training," credits the legendary Capt. W.E. Fairbairn of the Shanghai Municipal Police with the use of plastic bullet training in the 1920s, and Robert Welsch of the Ohio State Patrol with the use of cotton wad projectiles in training in the mid 1970s, but these early experiments were isolated and not widely adopted. Siddle, B.K. (1995). Sharpening the Warrior's Edge. Belleville, IL: PPCT Research Publications, p.100.

24. The excellent "Red Man" training suits went to market in 1984, but these early models were designed for a different mission—full-contact fighting with hands and feet, instead of force-on-force scenarios that involved firearms that shot projectiles. Later developments of the Red Man product would be optimized for Version 4.0 type simulations, after the highly successful Simunitions products entered use in the late 1980s and became popular in the early 1990s. Use of the proper protective gear is a critical element of force-on-force training, as the safety of the participants must be paramount. There is no training lesson so important that the safety and health of the students should be needlessly and recklessly put in jeopardy. Training and learning are best accomplished when the student's mind is not preoccupied with safety concerns.

25. Siddle, B.K. (1995). Sharpening the Warrior's Edge. Belleville, IL: PPCT Research Publications, p.99.

26. Siddle is quick to emphasize that the training needs to be carefully crafted and executed to encourage success and learning. Officers should not be exposed to no-win scenarios, as they are destructive and do little to program the proper survival response. An officer who is "killed" repeatedly in training because he is not given proper feedback or instruction will quickly lose confidence. Trainers are encouraged to consult Siddle's list of considerations when designing their own dynamic training exercises, as well as Gabe Suarez's outstanding text on the subject. Siddle, B.K. (1995). Sharpening the Warrior's Edge. Belleville, IL: PPCT Research Publications, pp. 100-101, and Suarez, G. (2005) Force on Force Gunfight Training. Boulder, CO: Paladin Press.

27. The FBI average for the prior decade (1991-2000) was even higher, with 71 percent of officers killed by attackers within 10 feet. Aveni, T.J. (2003, August). Officer-Involved Shootings: What We Didn't Know Has Hurt Us. The Police Policy Studies Council. <http://www.theppsc.org/Staff_ Views/Aveni/OIS.pdf> and, Federal Bureau of Investigation. (2010). Law Enforcement Officers Killed and Assaulted. Table 36: Law Enforcement Officers Feloniously Killed with Firearms, Distance Between Victim Officer and Offender, 2001-2010. http://www.fbi.gov/about-us/cjis/ucr/ leoka/leoka-2010/tables/table36leok-feloniously-with-firearms-distance-victim-offender-01-10. xls.

28. Givens, T. (2011, June 6). Shooting Incidents: Common Factors Among Different Groups. Tactical Talk. Volume 15, Issue 6. [Online]. <http://www.rangemaster.com/>.

29. *The CHP has embraced the use of Simunitions marking cartridges as part of Force On Force training for both initial and in-service training, but Force on Force training using this technology does not represent a significant part of its curriculum yet and has been one of the first victims of recent budgetary constraints. Academy cadets will train in limited amounts with the equipment during some phases of training, and in-service officers will also get exposure to it when they come back to the academy for Advanced Officer Safety Training (AOST), but most firearms training in the CHP is Version 2.0 level training. Simunitions training kits with marker guns, ammunition and protective gear are fielded at the Division level and available for checkout by Area Training Officers who have completed the appropriate CHP instructor training course, but budgetary, logistical and certification issues have limited their use in most Area level training in recent times. As of the date of publication, the CHP had just become fully funded for an "Active Shooter" training program (previously suspended, due to budget shortfalls) which plans to incorporate a large amount of Force On Force training with Simunitions equipment, so this is a positive development. All officers in the state are projected to receive this valuable training at the Area level, and it is hoped that it will lead to a greater emphasis on Force on Force training in other parts of the firearms and tactics curriculum. The CHP continues to demonstrate a zeal for enhancing its firearms training and continues to make steady progress in this area, setting a high standard for other agencies to imitate. Interviews with California Highway Patrol Academy Staff.*

30. *Indeed, some of the standard features in these qualification courses date back even further. For example, the five-round strings of fire found in many courses probably have their roots in U.S. Army standards developed around the 1873 Colt revolvers fielded in the latter part of the nineteenth century, which had six chambers, but were carried with the hammer resting on an empty chamber for safety. Similarly, the six-round strings of fire and the associated time limits in many of today's qualification courses were obviously structured to accommodate the double-action revolvers that became the quintessential law enforcement firearms in early twentieth-century America. Holdovers such as these have no place in modern law enforcement training standards, which should be based on the equipment, procedures, and tactics currently in use by the profession.*

31. *A training officer and S.W.A.T. team leader from a major Northern California agency advised that the officers on his department used to shoot quarterly as recently as 2009, but now only shoot biannually. The only officers on the department who shoot more than once every two years are the officers detailed to S.W.A.T. assignments, and even their training program has been reduced from a monthly activity to a quarterly activity. This particular case is representative of what most law enforcement agencies are experiencing as of this writing, in 2011.*
To its credit, the CHP has largely been able to resist these budgetary pressures. It continues to allocate 50 rounds of training ammunition every month for each officer, and continues to require quarterly shotgun and rifle training. At times, the CHP has been forced to suspend other training ("active shooter" training courses, for example), due to budget shortfalls, but has maintained a strong firearms training program, the benefit of a strong officer safety culture.
Ironically, in recent times the CHP has deemphasized its non-lethal training ammunition (Simunitions) program as a result of budgetary pressures. If the CHP were to consider an expanded use of the more affordable Airsoft-type training tools, it could actually accomplish even more training at a lower price.

32. *Aveni, T. In, Surefire Institute. (n.d.) Lowlight and Tactical Training. Study Reveals Important Truths Hidden in the Details of Officer-Involved Shootings, Reprinted from Los Angeles County Sheriff's Department, Operation Safe Streets. [Online]. <http://www.surefireinstitute.com/images/pdfs/Officer-Involved_Shooting_Study.pdf>.*

33. *Marshall, E. (n.d.) Stopping Power Forums. [Online]. <www.stoppingpower.net>.*

A History of CHP Firearms, Equipment and Firearms Training

Introduction

The early history of California Highway Patrol firearms, equipment, and training is similar to that of many law enforcement agencies in the United States, but the 1970 Newhall Shooting spurred a period of rapid changes in the CHP's training and equipment that was trend-setting within the law enforcement community. The CHP's firearms training and equipment continued to evolve after Newhall, and the CHP officer of today is still among the best equipped and trained of the nation's law enforcement officers.

The transitions between certain elements of training and equipment can be difficult to identify with precision, because little effort was made to chronicle them in the early years. Additionally, veteran officers on the Patrol have always been allowed some latitude to continue using equipment that had been purchased or issued earlier in their careers, even though it had been superseded and was no longer the current issue standard. For this reason, there has always been some overlap between generations of equipment, and exact transition dates can be elusive. However, with the assistance of photographs, written records, and the recollections of retired officers, the following reconstruction of CHP firearms history is possible.

Circa 1920s

From the time the first cars and motorcycles began rumbling down dirt roads up through the early 1920s, traffic laws were enforced by officers appointed by their respective cities or counties. The traffic laws and speed limits varied greatly from one location to the next, creating a patchwork quilt of conflicting ordinances that defied standardization and frustrated travelers.

Like the laws, the selection, training, funding, and employment of the traffic officers who worked in these county motor Squads also lacked uniformity. Officers were typically chosen for their riding skill or political connections, instead of any particular aptitude for law enforcement. They received no training and very little guidance on how to enforce the law. Most were paid out of the proceeds of the tickets they wrote, sometimes by salary, sometimes by commission. Some of the county motor squads were subject to control by powerful politicians, who used the squads to generate revenue, resulting in a high level of bureaucratic graft and corruption.

The officers were required to supply their own motorcycles, uniforms, equipment and weapons, the choice of which was left to the officer's discretion. As such, there was a great diversity in uniforms (sometimes, none at all), and equipment, even within each of the county motor squads. Over time, each of the county motor squads would eventually settle on a rough level of uniformity amongst their members, but wide variations still existed, particularly in choice of weaponry.

In an attempt to standardize enforcement practices and clean up graft and corruption, the various county motor squads were collectively organized as the State Motor Patrol under the Department of Motor Vehicles, on September 1, 1923. There were a few motor squads (notably, Los Angeles County's) that were not incorporated as part of the State Motor Patrol and continued to operate independently, but the remainder were placed under the unique "Dual Control System" (DCS) of the State Motor Patrol.

Under DCS, the county boards of supervisors would submit lists of traffic officer candidates to the Department of Motor Vehicles, which would choose the best qualified among them to become members of the State Motor Patrol. The salaries for the officers would be set by the county supervisors, but would be paid by the state Department of Finance, in an effort to cut some of the politics out of the operation.

While operational control of the officers and enforcement policy was split between the counties and the state, the officers of the State Motor Patrol were still responsible for choosing their own transportation, uniforms, and equipment, and they continued to identify themselves as members of county motor squads.

This first step towards professionalizing the traffic officers would be fol-

A picture of the original Grass Valley Motor Squad from the era of "Dual Control" in the CHP. From left to right, Officer Hammill, Captain J.E. Blake, and Officer Fowyer. The chest straps and ammunition loops would eventually disappear by the 1950s, but the swivel holsters would remain part of CHP uniforms well into the 1990s, and perhaps beyond. Photo courtesy of the California Highway Patrol Museum.

lowed up with the establishment of a new state Division of the Highway Patrol, on August 14, 1929. The Division of the Highway Patrol was part of the Department of Public Works, and it included all officers of the State Motor Patrol. The authorized strength of the new Highway Patrol was 280 uniformed men, who were distributed among 16 districts throughout the state.

With the establishment of the Division of the Highway Patrol, the first efforts at standardizing uniforms and equipment began to take shape. The state began to provide transportation for the officers, and adopted official insignia and uniform standards, but officers were still responsible for providing their own uniforms and weapons.

When the legislature created the Division of the Highway Patrol, in 1929, it also provided for the institution of a professional training academy. Prior to this time, the members of the county motor squads received little instruction beyond on-the-job training from veterans of the squads. A few members completed correspondence training that focused on traffic enforcement regulations, but the majority had no formal legal training whatsoever.

Therefore, in 1930, the Division of the Highway Patrol established its first academy and began to host classes of 40 officers each. The academy training provided training in laws and regulations, and by the end of the first year, every officer in the state had attended the short-duration training. The curriculum did not include any notable firearms training however, which was typical of American law enforcement training at the time.

FIREARMS

As noted, the first motor squad officers and highway patrolmen provided their own weapons and equipment according to their personal desires and financial abilities. Since the recently completed World War had interrupted the civilian supply of weaponry for an extended period, there were shortages of the most desirable arms. As a result, a broad variety of firearms were pressed into service.

The vast majority of these firearms were double-action revolvers from either Colt's or Smith & Wesson, with longer barrels (approximately six inches) being favored over shorter ones. However, photographic evidence indicates that semi-automatic pistols were used by a minority of officers, as well (several pictures from the era show officers armed with 1911-pattern pistols).

A broad range of calibers was used by these early motor squad officers and highway patrolmen. There is evidence that indicates some number of the Los Angeles County Motor Squad was principally armed with .32-caliber revolvers. With the close of World War I and the availability of surplus weapons, there were undoubtedly examples of .45 ACP Colt and Smith & Wesson Model 1917 revolvers being used by the early lawmen as well, alongside a few .45 ACP 1911-pattern pistols and .45 Colt revolvers. Perhaps even a sprinkling of various .44-caliber revolvers were used by the early officers, but it appears that .38-caliber revolvers were the dominant arm throughout the state.

The .32-caliber revolvers were most typically chambered in .32 S&W Long, which was relatively popular in American police service during the early part of the century, particularly in the East; for example, in 1903, Police Commissioner Theodore Roosevelt armed the New York Police Department with Colt's revolvers chambered in the identical .32 Colt New Police cartridge. However, the .32-20 Winchester (.32 WCF) was probably used, as well. The .38-caliber revolvers were typically chambered for the .38 Special, which would go on to become the dominant police cartridge of the twentieth century.

AMMUNITION

Ammunition was supplied by the individual officers in the 1920s. The .32 S&W Long (alternately, .32 Colt New Police) cartridge had a 98-grain lead round-nose bullet that reached about 705 feet per second (fps), and the .32-20 Winchester had a 100-grain lead bullet that reached about 750 fps. The .38 Special ammunition largely consisted of 158-grain round-nose lead loaded to around 775 fps, but some 200-grain "Super Police" loads around 650 fps (advertised at 750 fps), were undoubtedly used by officers who wanted more punch. The .45 ACP ammunition of the time was standard military issue, a 230-grain jacketed bullet at 850 fps.

LEATHER

A variety of makes and designs were used, including big names like S.D. Myres, H.H. Heiser, and George Lawrence, plus generic military surplus and locally produced rigs. The motor squads of the 1920s typically wore Sam Browne belts with diagonal chest straps and a flap holster. The flap holsters were especially helpful in protecting the exposed guns of the motor riders and retaining them as the officers rumbled down rough dirt roads on bikes with primitive suspensions. Spare ammunition was typically carried in loops on the belt, although some pouches were also used. This pattern continued throughout the 1930s, as the CHP was almost entirely composed of motorcycle officers wearing the same (officer-supplied) uniforms and leather gear.

TRAINING

Formal firearms training was nonexistent in most American law enforcement agencies throughout the 1920s, including the California county motor squads and State Motor Patrol. An officer's proficiency was dictated by whatever training he sought himself. Even when the new Division of the Highway Patrol instituted its early academy, in 1930, the curriculum did not include formal firearms training.

Circa 1930s

The Division of the Highway Patrol was transferred to the Department of Motor Vehicles in 1931, and in July 1933, the Los Angeles County Motor Squad was absorbed and became the seventeenth district in the fledgling organization. But despite the bureaucratic maturation of the Highway Patrol in the early 1930s, there was little attempt to standardize the weapons and equipment of the officers, who continued to provide their own.

There were some notable advances in ammunition during the period. The enactment of Prohibition in the United States at the end of 1919 spurred the development of organized crime, and as these gangsters grew increasingly violent throughout the 1920s, the need for a police cartridge that could defeat the bulletproof vests and armored vehicles of gangsters grew increasingly important. In response, Colt's offered the .38 Super in its 1911 pistol, and Smith & Wesson offered the .38-44 S&W Special in the large frame Heavy Duty revolver, in late1929 to early 1930. The .38-44 became popular with lawmen, but never replaced the .38 Special, which was fast becoming the law

In this 1936 photo, California Highway Patrol Chief E. Raymond Cato inspects the Bay Bridge Squad prior to the opening of the San Francicso-Oakland Bay Bridge. High level appearance standards were critical to maintaining the image of the infant Patrol. Photo courtesy of the California Highway Patrol Museum.

enforcement standard of the century. Attempts to boost the performance of the .38-44 led to the development of the .357 Magnum cartridge, in 1935, which achieved even greater popularity than the .38-44 and .38 Super, but still never displaced the .38 Special as the king of police cartridges.

As in the prior decade, highway patrolmen were given great latitude to select their own firearms and personal equipment, so there was a diversity of types in service. With the onslaught of the Great Depression, there was often little money to go around for new firearms and ammunition, so there were few changes in firearms, ammunition, and equipment for most officers from one decade to the next.

FIREARMS

The odd mix of firearm types and calibers continued throughout the new decade, with various models of Smith & Wesson and Colt's .38 Special revolvers appearing to be the most popular weapon of choice. With the introduction of the Smith & Wesson Heavy Duty revolver, in early 1930 (and the adjustable sights Outdoorsman late the following year), the high velocity .38-44 cartridge also began to see limited use on the highways. These large, .44-caliber framed guns typically had five-inch barrels, but small numbers of four-inch and 6½-inch guns were produced as well. The 1935 introduction of the Smith & Wesson .357 Magnum revolver was widely heralded, and even in this depression era some officers probably found a way to afford the "World's Most Powerful Handgun" for service use, but the high cost and limited production of these arms prevented them from becoming too popular with the poorly paid lawmen.

AMMUNITION

Ammunition was still supplied by the individual officers. The 158-grain round-nose lead .38 Special ammunition continued to be popular in that caliber. The hot new .38-44 ammunition, designed to offer increased penetration through automotive bodies and the body armor that was becoming popular with gangsters of the era, typically had a 158-grain, pointed full metal jacket bullet loaded to about 1,175 fps, although some 150- and 110-grain loads of different shapes existed, as well. The even hotter .357 Magnum debuted, in 1935, with a 158-grain lead Sharpe semi-wadcutter style bullet loaded to over 1,400 fps, and this was certainly the load used by officers who could afford the expensive new revolver.

LEATHER

No changes. A variety of colors, patterns, and styles were used by the officers. Flap holsters, Mexican loop holsters, drop shank holsters, and swivel style holsters are all in evidence in the photographs of the era. Spare ammunition, when evident, was typically carried in cartridge loops on the belt, although a few pouches are seen in photographs, as well.

TRAINING

There was still little to no formal training during the era. The county motor squads would occasionally challenge each other in shooting matches, but formal training was sparse, particularly in the first half of the decade.

Handgun shooting techniques of the era were almost all derived from military match-style protocols. The handgun was typically fired with a single hand in a formal target shooting stance that had the strong side of the body bladed towards the target, while the non-shooting hand was placed on the hip or in a pocket. Single-action fire predominated, even with the double-action revolvers of the time, because the light trigger stroke made it easier to hit the target from this unstable position, and because single-action fire was a holdover from military training that had its roots in single-action arms like the 1873 Colt's revolver.

The arming of the FBI, in 1934, and that agency's subsequent adoption of the Practical Pistol Course (PPC) brought some short-range techniques that involved firing from a single-handed position at the hip. Double-action fire was emphasized at these short distances, although some officers undoubtedly reverted to single-action fire habits at these seven-yard distances.

Sacramento officers demonstrating the classic single handed firing stance of early to mid 20th Century law enforcement. Some weapons are visibly cocked in single action mode, and all shooters have rested the non-shooting hand on a hip or in a pocket, in true "Camp Perry" fashion. Ammunition is loaded from the cartridge boxes on the bench instead of from the pouches on their Sam Browne rigs. Except for the uniforms, this 1939 scene would be indistinguishable from similar images of CHP training through the 1960s. Photo courtesy of the California Highway Patrol Museum.

Very little "combat" training existed in this era. Courses of fire began with the gun in hand, not in the holster. Officers mostly fired at match-style "bull's-eye" targets in training, and loaded from trays or cans of ammunition that were frequently located on a waist-level table in front of the shooter. They were expected to police their brass during the course of fire and neatly collect it for disposal later. Some humanoid silhouette targets were introduced to police training later this decade, but it appears the majority of Highway Patrol training (when it occurred) was done on bull's-eye targets.

Circa 1940s

In the 1940s, the highway patrol continued to evolve and made the transition from being a loose confederation of independent county motor squads to a centrally controlled, statewide organization with common standards, policies, and practices.

The autonomy given the county motor squads in the areas of uniforms

Full dress inspection for the "Princes of the Highway." The trend towards increasing standardization of uniforms and equipment is evident in this image. The "spoked wheel" shoulder patch was replaced in 1947 by the current "shield-style" emblem, adopted when the CHP achieved "Department" status within California's government structure. Photo courtesy of the California Highway Patrol Museum.

Helmets, gas masks and Thompson submachine guns were added to the CHP inventory during World War II to help officers defend California against possible Japanese attacks or acts of sabotage. While the Thompsons made for an impressive photo opportunity, they actually saw little use on the Patrol and disappeared from the inventory by the early 1960s. Photo courtesy of the California Highway Patrol Museum.

and equipment was gradually eliminated during this decade. The uniform standards adopted in the 1930s were now enforced, and a greater level of standardization in uniforms, weapons, and equipment is observed in the photographs of the era.

In 1947, the Highway Patrol became a full department of the state government, bringing the organization to full bureaucratic maturity. The Department of the California Highway Patrol adopted a new uniform patch and made other changes to the duty uniform. Additionally, the department began to publish and enforce regulations that governed the weapons and equipment used by highway patrolmen, which eventually eliminated the odd mix of firearms used by the officers.

FIREARMS

With the declaration of war in 1941, Colt's and Smith & Wesson focused their efforts on the production of military arms; very few were produced for the civilian population. Production of some models, such as the handguns chambered for .38-44 and .357 Magnum, was suspended entirely. The demands of the wartime economy meant that the majority of highway patrolmen were armed with a mix of pre-war handguns during the first part of this decade.

However, sometime during this decade (presumably after the war's end), the department issued regulations that began to standardize firearms used by the officers. The regulations required officers to be armed with Colt's or Smith & Wesson double-action revolvers chambered in .38 Special or .357 Magnum calibers. These revolvers were required to have six-inch barrels, and the officers were responsible for purchasing their own revolvers.

Long guns (rifles and shotguns) had not been issued or used by the department prior to the war, but, beginning in 1942, the CHP began to supply limited numbers of Thompson M1928 and Reising M50 submachine guns (both in .45 ACP) for anti-sabotage patrols along the coastlines, strike and riot control, and military convoy escort missions (helmets and gas masks were issued, as well). Some of these submachine guns remained in inventory into the early 1950s (photographic evidence shows them being used in training at the McClellan AFB Academy location, in 1951), but were eventually removed from stock.

AMMUNITION
No changes during this period. The demands of the wartime economy meant that ammunition was scarce on the home front, so it's likely some officers continued to carry the same cartridges that had been in service for many years.

LEATHER
By the end of the 1940s, the Highway Patrol had adopted a uniform pattern for leather gear. The new standards called for black leather gear stamped with a basket-weave pattern and having brass hardware. The odd assortment of old colors, patterns, and styles was phased out by the end of the decade.

Open-topped, drop shank holsters with simple straps (and sometimes with a metal tab that bore against the triggerguard to keep the gun in the holster in lieu of a snap), became the norm, especially for officers who patrolled in sedans. Many of these holsters incorporated a swivel on the shank, which allowed the holster body to swing back and forth—a significant aid to officers seated in cars. Additionally, by the late 1930s and early 1940s, the "clamshell" style of holster, in which the two spring-loaded halves of the holster pop open to release the handgun (after a hidden button is activated through the trigger guard), began to see service on the Patrol. Ammunition loops mostly disappeared, and officers were now seen carrying their spare ammunition in simple spill or dump pouches with a snap on the bottom that released the cartridges to fall out by gravity.

TRAINING

There were no significant changes in CHP firearms training during this period. The wartime economy made the ammunition supply scarce, and this discouraged the expenditure of ammunition for training. Match-style shooting courses and techniques predominated where any training was taking place.

Three Colt Officer's Models and a single Smith & Wesson (which appears to be an N-Frame .357 Magnum) in action during training. Note the box of low powered Remington 148 grain wad cutter ammunition and the clamshell holster in use by the officer on the right--two items which would eventually disappear from the Patrol. Photo courtesy of the California Highway Patrol Museum.

Circa 1950s

By the 1950s, the California Highway Patrol had clearly broken from its county motor squad past. It bore all the marks of a modern law enforcement agency, and uniforms, equipment, weapons, and training were highly standardized throughout the state.

FIREARMS

The department still required all officers to carry six-inch barreled .38 Special or .357 Magnum caliber revolvers from Colt's or Smith & Wesson, but sometime during this period the department began to issue this equipment to new cadets instead of requiring them to purchase their own.

Circa 1957, new academy cadets were issued either Colt Officer's Model Match (.38 Special) or Smith & Wesson Model 14 (.38 Special) revolvers on a "luck of the draw" basis. One report from this era indicates that department policy required all officers to carry .38 Special revolvers, with the exception of early members of the Patrol, who were grandfathered to carry their .357 Magnum revolvers with .38 Special ammunition on duty. However, other reports indicate that .357 Magnum revolvers were approved for all officers who wished to purchase them (and the ammunition) on their own. Since this trend is observed in later years, it is probably correct that officers were allowed to provide their own .357 Magnum pistols and ammunition in this era without restriction, after they had graduated from the academy.

With the cessation of international hostilities and a booming economy, Smith & Wesson and Colt's began to reintroduce products discontinued during the war, and also began to market new designs, especially in the popular .357 Magnum chambering. It wasn't until the early to mid-1950s that .357 Magnum revolvers truly became widely available to the consumer and common on the Patrol. New designs such as the Smith & Wesson Combat Magnum (known after 1957 as the Model 19), and the Colt Python, both introduced in 1955, were immediately popular with the lawmen who could obtain them.

The Thompson M1928 and Reising M50 submachine guns that had been issued in the 1940s for military missions went back into storage for the most part, typically used only in Academy familiarization training. There was no attempt to keep the weapons serviceable, and, as they broke, they were eventually removed from stock. By the late 1950s or early 1960s, the few remaining weapons were removed from inventory entirely, and the only traces of these firearms today are the few samples on display at the CHP Academy Museum.

AMMUNITION

The Highway Patrol began to issue duty and training ammunition during this period, instead of requiring officers to supply their own. Issued duty am-

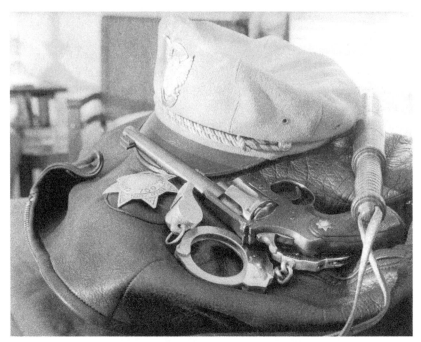

The tools of the trade. The "759" badge number is an early one, denoting a veteran member of the Patrol. This style of uniform cap would be phased out in 1957, but the Colt Officer's Model would have looked right at home in a CHP officer's holster for another 3 to 4 decades after this photo was taken. Photo courtesy of the California Highway Patrol Museum.

munition was .38 Special 158-grain round-nose with a copper jacket during this period. Issued training ammunition was Winchester-Western .38 Special 148-grain wadcutter. Officers who chose to carry .357 Magnum ammunition in lieu of .38 Special had to provide their own ammunition for both duty and training.

LEATHER

The CHP began to issue leather gear during this era. The issued holster was a drop shank swivel design (made by various manufacturers) and it was prone to failure. The swivel was a peened rivet that would break, frequently leaving the holstered gun behind on the seat of the car. The holster became known as a "suicide pouch," and many officers elected to purchase their own Hoyt, Safety Speed, Lawrence, Tex Shoemaker, or others of superior construction. Spare ammunition was carried in dump pouches.

Many officers began using "clamshell"-style holsters in this era from makers such as Jewett Safety Holster/Stanroy, Hoffman & Sons, or Safety Speed. The clamshell holsters were popular in the 1940s through the early 1960s, but, in 1962, two officers equipped with these holsters shot themselves in the leg in separate incidents, and the department put new restrictions into place. New officers were prohibited from purchasing clamshell holsters for duty. Older officers were grandfathered and allowed to wear them as long as they remained serviceable, but were not allowed to replace them with a new clamshell. Many of these veteran officers elected to have their old holsters refurbished by local shops or large police supply outfits such as the F. Morton Pitt Company, so they could continue to wear them beyond their original service life, and they became a status symbol of sorts among the old timers.

TRAINING

In-service firearms training for CHP officers started to become more common during this period, as ammunition supplies rebounded from the war years. Match-style shooting courses and techniques still dominated the scene, but the FBI's Practical Pistol Course influence began to rise, and photographic evidence indicates a limited amount of combat-style instruction was provided, with Academy cadets shooting at humanoid silhouettes from a crouched, single-handed, hip-level shooting position. The use of the Colt Police Silhouette Target (usually the 35x45-inch T-8, with the smaller 22x32-inch T-6 reserved for firearms ranges with a maximum shooting distance of 50 feet), became increasingly common during this period. This famous target, a staple of law enforcement training for decades, incorporated a blackened humanoid silhouette that appeared to be drawing a gun from the waistband area with its right hand. Subtle white scoring rings separated the target into scoring zones, with a bowling pin-shaped "K5" zone running from head to torso, and a bull's-eye ring in the sternum area.

Circa 1960s

FIREARMS

The department still required all officers to carry six-inch barrel, .38 Special or .357 Magnum revolvers from Colt's or Smith & Wesson. It appears the department alternated back and forth between policies that required new cadets to choose and purchase from an approved list of weapons, and policies that required the department to issue .38-caliber guns directly to the new cadets.

After academy training had been completed and officers were in service, it appears the department's regulations allowed officers to replace equipment at their own expense as desired. The .357 Magnum was a popular choice among officers during this period.

AMMUNITION

Issued duty ammunition was .38 Special 158-grain round-nose lead. Thirty rounds were issued to officers each year by the department (six for duty weapon, 12 for dump pouches, and 12 spares). Many officers purchased their own .357 Magnum 158-grain semi-wadcutter or jacketed soft-point ammunition for duty use in privately purchased guns, but some reports indicate officers felt compelled or pressured to load the state-issued .38 Special ammunition for inspections. Training continued to be conducted with state-supplied .38 Special 148-grain wadcutter ammunition and officers who chose to carry .357 Magnum ammunition on duty were not compelled to practice or train with it. Peters, Remington, Smith & Wesson, and Winchester brands were all used.

LEATHER

The drop shank swivel holster predominated throughout this period and remained the issued holster design, but the clamshell designs also remained popular with officers who were grandfathered to use them. Crossdraw holsters enjoyed some limited popularity within the department, as well, during this period, but they were never issued by the Patrol and were strictly an optional, approved item. Spare ammunition was carried in dump pouches.

TRAINING

In-service firearms training for CHP officers became increasingly standardized during this period. In early 1965, Academy training (Meadowview location, 1954 to 1976), included the so-called Police Pistol Combat (PPC) course on bull's-eye targets, as well as limited amounts of rapid fire training on T-8 Colt Police Silhouette Targets.

PPC training emphasized double-action shooting at seven yards and single-action shooting at 15 and 25 yards (it appears the CHP deleted the PPC's standard 50-yard stage). The seven-yard stage was shot from a variation of the "FBI crouch," with the gun extended to the target from waist to chest level, below the line of sight. The 15-yard stages used a stance that was traditional "Camp Perry" or match-style, with the revolver extended at arms length with a single hand, while the free arm was placed with hand on hip. Sights were used to align the revolver.

Targets were typically bull's-eyes or T-8 Colt Police Silhouettes. Reports indicate that the PPC course was typically shot from the standing position only (traditional PPC involves some prone and kneeling), in deference to keeping cadet uniforms clean and undamaged. This static-position firing was done from covered positions at the Meadowview Academy location. Spent brass was collected neatly in cans at the officer's feet during firing.

Limited training in combat shooting techniques was incorporated sometime in the early 1960s, under the direction of CHP Academy firearms instructor Officer John Pedri, with pointers on such topics as sitting, kneeling, crouching, shooting from cover, and so forth. Typical stance during this training involved a deep crouch with the firearm extended single-handedly about hip to chest level and below the line of sight (the "FBI crouch."). Point-shooting technique was used in lieu of using the revolver's sights. Some rapid-fire instruction was given. Targets for this phase of instruction were the aforementioned Colt Police Silhouette Target. Notably, support/weak-hand only firing and barricade firing were not part of the instruction.

Circa 1963-1965

FIREARMS

In 1963, the Directors of the California Association of Highway Patrolmen asked the CHP Commissioner to approve shotguns for officers on patrol in cars, but the Commissioner demurred, stating the idea would not be supported by the legislature. On November 15, 1963, Officer Glenn W. Carlson was fatally shot by one of three parolee bank robbers in Truckee. As a result, Assemblywoman Pauline Davis, of Portola, introduced an Assembly bill to provide the CHP with shotguns. The bill passed, and the CHP was provided with a limited number of Remington 870 shotguns (six guns per every 10 patrol vehicles, about one for every five to 10 officers), beginning in 1964.

Training was conducted in late 1964 and early 1965. One report from Zone VI (San Diego) stated the weapons training officer had "trained 50 local officers" between February and April 1965, and the Patrol was on course to arm most of the 3,000 patrolmen in the state with shotguns that year.

Although limited in number, the shotguns were very valuable during the August 1965 Watts Riot near Los Angeles. In the wake of the riot, the legislature provided the CHP with enough funds to include one Remington 870 shotgun in a dashboard-mounted, electrically operated, Lektro-Lok rack in every patrol car.

AMMUNITION

Issued ammunition for the Remington 870 shotgun was nine-pellet 00 Buckshot, typically Winchester-Western Super X. Four rounds were loaded in the magazine of the shotgun, and the chamber was left empty. No spare rounds were carried on the gun.

LEATHER

There were no changes to the leather of the Patrol during this time.

TRAINING

Shotgun training was limited within the CHP. Aside from the initial training when the weapons were first issued, there was no recurrent training for in-service officers for a long time in the CHP. Academy cadets received limited basic training as part of the curriculum, but once they got to the field, there was little recurrent training to be had for several years.

The Patrol's early shotgun training curriculum focused on administrative practices such as loading and unloading the weapon, function checks, approved carry positions, procedures for "sealing" the weapons, and the use-of-force policy. Cadets and officers were given the opportunity to practice firing the shotgun from the shoulder and hip positions as taught by the CHP, but did not train in street-relevant environments and did not get the chance to practice skills beyond entry-level operation of the weapon. Since spare ammunition was not carried on the gun, cadets and officers were not trained to reload and sustain the weapon in a tactical environment.

Circa 1965 and 1968

FIREARMS

New Academy cadets purchased their own Colt's or Smith & Wesson revolvers, typically from selected vendors that visited the academy, such as the F. Morton Pitt Company (of San Gabriel), or the George F. Cake Company (with stores in Berkeley and the greater Los Angeles area). A six-inch barrel was required, but the guns could be chambered in either .38 Special or .357 Magnum. The Smith & Wesson Model 19 was the most popular choice.

AMMUNITION

There were no changes to the ammunition of the Patrol during these two time periods.

LEATHER

No changes. The drop shank swivel design holster remained standard issue, clamshell holsters were grandfathered, and crossdraw holsters were authorized as an optional item. No "high-ride" designs were officially allowed by the Patrol in 1965, but they were soon to come. By this era, Hoyt and Safety Speed were the preferred holster brands. Spare ammunition (12 rounds) continued to be carried in dump pouches. Some enterprising officers soaked the pouches in water to stretch them out, allowing a total of 18 rounds to be carried if they were stacked in an alternating fashion in the pouch.

TRAINING

Shotgun training continued to be limited for CHP officers. Academy cadets received some training on the shotgun, firing it on silhouette targets, but training for officers already in the field remained spotty. More disturbing was the introduction of perforated, adhesive, yellow evidence seals to the shotguns, which were applied around the barrel and forearm of the shotgun. If the shotgun was "racked" and a round was loaded into the chamber, the seal would break and it would become apparent to all that the gun had been loaded. Officers were required to write and submit memos each time they broke a shotgun seal to justify why their actions were necessary. The shift sergeant would receive and review the report, inspect the gun, unload it if necessary, and re-apply a new seal. This procedure discouraged the use of shotguns among CHP officers, who were reluctant to write the memos and face irritated sergeants.

Circa Late 1960s, Early 1970s

FIREARMS

No known changes. At some point in this period, perhaps the early 1970s, the California legislature passed a bill that required the department to provide all new-hire officers with safety equipment, to include Sam Browne belt, handcuffs, and revolver. Veteran officers could keep their existing personal gear in service, or could choose to be retrofitted with the department-issued equipment. All new officers received state-issued equipment when they began the academy and could elect to buy other department-approved gear after they graduated.

AMMUNITION

No changes. Ammunition standards were loose, and .357 Magnum ammunition was officially authorized, but not issued. Issued duty ammunition was .38 Special 158-grain round-nose lead.

LEATHER

Some officers began to use "high-ride" design holsters that omitted the drop shank and carried the revolver closer to the belt line. These designs became increasingly popular, since the Patrol had moved away from motorcycles as the primary vehicle and most officers were now driving cars that made the drop shank holsters awkward. The swivel design had been an early solution for that problem, but increasing dissatisfaction with the strength of the swivel encouraged some officers to switch to the high-ride design.

"Break-front" holsters, patterned after the original 1930s Berns-Martin design, also became popular on the Patrol, during the 1960s. These break-

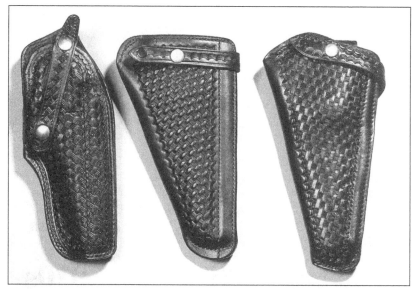

Holster tech, Circa 1960s - 1970s. Three popular "breakfront" designs evaluated by the CHP included (left to right) the Hoyt "Breakfront," Bianchi Model 27, and Safety Speed "Full Breakfront." The Model 27 would become standard CHP issue and launch a longstanding relationship with the company, but all three models were exceptionally popular with CHP officers of the era. Photo courtesy of the California Highway Patrol Museum.

front holsters were split down the front seam and the holster halves were held closed by means of a spring incorporated into the design. Drawing the revolver was accomplished by levering it through the split front of the holster against the spring tension. In practiced hands, these designs were very quick and became very popular among CHP officers, who purchased many of the Berns-Martin, Hoyt, or Bianchi Model 27 break-front holsters with their own funds. Spare ammunition was still carried in dump pouches.

On August 5, 1972, Officer Kenneth D. Roediger, from the East Los Angeles area, was fatally shot, when an ex-con he was trying to arrest became violent and disarmed him. The struggling arrestee had been pulled from his car and landed flat on his back. The officer sat on his stomach and tried to pin the con's shoulders to the ground in preparation for rolling him over for handcuffing. While the officer's hands were occupied, the con easily drew the officer's revolver from his crossdraw holster and shot him through the heart with his own gun, killing him. Tragically, the holster had been given to Officer Roediger by his highway patrolman father. As a result of this incident, all crossdraw holsters were immediately banned by the department.

TRAINING

The PPC shooting format evolved into something moderately more practical and known as the "Modified Police Pistol Combat" course. Officers conducted training in coveralls or street clothes and began to fire from stances other than standing. There was more emphasis on double-action shooting. Brass was still policed during the course of fire.

A new "75 Foot Silhouette" B-21E style target was adopted sometime during this period. This target has the same general shape as the T-8 Colt Police Silhouette target and retains the coke bottle-shaped "K5" zone of that target, but eliminates the "5X" scoring ring in the center of the chest and the vertical "spinal cord" scoring zone that appeared on some versions of the T-8. The target has "CHP" stamped in the upper left corner and is labeled "75 Foot Silhouette" in the upper right corner. Another version of this same target would soon appear, with the "5X" scoring ring included.

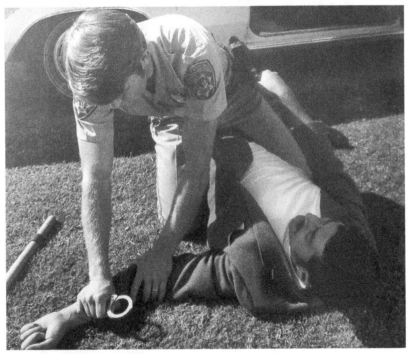

This training photograph recreates the 1972 killing of Officer Kenneth D. Roediger, who was killed with his own gun after the suspect removed it from the officer's crossdraw holster. The CHP banned the use of crossdraw holsters in the wake of the killing. Photo courtesy of the California Highway Patrol Museum.

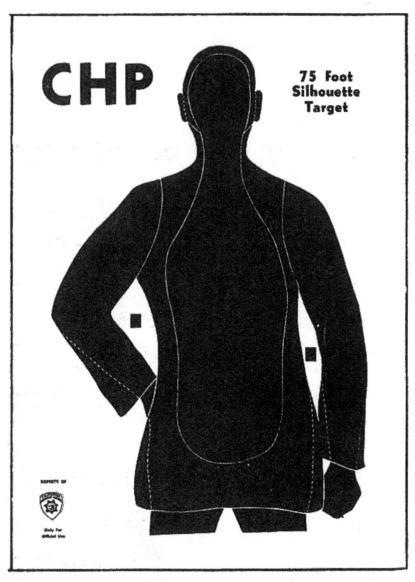

The CHP 75 Foot Silhouette Target was modeled after the earlier T-8 Colt Police Silhouette target. Later versions of this target included a "5X" scoring ring in the center of the target area which looked good, but encouraged shooters to aim too low, missing the critical anatomical features/targets of the upper chest area. Photo courtesy of the California Highway Patrol Museum.

Circa Early to Mid-1970s

FIREARMS

Sometime after the arrival of the Ruger Security Six revolver, in 1970, Ruger was added to the approved list of manufacturers for private-purchase weapons. Additionally, after the 1970 introduction of the stainless steel Smith & Wesson Model 66 and the 1972 introduction of the stainless steel Smith & Wesson Model 67, department policies were altered to allow officers to purchase stainless steel revolvers. Dan Wesson revolvers were still not permitted for duty use, due to the front-actuated cylinder release that was awkward to effect with a single hand.

Many officers began to purchase their weapons from a new vendor, the Bill Davis Co., in Sacramento. Davis, a retired CHP Academy firearms instructor and acclaimed competitive shooter on the CHP Blue and Gold Team, entered the industry as an employee of the George F. Cake Co., a business with long-established ties to the CHP. The name of the business soon switched to Cake-Davis Company, and eventually to just the Bill Davis Company. The Bill Davis Company would last for several decades and maintained a very close relationship with the CHP throughout its life. It also made a name for itself throughout the industry as the birthplace of the "Smython," a hybrid revolver popular with match competitors that mated a Colt Python barrel to a Smith & Wesson K-frame.

Sometime in the mid-1970s, after the Newhall Shooting, the department approved officers to carry secondary (backup) revolvers chambered in .38 Special and produced by Colt's or Smith & Wesson. The weapons had to be inspected by CHP armorers for proper function and safety and had to be carried in a holster with a safety strap that also had to be inspected by CHP personnel. Previous to this policy, some officers had carried unofficial backups of various designs, calibers, and quality, but they did so in contradiction to CHP standards. The new program was a critical change in the department's culture and normalized this important officer safety habit.

In the wake of the April 6, 1970, Newhall shooting, the yellow evidence seals were removed from the CHP shotguns, and the practice of writing memos when they were loaded was discontinued. In another post-Newhall development, five rounds of spare ammunition began to be carried on the shotgun in a canvas pouch that was wrapped around the buttstock, this addition taking place in late 1971 to early 1972. In later years, the canvas pouch would be replaced by a leather carrier with five loops that were laced onto the buttstock. These leather carriers were in widespread service by 1976.

AMMUNITION

In light of the April 6, 1970, Newhall Shooting, the CHP recognized that its policy of allowing officers to carry .357 Magnum ammunition on duty, but training these same officers with low-powered .38 Special ammunition, was unsatisfactory. A new policy was enacted that required officers to train with the same ammunition they used on duty. Since the department still did not issue .357 Magnum ammunition for training, this meant that officers who wanted to carry the more powerful ammunition on duty had to supply their own training ammunition.

The new training ammunition policy took a while to fully implement, as many CHP Area offices had an ample supply of .38 Special wadcutter ammunition that had to be disposed of first. As such, some areas lagged behind on the transition to shooting duty ammunition during training, but, eventually, all area offices made the switch.

Sometime around 1975, probably coincident with the issue of the new Model 67 and 68 revolvers in 1976, the CHP began to issue and mandate a new load for all training and duty purposes. The new load was the Winchester-Western .38 Special 110-grain +P+ jacketed hollow point, commonly referred to as the "Treasury Load" (Catalog #Q4070). This ammunition was favorably regarded by the National Institute of Justice in the 1975 report of its "Relative Incapacitation Index" (RII) study, and it was subsequently adopted by the Secret Service, the Treasury Department, and the Los Angeles County Sheriff's Department, among others.

The department apparently chose to issue and mandate .38 Special ammunition in lieu of .357 Magnum, because of nagging concerns that persisted about the ability of officers to handle the powerful Magnum ammunition. After the 1970 Newhall shooting, many in law enforcement felt that, perhaps, this ammunition was too powerful for the average officer to control, especially without frequent practice. Additionally, the demographics of the department were changing—female officers entered the Academy in 1974-'75, and there were significant concerns that these officers with slighter builds would not be able to control the Magnum ammunition at all.

Sometime in the early to mid-1970s (photo evidence indicates by late 1971 to early 1972), speedloaders were adopted by the CHP in lieu of dump pouches. This, too, was a reaction to the 1970 Newhall shooting, in which the horribly wounded Officer Pence was killed while he struggled to load his revolver from the problematic dump pouches. Various models of speedloaders were issued by the department, to include Second Six, Dade Machine Co., and HKS models. Other models from Safariland and other vendors were authorized for private purchase. Speedloaders were issued in pairs and carried in a flapped leather box or pouch on the Sam Browne.

Two sharp officers from somewhere around the mid 1970s to early 1980s. The officer on the left has a high ride breakfront holster, while the officer on the right has a swivel. Both have the speedloaders which came about as a critical post-Newhall reform. Photo courtesy of the California Highway Patrol Museum.

LEATHER

Bianchi Leather Products, Inc., was contracted to supply the issue leather for the CHP during this era. In April of 1974, John Bianchi had acquired the Berns-Martin Holster Company and, in the process, had secured the rights to its legendary designs and patents, including their front-draw break-front model. The Bianchi Model 27 "Breakfront" holster became standard issue for the CHP in the early 1970s, followed by the 1974 introduction of the Model 2800 ("The Judge"), that also became official CHP issue, perhaps concurrent with arrival of Model 67 and 68 revolvers, in 1976.

TRAINING

In the wake of the Newhall shooting, CHP officers began to receive more in-service training on the Remington 870 shotgun. Experiences varied from office to office, but some officers reported quarterly training with the shotgun, while others reported only annual qualifications. Training ranged from inappropriate aerial target practice (shooting clays), to more effective combat-oriented training involving the shooting of paper CHP silhouette targets. for the first time, officers were taught how to reload the weapon from the spare ammunition carrier on the gun.

Handgun training became more street relevant. Reloading via speedloaders was taught, CHP silhouette targets completely replaced bull's-eye targets, and more practical handgun shooting stances (two-handed Weaver and Isoceles stances and weak-hand only shooting), took up an increasing part of the curriculum.

Handgun cartridges loaded with plastic or wax bullets and powered solely by primers were introduced for training in some areas. Training with this ammunition was done at the office grounds, in the parking lot or car port, in an informal setting. No qualifications were fired with this ammo, and no record of training was kept, as it was designed only as optional, supplemental training.

On September 17, 1974, the CHP held a groundbreaking ceremony for its new Academy in Bryte (later to become West Sacramento). The new facility began training cadet classes in 1976. This modern facility incorporated a state of the art firearms range with moving target capability.

Circa 1971 and 1973

FIREARMS

Academy Cadets were issued Smith & Wesson K38 (Model 14) revolvers with six- barrels (.38 Special). Once in the field, officers were still allowed to purchase .357 Magnum revolvers with their own funds, with the Smith & Wesson Model 19 Combat Magnum being most popular choice.

AMMUNITION

Reports from one officer who came on in 1971 confirm that he had to provide his own (optional) .357 Magnum ammunition for duty and training. Dual dump pouches were still being issued as late as January 1971, over half a year since the Newhall Shooting. Photo documentation from the period indicates that speedloaders were finally issued to officers by perhaps late 1971 to early 1972.

An officer assigned to the Westminster Area office from 1972 to 1977 indicated that Secret Service personnel trained with them at the same location (Seal Beach Naval Weapons Station), and unofficially provided the CHP officers with large quantities of Winchester-Western .38 Special 110-grain +P+ jacketed hollowpoint ammunition ("Treasury Load"-Q4070) for training,

A CHP Cadet from Class III-73 scores his target on the old Meadowview Academy outdoor range. The target is the old CHP Silhouette target, the holster is a Hoyt Breakfront, which carries a Smith & Wesson. Photo courtesy of the California Highway Patrol Museum.

used in lieu of the wadcutter ammunition that was still being provided by the department for training. Furthermore, the officer indicated that the wadcutters did not fully disappear in training until the adoption of speedloaders (around early 1972), which made it difficult to feed the blunt cartridges into the cylinder.

LEATHER

Academy cadets were issued swivel holsters of unknown make, still colloquially referred to as "suicide holsters," because of weaknesses in the swivel design and because they offered no retention capability in a struggle. Many officers later purchased their own swivel holsters from other manufacturers, such as Hoyt or Safety Speed.

TRAINING

Handgun training at the academy was starting to evolve. Officers continued to shoot from covered static positions at the Meadowview Academy location, but two-handed firing grips were now being taught as part of the curriculum. A mix of bull's-eyes and CHP silhouettes were being used. Quick draw training was conducted with cadets, who would draw and fire revolvers loaded with blanks against a time clock.

Shotgun training at the Academy was conducted in the bermed, open field range at Meadowview, in addition to some combat-type handgun training. There was still no emphasis on weak-hand firing with the handgun.

Circa 1976

FIREARMS

Smith & Wesson Model 67 and 68 revolvers (.38 Special revolvers in four- and six-inch barrels, respectively) became standard issue, ushering in a new era of stainless steel and four-inch barreled firearms for the CHP. Officers were now approved to purchase four-inch or six-inch barreled .38/.357 revolvers in either stainless or blue steel from the approved list of manufacturers (Colt's, Smith & Wesson, or Ruger) for duty use. Veteran officers were permitted to continue using their presently owned, department-authorized equipment. All .357 Magnum revolvers were required to be loaded with the state-issued .38 Special load for duty after 1976.

Early reports on the new Model 67 revolvers indicated they did not withstand the high pressures of the newly issued Winchester .38 Special 110-grain +P+ load very well. Ejection rods backed out and tied up the guns. Some rear sight screws backed out, causing the rear sights to depart the guns during firing. Some of these .38 Special-rated frames were torqued by the excessive pressures of the +P+ cartridges and were damaged. As a result, some officers traded their four-inch Model 67 revolvers for six-inch Model 68s, because the Model 68s were built with stronger, .357 Magnum rated-frames (the Model 68 was actually a .357 Magnum Model 66 retrofitted with a .38 Special cylinder and forcing cone). Others chose to remain with privately purchased .357 Magnum-chambered guns.

AMMUNITION

By 1976, the issued load was the Winchester-Western .38 Special 110-grain +P+ jacketed hollowpoint ("Treasury Load") in nickel cases. A version of this same cartridge, loaded by Federal, was also issued for a short period around the late 1970s. The Federal version of the load had slightly less velocity than the Winchester version, and the bullet tended to fragment more easily and offered less penetration. Depending on the contract, either the Winchester or Federal load could be loaded in brass cases instead of nickel-plated cases. It has been suggested that the brass cases were requested by the department so that they would be more visible in the stainless steel cylinders of the issued Model 67 and 68 revolvers (in comparison to the silver color of the nickeled cases), following some accidental discharges, but it is more likely that the selection of brass cases was simply a matter of economy or inventory at the factory.

HKS speedloaders became standard issue by 1976. Some officers continued to use Dade Machine Company and other previously issued designs, but all new officers received HKS loaders during the academy.

LEATHER

No known changes. Bianchi International leather gear was standard issue, but officers could purchase department-approved gear from other vendors.

TRAINING

Although methods and facilities varied from office to office, training was becoming more and more street relevant. In example, at the Laguna Hills/San Juan Capistrano office, the rangemaster developed a "Hogan's Alley" course that involved officers running from position to position to engage targets on the contracted San Clemente PD range. Officers were required to fire from positions of cover (including vehicles) and reload using speedloaders. Brass was dumped onto the ground and was not policed until after the course was completed and the targets had been scored. Officers were also required to fire the shotgun dry, then demonstrate the ability to load one-shoot one from the spare ammo carrier on the buttstock as a means of keeping up continuity of fire. Training was entirely conducted on the CHP-issue silhouette targets. The use of two hands and the use of sighted fire was emphasized throughout the course, and all training was conducted using duty ammunition (W-W Treasury load, W-W Super X 00 Buckhot). The era of advanced "square range" training had arrived at the CHP.

Circa 1978 and 1981

FIREARMS

No known changes. The Smith & Wesson Model 67 and 68 (cadet's choice) remained standard issue guns for Academy cadets, but officers could purchase their own blue or stainless Colt's, Smith & Wesson, or Ruger revolvers in either four-inch or six-inch barrels and chambered in either .38 Special or .357 Magnum once they were out of the academy.

AMMUNITION

No known changes. Officers were issued Winchester-Western or Federal .38 Special 110-grain +P+ jacketed hollowpoint ("Treasury Load") ammunition, depending on the contract.

A CHP Cadet from Class II-81 training with the 12 Gauge Remington 870 shotgun. The CHP was slow to adopt the shotgun, but it quickly became an essential part of an officer's safety equipment. Cadets and officers receive excellent training with their shotguns and patrol rifles today. Photo courtesy of the California Highway Patrol Museum.

LEATHER

No known changes. The Bianchi International Model 2800 "Judge" holster remained standard issue into the 1980s.

TRAINING

More combat-relevant training was introduced and formalized at the Academy, including scenario training. Interestingly, some cadets of the era reported they were still required to deposit spent brass neatly during static-position firing on range, but were encouraged to dump it on the ground during so-called combat training. Class III-81 was the last to hit the field with straight batons and without portable radios. It was also among the first of the classes required to wear issued body armor during the Academy.

Circa Early 1980s

FIREARMS

No known changes. The Smith & Wesson Model 67 and 68 (cadet's choice) remained standard issue guns for Academy cadets, but officers could purchase their own blue or stainless Colt's, Smith & Wesson, or Ruger revolvers in either four- or six-inch barrels and chambered in either .38 Special or .357 Magnum, once they were out of the Academy.

Officers in some special assignments, such as auto theft investigation and the Protective Services Detail (the Governor's drivers and bodyguards), were issued J-Frame Smith & Wesson Model 60 revolvers. These firearms were also issued to some senior members of the chain of command assigned to positions where a duty-sized firearm was not required or desired. This was helpful for these senior leaders because many of their duties involved meetings with outside agencies and community groups, where plain clothes were the uniform of the day and the small revolvers were more discreet.

AMMUNITION

No known changes. Officers were issued Winchester-Western or Federal .38 Special 110-grain +P+ jacketed hollowpoint ("Treasury Load") ammunition, depending on the contract.

LEATHER

No known changes. The Bianchi International Model 2800 "Judge" holster remained standard issue for service revolvers well into the 1980s.

TRAINING

There were no known changes in the training regimen of the CHP during the early 1980s.

Cadets from Class IV-88 shoot their Smith & Wesson Model 67 revolvers on the range at the CHP Academy in West Sacramento (used 1976 - Present). Note the Bianchi Model 2800 "Judge" holster and the PR-24 side handle baton on the gun belt. The ammunition in use is the Federal .38 Special +P+ 110 grain jacketed hollowpoint. Photo courtesy of the California Highway Patrol Museum.

Circa 1986

FIREARMS

Influenced by their close associations with international, federal, and municipal S.W.A.T. teams during the 1984 Olympic Games in Los Angeles, the CHP began to issue the popular Heckler & Koch MP5 submachine gun (9mm) to the Patrol's Incident Response Team of the Protective Services Division. Photographic evidence indicates AR-15/M-16-pattern rifles were also in use by the team.

Circa 1989

FIREARMS

The CHP began to study alternatives for its issue handgun. In February 1989, a field trial of five different 9mm pistols was initiated. Limited numbers of Glock 17, Beretta 92, Smith & Wesson 5906, Sig Sauer P226, and Heckler & Koch P7 pistols were issued to three patrol areas and one investigative area, but, at the completion of the trial, none were selected for duty use. Other designs were evaluated by Academy staff, to include oddballs such as the

California Highway Patrol officers stand watch during the 1992 Rodney King Riots in Los Angeles. The officer in the foreground is armed with the .223 caliber Ruger Mini-14 rifle and the new .40 caliber Smith & Wesson Model 4006 handgun, while the officer in the background is backing up his S&W 4006 pistol with a 12 Gauge Remington 870 shotgun. Photo courtesy of the California Highway Patrol Museum.

Smith & Wesson Model 25 revolver in the .45 Colt chambering. None of these designs were formally adopted at the completion of testing and trials.

Also in 1989, the CHP began to issue limited numbers of Ruger Mini-14 rifles in .223 Remington, along with 20-round magazines, primarily to officers in rural areas. Initially, the rifles were carried in the trunks of sergeants' cars, but eventually they were stored in a rack alongside shotguns within the patrol cars. The push for patrol rifles was attributed to the rise in heavily armed criminals, such as the May 9, 1980, Norco bank robbery in Southern California, in which five robbers armed with explosives and rifles led police, sheriff, and CHP forces on a prolonged chase, destroyed 33 law enforcement vehicles, damaged a helicopter, killed one officer, and wounded eight others.

AMMUNITION

The CHP began to study alternatives, including 9mm, .45 ACP, and 10mm. The FBI was simultaneously conducting extensive ammunition research and development following its April 11, 1986, Miami shootout, and had developed a strong interest in the 10mm that influenced CHP testing and evaluation.

In the meantime, the CHP began to authorize Remington (and later, Winchester) .357 Magnum 125-grain jacketed hollowpoint ammunition for those officers who carried privately purchased department approved .357 Magnum revolvers. These officers were required to shoot the .357 Magnum ammunition during training and qualification. The Winchester .38 Special 110-grain +P+ jacketed hollowpoint ("Treasury Load") remained standard issue for most personnel, including all those who carried the department-issued Model 67 and 68 .38 Special revolvers.

LEATHER

There were no known changes in the leather issued in 1989.

TRAINING

Scenario training continued to mature at the Academy and during in-service training. By the mid-1970s, department policies required all officers to shoot quarterly.

Sometime around the mid- to late1980s, the CHP B21-style silhouette was replaced by a series of animated silhouette targets. The new "CHP Combat Target" silhouettes featured armed persons in realistic threatening postures, and some had the persons standing at oblique angles to the shooter. The persons (both male and female), were armed with guns, knives, and a variety of other deadly weapons. Subdued scoring rings that rewarded hits in a bowling pin shape that covered the head and torso were featured. The CHP Combat Target silhouette continues to be used through the present.

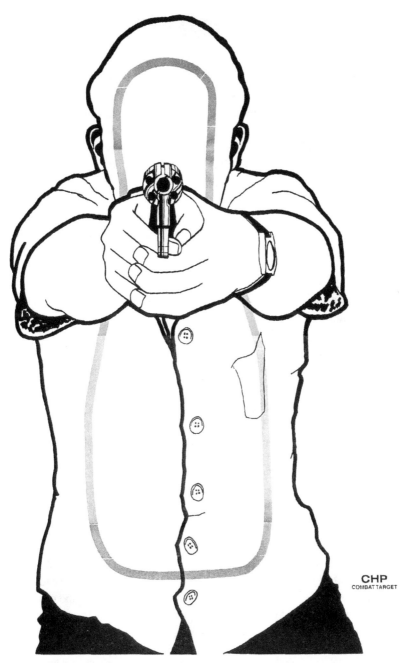

CHP
COMBAT TARGET

The "CHP Combat Target" in various styles replaced the old "CHP Silhouette Target" for training in the mid-to-late 1980s and is still in use. The new target features more realistic images, including the use of weapons by the aggressors. The bowling pin-shaped vital area does a better job of encouraging well-placed hits than the scoring rings on the previous target. Photo courtesy of the California Highway Patrol Museum.

Circa 1990

FIREARMS

The CHP conducted a test on 10mm and .40 S&W firearms, requesting samples from 23 manufacturers. Three manufacturers responded, submitting a total of eight pistols, to include: Colt's Double Eagle (10mm); Glock Models 20 (10mm), 22 (.40 S&W), and 23 (.40 S&W); and Smith & Wesson Models 1006 (10mm), 1076 (10mm), 4006 (.40 S&W with a frame-mounted decocker), and 4006 (.40 S&W with a slide-mounted safety/decocker).

At the completion of testing, the Smith & Wesson 4006 with the slide-mounted safety/decocker was selected as the new issue pistol for CHP. The CHP specified a flush hammer without a protruding spur on the new pistols. Officers were allowed to choose factory stocks with either straight or arched backstraps.

AMMUNITION

With the introduction of the .40 S&W cartridge, in January 1990, at the SHOT Show, the CHP decided to test it alongside the 10mm. After the testing was complete, the CHP decided to adopt the .40 S&W as its new issue caliber, becoming the first major agency to do so.

LEATHER

The Bianchi International Model 98 "Top Draw I" holster was selected as standard issue for the S&W 4006. Additionally, a Bianchi double magazine pouch was selected as standard issue. The magazine pouch was slotted to allow vertical or horizontal carry on the belt.

Circa 1990 to 1991

FIREARMS

The Smith & Wesson Model 4006 entered service as the standard CHP firearm, and all officers were required to transition to it. Academy cadets received it as their standard issue from the start of their careers, and officers in the field were required to replace their revolvers with the new pistol.

The cost for 7,000 of the new sidearms was $3 million. The total cost of the new weapons system (pistols, holsters, ammunition pouches, ammunition) was approximately $6.5 million.

While the new pistols were generally welcomed by the troops, reports from the period indicate that some of the veteran officers didn't like the new handgun. This was unsurprising, given their extensive training and experience with revolvers. Some officers felt the new 39 ounce pistol and its pair of spare magazines (which nearly doubled their standard ammunition loadout) were too heavy on the belt, nicknaming it "the boat anchor." Others complained that the weapon was prone to malfunctions, but it's likely that many of these were attributable to shooter error, rather than a defect in the design, because the complaints disappeared relatively quickly as officers received more training and gained more experience operating and maintaining the new weapon.

Some officers reported that early guns may have had some durability issues and that CHP armorers were initially required to inspect each weapon quarterly for frame and barrel cracks, but again these problems seemed limited and did not appear to last long.

All of these early issues were suitably dealt with, and the 4006 quickly evolved into an excellent and very durable weapon for the CHP which provided greater hit potential, increased capacity, faster reloads, and greater power than the revolvers they replaced.

The 27 ounce Model 4013 pistol also entered service as the replacement for the Model 60 revolvers used by special details and by senior leadership who required a more compact duty weapon.

AMMUNITION

The original formula of the new .40 S&W round, the Winchester 180-grain jacketed hollowpoint, entered service as standard issue.

LEATHER

Bianchi Model 98 "Top Draw I" holster and a double magazine pouch entered service as standard issue. Officers were authorized to purchase leather gear that met department standards from other vendors such as Aker Leather and Safariland.

TRAINING

Officers in the field were transitioned to the new firearm throughout the 1990-'91 period in three-day classes taught locally by Area training officers. Each of the 6,226 uniformed officers on the Patrol fired approximately 1,000 rounds through the pistol during the concentrated transition training, which allowed them a good start towards building a new set of weapon handling skills and "muscle memory." These new skills would be further engrained during quarterly area-level firearms training and periodic in-service training at the academy.

Circa 1992

FIREARMS

Limited numbers of Ruger Mini-14 rifles were seen in the hands of CHP officers sent to the Rodney King Riots, in April 1992. Throughout the remainder of the 1990s, the CHP expanded use of the rifles throughout the state, to the point they became relatively common in patrol cars.

Circa late 1990s to early 2000s

FIREARMS

The Smith & Wesson Model 4006 remained the standard sidearm. In fiscal year 1997, the National Defense Authorization Act, Section 1033, established a program whereby the Secretary of Defense could authorize the transfer of surplus military weapons to federal and state law enforcement agencies that needed the equipment. Under the 1033 program, the CHP began to replace its Ruger Mini-14 rifles with military-loaned M-16A1 rifles (which were converted to semi-automatic fire only), and also began to procure its own AR-15-pattern rifles from Colt and Bushmaster.

In the early 2000s, officers who wanted to take a rifle on patrol had to check one out from the sergeant, as the cars were not routinely equipped with them. However, as more rifles were acquired, the CHP transitioned to a policy where rifles were routinely carried in every cruiser. The M-16A1/AR-15 was mounted side by side with the Remington 870 shotgun in a cradle located in the middle of the front seat of the patrol car. It was equipped with a 20-round magazine. Two 20-round spare magazines were mounted to the butt of the rifle in a pouch.

AMMUNITION

The Patrol continued to issue 180 grain jacketed hollow point ammunition from a variety of vendors, depending on contract. The original Winchester .40 S&W 180-grain jacketed hollowpoints remained popular, but some contracts were also issued to Remington, which provided its own 180-grain jacketed hollowpoint load for duty and training use.

TRAINING

The Task Oriented Qualification Course (TOQC) now becomes the standard course of fire for qualification. In the TOQC, each required skill set (task) is individually tested, and a minimum standard (time and

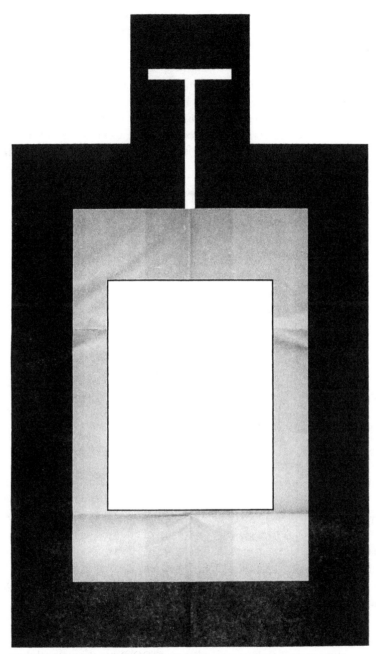

The Task Oriented Qualification Course (TOQC) target above is reserved for CHP qualification exercises today, while the CHP Combat Target is used for training. The "T" shape represents critical target areas of the central nervous system. Photo courtesy of the California Highway Patrol Museum.

score) is established for passing. Officers must pass all the individual tasks in order to qualify on this exam. If one or more tasks are failed, the officers can receive retraining in those particular skills and must be reevaluated at a later time for proficiency.

The TOQC is shot on a special TOQC target (CHP 241) printed on the back of the CHP Combat Target. The TOQC target incorporates an 8x11-inch target zone in the torso area, as well as a narrow, half-inch wide, T-shaped scoring zone in the face and spinal area. The CHP Combat Target continues to be used for training, while the TOQC target is reserved for qualification.

Circa 2006 to Present

FIREARMS

The Smith & Wesson Model 4006TSW was adopted as the new standard issue and replacing aging Model 4006 pistols in service, after a non-competitive bid that raised complaints from competitors and state politicians. Shipments of 9,730 guns, purchased in a $6.6 Million contract, began in June 2006. The new TSW version included an accessory rail on the dustcover, but the Patrol did not (and currently does not) issue weapon lights to their personnel. The new pistol featured ambidextrous decocker-only levers, an improved hammer and trigger group, and was a "Performance Center" gun built to tighter tolerances than the standard 4006 it replaced.

Some minor issues accompanied the introduction of the TSW pistol. A subcontractor to Smith & Wesson delivered a batch of sears that did not meet specifications, so the CHP recalled approximately 3,000 pistols to be retrofitted with replacement parts in March 2007 as a precautionary measure. Additionally, it quickly became apparent that the magazines used in the earlier 4006 service pistol were not always compatible with the new TSW version, due to the tighter tolerances of the Computer Numerically Controlled (CNC) machined frames of the new gun. In August of 2007, many of these older magazines were recalled and modified to fix the feed problem that resulted when the older magazines (which fit fine in the more generous magazine well of the classic, hand-milled, 4006 frames) were inserted into the tighter and more uniformly cut magazine well of the new TSW pistol.

These early issues with the pistols were quickly fixed and the TSW remains the standard issue weapon for the CHP today, who is very satisfied with its performance and reliability. While there is considerable speculation about a potential replacement program for the TSW pistol, this durable weapon has a lot of service life remaining and there are no immediate plans to retire it. However, when that time eventually comes, it would seem that the lighter weight, polymer-framed Smith & Wesson M&P pistol would be a natural replacement, given the department's historical proclivity to the brand and the potential for a favorable exchange program with the manufacturer. Although the 4006TSW pistols are equipped with an accessory rail, weapon lights are not issued by the CHP. Individual officers are permitted to purchase their own weapon lights and use them on duty, but they must supply both the light and a compatible holster at their own expense. Additionally, the officers must complete a CHP training course with the new lights prior to using them in service for the first time, and are prohibited from removing them from the pistol during future training if they intend to continue using them on duty.

Commercial or military AR-15-style rifles continue to serve alongside Remington 870 shotguns, and every CHP cruiser is routinely equipped with both weapons. As of press time, the CHP was set to begin replacing the standard 20-inch barreled AR-15 and M-16-style rifles with a shorter, barreled version patterned after the military M-4 carbine. The shorter 16" barrels on the new Sig Sauer M400 carbines procured by the CHP will make them easier to get in and out of cramped patrol cars without sacrificing any capability at the short ranges typical of CHP engagements. Furthermore, standardizing the entire department on a single platform will be a tremendous improvement from a logistical and maintenance standpoint.

AMMUNITION

Issued handgun ammunition changes frequently, depending on which company has the current contract. In recent years, the CHP instituted performance standards for its duty handgun ammunition that specified penetration, velocity and expansion requirements which have driven the adoption of more advanced 180 grain projectiles, such as the CCI-Speer Gold Dot, Winchester Ranger T Series, and Remington Golden Saber bullets. These rounds are more sophisticated than the plain jacketed hollowpoints of earlier years. Officers are required to carry at least two spare magazines of ammunition on duty, but may carry more at their option.

Both the military surplus M-16A1 and commercial AR-15 rifles are currently issued with three 20 round magazines of Winchester 64 grain soft point ammunition, but as with the handgun ammunition, this will vary depending on the active contract. The two spare 20-round magazines are located in a pouch attached to the buttstock of the rifle.

The Remington 870 shotguns continue to be issued with 00 Buckshot ammunition from various manufacturers, depending on the contract. Five spare rounds continue to be carried in a cuff on the buttstock.

LEATHER

A number of different holsters have been issued by the CHP in various contracts. New cadets are issued basic holsters during academy training (such as the Safariland Model 200 or 2005 "Top Gun," or the Aker Leather Model 118 "Blue Line Drop Loop") but they are encouraged in the early part of the program to procure their own holsters with advanced retention systems or other desirable features such as weapon light compatibility. By purchasing these holsters early, the cadets can train with their gear from the start and develop their skill with this critical piece of safety equipment. Officers already in service may similarly purchase their own holsters to replace the issued item. The CHP does not maintain an "approved holster list," but instead mandates certain key features and allows its personnel to choose a holster that meets the requirements and satisfies their own personal needs.

As a result of this progressive policy, a wide variety of holsters are found in service. A multitude of designs from industry giants Safariland and Aker Leather are popular with the CHP lawmen, but they are not limited to these brands and others can be found as well. The Safariland 6280 (mid ride) and 6285 (1.5" drop) holsters as well as the Aker Leather Model 118 "Blue Line Drop Loop" holster are well represented. Safariland ALS-equipped holsters are very popular, as are the "Patrolman" and "Sentinel" models by Aker Leather.